Ode to the
Front End

Ode to the Front End

Ode to the Front End

Library of Congress Control Number: 2021945351

ISBN: 9781662928550 Paperback
ISBN: 9781662928567 eBook

To **Jesus Christ my Lord and Savior** who has entrusted me as a Steward over this project, a most unlikely servant.

To **Susan Marguerite Gordon**: I will always love you and your twin brother. I hope you can forgive me for not having courage then to marry you at Wake Forest.

To **Christy Lea Miller**: I hope one day you choose to have me in your life.

Quota pars operis tanti nobis committitur
Velikovsky

Foreword

I am not the author but steward of what is contained in this book. Never written a line of poetry in my life and many readers have far better skill sets for this. The author is God who has used me as a practicing Christian to be His steward over this project.

I am a kingdom dweller. God brought me in one night by literally pulling my leg. He grabbed my congenitally short leg and pushed it out to the same length of my other leg. I have never recovered.

Anyone reading this has a choice and the freewill to make it. You can receive Jesus as Lord in your heart and believe that the Father raised Him from the dead. He died to create this inheritance for you. Name it and claim it. That is your right paid for by the sacrifice and death of God incarnate to provide you this inheritance.

The journey begins when I retired from a consultancy in risk management and wanted something to do that involved people contact. I joined the Home Depot as a front-end cashier in late January of 2019.

I discovered a collection of people living very difficult lives in an extraordinary manner that greatly humbled me. They are far better human beings than I can ever be as I quickly discovered. Earning their trust and business friendship means more to me than anything ever in my half century insurance career. This is a blessing beyond measure more valuable than any amount of gold or silver.

About six months ago returning home from work a little ditty entered my mind set from a short poem written by the defenders of Bataan. It was titled Battling Bastards of Bataan written by Frank Hewlett bureau chief at Manila when Japan attacked. He is credited with the following short poem. "…We are the battling bastards of Bataan No aunts, no uncles, no nephews, no nieces. No pills, no planes, no artillery pieces and nobody gives a damn."

I used the last piece as a tag line that appears throughout each stanza and quatrain. Initially the poem was to have been a page or two and then be shared with employees for a good laugh. Little did I know the Lord had other plans that turned this project into the work that follows. Doing the writing used every ounce of my limited intellectual and creative ability. At times I was almost driven to keep going when exhaustion had overcome effort. When stopping late at night and early morning I collapsed in bed unable to even move.

The work has curb appeal. Home Depot is a household name throughout the United States. It reflects the good and bad and dark and light in America. Anyone that comes across this title will have their curiosity piqued.

The book is unique. A 2,500 plus quatrain poem. Are you serious? The Lord revealed to me one night why this format. He asked me to pick a quatrain and read it. I did. He then asked could I write a narrative expanding it. I said yes. For some could I write a chapter or even a book and I said yes. He then said exactly. That writing encompassing all the quatrains would exceed 10,000 pages. Why he chose me to be His conduit for this project I will never know and trust me I resisted Him just as much as Moses back in the day.

Who is the audience? Everyone. No matter who you are or where you are or even what you are there is a lot in this work for you. Warning, it is not always easy reading. The poem runs from humor of various types to specification applications of humans struggling to callous corporate indifference and most anything in between. A preacher can find many opportunities to make a sermon. A reader looking for a laugh will be well served. An investment banker will find some of the quatrains a major source of disbelief if not heart burn. Just look at the cover.

The appendix provides some real-world examples of corporate disdain for employees and anything else not found on a spread sheet or profit and loss statement. The big box store crushes human spirit into fear and loathing. Control is maintained through systemic disparagement, denial, and dismissiveness. Depot is simply a prime example. Will there be a volume 2? No beginning and no end indicate that this will be the case but that is up to Him. I am His steward and nothing more.

Ode to the Front End

Oh where does this Bard begin much less end
We the front end of store 0884 have
No Mamma No Pappa No Uncle Sam
And no one in corporate gives a Damn.

We struggle and serve to serve and struggle
Dreams transformed into nightmares of grovel
No Mamma No Pappa No Uncle Sam
And no one in store 0884 gives a Damn.

They bring their throngs flood our floors
Flat cars and lumber carts strewn as if war
No Mamma No Pappa No Uncle Sam
And still no one to give a Damn.

We stand as one alone strickened in woe
Still they come with ceaseless flow
No Mamma No Pappa No Uncle Sam
And no one else to give a Damn.

Never remembered rewarded nor appreciated
Morale droops becomes constipated
No Mamma No Pappa No Uncle Sam
What are these to give a Damn.

No carts buggies gurneys systems to help our stay
We battle but lose each day
No Mamma No Pappa No Uncle Sam
No one cares to give a Damn.

We do our best alas futilely failed no repose
Forgotten forlorn never forgiven exposed
No Mamma no Pappa no Uncle Sam
Nor do unforgiven give a Damn

Disparaged dismissed denied hung out to dry
Eyes dulled ears stopped Gotterdammer rye
No Mamma No Pappa No Uncle Sam
What human could give a Damn

Toil and sweat increasing regret trudge through day
Not quite dead but no longer alive in ever darkening quay
No Mamma No Pappa No Uncle Sam
Who cares if chattel gives a Damn.

Deliberate indifference or indifferent deliverance each day
Home Depot demands all employees fall in this way
No Mamma No Pappa No Uncle Sam
And Burt Reynolds does not give a Damn.

They bring them in to have them leave
Do what will don't what won't as pleased
No Mamma No Pappa and No Uncle Sam
You think they give a Damn.

Last first wrong right 0884 blue
Work system or it shall you
No Mamma No Pappa No Uncle Sam
Who in this system gives a Damn.

They build up to tear down
Aspiration hope strangled wretches bound
No Mamma No Pappa No Uncle Sam
Wretches bound don't give a Damn.

They say treat customers best way
While relate to us another way
No Mamma No Pappa No Uncle Sam
And they don't give a Damn.

They cut our hours because they can very rude
Consumed we are like toothpaste from a tube
No Mamma No Pappa No Uncle Sam
Squeezed tubes do not give a Damn.

Suggestions from horde sprawl on floor
Senseless wrong crushed their box smashed like a boar
No Mamma No Pappa No Uncle Sam
Suggestions never did give a Damn.

Failure to schedule schedules failure
Impaled often employed seldom enjoyed behavior
No Mamma No Pappa No Uncle Sam
Impaled do not give a Damn.

They schedule five for all to see when need only three
Three becomes one or two because do not see
No Mamma No Pappa No Uncle Sam
Five or three who gives a Damn.

Middle open during day only three for coverage stay
During night five for coverage in way
No Mamma No Pappa No Uncle Sam
And scheduling does not give a Damn.

Control narrative essential for fun
Then wonder why they the pun
No Mamma No Pappa No Uncle Sam
Puns don't give a Damn.

Hired from Lowes thrust into Customer Service
Sent paddle buyer to Garden not PRO for purchase
No Mamma No Pappa No Uncle Sam
Depot not Lowes Damn.

See something say something be unappreciated
Denied dismissed disparaged never vindicated
No Mamma No Pappa No Uncle Sam
Whistles throttled don't give a Damn.

Caesar his Brutus Lincoln his Booth Kennedy his train
Store 0884 would do well to profit learn from same
No Mamma No Pappa No Uncle Sam
These never knew to give a Damn.

Promote by plumbing and melanin because they can
Melanin deprived with plumbing pound sand
No Mamma No Pappa No Uncle Sam
Melanin deprived do not give a Damn.

Selected new HC based on plumbing
Told rest to keep on slumming
No Pappa No Mamma No Pappa No Uncle Sam
No way having three male HCs Damn.

Algorithms leave part-time employees adrift
No rhyme nor reason always confusion on shift
No Mamma No Pappa No Uncle Sam
Algorithms do not give a Damn.

They use texts to act as pests
On call whenever suits geste
No Mamma No Pappa No Uncle Sam
Endless texts do not give a Damn.

Godot waits in Spain for rain to fall on plain
Not entering this store for gain nor fame
No Mamma No Pappa No Uncle Sam
Beckett does not give a Damn.

Women come and go there were servants too
Home Depot often acts like Timbuktu
No Mamma No Pappa No Uncle Sam
Timbuktu does not give a Damn.

Caught a break on four hours today
First time in four shifts came that way
No Mamma No Pappa No Uncle Sam
Break when convenient only Damn.

The Old Man and the Sea catch sharks steal
Work at Home Depot know how he feels
No Mamma No Pappa No Uncle Sam
Hemingway does not give a Damn.

Christy Lea no kingdom by the sea on this lifeless shore
Imprisoned by ginseng and drinks that bore
No Mamma No Pappa and No Uncle Sam
And who is this to give a Damn.

A Rabid squirrel she locked in frenzies seizes wheel castor
Turning faster and faster going forward only to disaster
No Mamma No Pappa and No Uncle Sam
Rabid squirrels do not give a Damn.

Roaming store with customers in tow
Self checkout abandoned a disastrous row
No Mamma No Pappa No Uncle Sam
Towed does not give a Damn.

Imprisoned like flies in glass web bin
Christy Lea's chatter drones on no hope for end
No Mamma No Pappa and No Uncle Sam
Endless chatter does not give a Damn.

Christy leaves notes for ponder and wonder
Thrown rock with hidden hand often plan auger
No Mamma No Pappa No Uncle Sam
Ponder and wonder do not give a Damn.

Hatchet to back bus to under
Christy habit of tearing asunder
No Mamma No Pappa No Uncle Sam
Hatchet and bus don't give a Damn.

Christy takes care of Christy rarely gets hurt
Ever frisky leaves others in lurch or dirt
No Mamma No Pappa No Uncle Sam
Frisky never gives a Damn.

0884 has record no other store can match
No functioning front end supervisor in three years natch
No Mamma No Pappa No Uncle Sam
What's a FES who knew to give a Damn.

Leadership by example right out the door
Queen Christy of absence excuses galore
No Mamma No Pappa No Uncle Sam
Since when did excuses give a Damn.

Marley dead this must be known
Christy wants not this job and groans
No Mamma No Pappa No Uncle Sam
Old Marley does not give a Damn.

Returned from vacation stomach pummeled by virus
Upset whole front end by not being among us
No Mamma No Pappa No Uncle Sam
Vacation extended does not give a Damn.

Christy lives grief for all to see naturally
In drama scenes acts and lies beautifully
No Mamma No Pappa No Uncle Sam
Unwed but has mother in law Damn.

Bennies and speed by gross Christy consumes
Roils floor out the door even to doom
No Mamma No Pappa No Uncle Sam
Speed freaks do not give a Damn.

Flummoxed and flustered not kind to rote
Sometimes circumstances run over goat
No Mamma No Pappa No Uncle Sam
Goats ram but never give a Damn.

When not entombed Christy leaves room for care
From time to time does for others dare
No Mamma No Pappa No Uncle Sam
This Christy can give a Damn.

A cash register genius for all to see
Customer engaged made special indeed
No Mamma No Pappa No Uncle Sam
Customers know this Christy Damn.

Christy perishing grieve to see
Incredible thoroughbred exhausted muddy lee
No Mamma No Pappa No Uncle Sam
A tragedy this an awful Damn.

Horse with limp knee makes grimace and gimp
Buckling one step at a time in hope of a splint
No Mamma No Pappa No Uncle Sam
Palominos doomed Damn.

Cortisone injected for knee treatment
Christy recovered believed an achievement
No Mamma No Pappa No Uncle Sam
Cortisone dissolves bone Damn.

Called out to Garden that we might receive
Made sure help came in cold to relieve
No Mamma No Pappa No Uncle Sam
Christy kind to give a Damn.

Her car entwined in late night rumble
Christy protected by escort ensemble
No Mamma No Pappa No Uncle Sam
Escorts do give a Damn.

Christy on vacation spied weather fluxation
Used to extend with call out vexation
No Mamma No Pappa No Uncle Sam
Christy stays home Damn.

Christy saw hole in SCO niche switched to stitch
Unplanned appeared put money to bed with fix
No Mamma No Pappa No Uncle Sam
Christy did once more give a Damn.

This FES horse calls out more from this store
Christy legions of reasons to leave us poor
No Mamma No Pappa No Uncle Sam
Don't fence her in who gives a Damn.

Twelve out of thirteen bit much for part time to hoe
No one cares nor thanks stay until they say go
No Mamma No Pappa No Uncle Sam
Part times should never give a Damn.

Register in Garden went away
Customers gladly waited for return to pay
No Mamma No Pappa No Uncle Sam
This cash register did not give a Damn.

Gimme shelter Stones used to wail
At Home Depot another revenue source to hale
No Mamma No Pappa No Uncle Sam
Stones rolling do not give a Damn.

Rumors swirl all through store about Christy's fate
Is there a need is she peeved or is it just too late
No Mamma No Pappa No Uncle Sam
No one anymore gives a Damn.

Nineteen straight and Christy can skate
It seems nothing left on her plate
No Mamma No Pappa No Uncle Sam
Poor Christy must be Damned.

Tin soldiers and Nixon coming finally on our own
Home Depot actions make us feel alone
No Mamma No Pappa No Uncle Sam
Kent State does not give a Damn.

Christy returned as if from the dead
Blonde hair streaked fiery red causing dread
No Mamma No Pappa No Uncle Sam
Dread red does not give a Damn.

Donna been in weeds for days
No Round Up found for her to spray
No Mamma No Pappa No Uncle Sam
Even Round Up does not work Damn.

Christy chirped knew successor
April if chosen a very good confessor
No Mamma No Pappa No Uncle Sam
April as FES will give a Damn.

On Monday Christy said leaving front part of store
Moving to flooring and painting next door
No Mamma No Pappa No Uncle Sam
Christy leaving Damn.

Her voice heard all over store
Three energy drinks laced with ginseng restore
No Mamma No Pappa No Uncle Sam
Energy drinks do not give a Damn.

A customer asked of her said I like cash
When contacted Christy knew who this trashed
No Mamma No Pappa No Uncle Sam
Christy or cash who gives a Damn.

Christy told Bard could not stay
Hated beans wanted to get far away
No Mamma No Pappa No Uncle Sam
Christy wants again to give a Damn.

Three cashiers but no Christy Lee just a stand-in for Saturday's eve
One cashier counted when store closed took leave
No Mamma No Pappa No Uncle Sam
No HC three cashiers one hour past close Damn.

Christy offered coke to Bard for delight
Had to decline because too white
No Mamma No Pappa No Uncle Sam
Crawford Johnson does not give a Damn.

Bonfire of vanities delight as place quakes
Christy burned at stake for mistakes
No Mamma No Pappa No Uncle Sam
Vanities and bonfires don't give a Damn.

Legions or more work in this big box store
Not saintly consumed by fear or bored
No Mamma No Pappa No Uncle Sam
You think these give a Damn

April knew who spied and fled reprise
When confronted repented gave surmise
No Mamma No Pappa No Uncle Sam
And spied does not give a Damn.

They called April to work some more
Wanted to reduce other time on floor
No Mamma No Pappa No Uncle Sam
Base pay no overtime Damn.

Management seeks respect with blatter
Fails to supervise FES does not matter
No Mamma No Pappa No Uncle Sam
Failure to manage managing failure Damn.

Receiving can schedule and be stable no one else able
Associates flock there to be like Mabel Black Label
No Mamma No Pappa No Uncle Sam
Mabel Black Label does not give a Damn.

Home Depot abuses part-time employees with clock
When full-time customers remember this shlock
No Mamma No Pappa No Uncle Sam
These full-time customers won't give a Damn.

Lowes bought Stain Master Carpet to sell
Home Depot buys back stock swell
No Mamma No Pappa No Uncle Sam
Stock buy backs don't give a Damn.

Home Depot speaks of their culture
More like petri dish in sulfur
No Mamma No Pappa No Uncle Sam
Petri dishes are not culture Damn.

Christy in Paint helping customers mix
Hair and face covered with spilled paint tricks
No Mamma No Pappa No Uncle Sam
Spilled paint does not give a Damn.

Coverage for SCO middle and keys simultaneously
Then wonder why we seized and drop into freeze
No Mamma No Pappa No Uncle Sam
Seized and freezed do not give a Damn.

Christy helped key complex lock
Three customers left in flooring no John Locke
No Mamma No Pappa No Uncle Sam
New Atlantis does not give a Damn.

The cross of multicultural inclusive tolerance awaits unwary
Open door inclusivity snared by sensitivity's dark stained Avery
No Mamma No Pappa No Uncle Sam
Multicultural does not give a Damn.

Seven days in a row legs start to go
One day off move very slow
No Mamma No Pappa No Uncle Sam
Seven days in a row Damn.

Taking care of business in this steel can
Do your stinking job part of Depot's brand
No Mamma No Pappa No Uncle Sam
BTO does not give a Damn.

Customer service pronounced by sign
Nowhere else in store to align
No Mamma No Pappa No Uncle Sam
You think this sign gives a Damn.

Buggies carts and returns clog Customer Service land
No one knows where may eventually hang
No Mamma No Pappa No Uncle Sam
Hang and land do not give a Damn.

Inside out up down management ruse
Punish that do reward that don't abuse
No Mamma No Pappa No Uncle Sam
Abused don't give a Damn.

We provide customer satisfaction
Management demands to know why for such action
No Mamma No Pappa No Uncle Sam
Demands do not give a Damn.

They ask questions we don't know
Require their answers before we go
No Mamma No Pappa No Uncle Sam
And why do questions give a Damn

They stuff our face with useless diapers
Wash us with their stinky alkie wipers
No Mamma No Pappa No Uncle Sam
Diapers and alkies Damn.

Big Blue up the street closed $90,000 deal sweet
That customer would not let Depot compete
No Mamma No Pappa No Uncle Sam
Big Blue wiped street with Depot again Damn.

Depot hates unions indoctrinates their way
Makes requirement for us to stay
No Mamma No Pappa No Uncle Sam
Unions or Depot Damn.

Alle alle in free heralds this endless drama
We work as we choose as if in coma
No Mamma No Pappa No Uncle Sam
Comatose and don't give a Damn

Shayla Smith as HR squared kept schedule score
One day Depot moved to another store
No Mamma No Pappa No Uncle Sam
And that ended scheduling Damn.

PRO appreciation day came and went inside store
Now we don't have to like them anymore
No Mamma No Pappa No Uncle Sam
And the biscuit received does not give a Damn.

Call out call in how this process transmits
A show that seemingly knows no end you twit
No Mamma No Pappa No Uncle Sam
Vaudeville shows do not give a Damn.

Melanie came in like Brothers Grimm
Assumed HR squared things began to dim
No Mamma No Pappa No Uncle Sam
Dim does not give a Damn.

Cashiers in play have a say
Want Bard to make their day
No Mamma No Pappa No Uncle Sam
Bard makes their shifts Damn.

Allocate hours because they rule
Coverage needs grow like Kudzu
No Mamma No Pappa No Uncle Sam
Kudzu does not give a Damn.

Ownership and Accountability laid in nest
Those that contest lost with rest
No Mamma No Pappa No Uncle Sam
And why should they give a Damn.

Emily Bo Peep tends sheep that never sleep
Shepherd's hook silences their bleep
No Mamma No Pappa No Uncle Sam
Sheep do not give a bleating Damn.

Bo Peep bleeps shift to fill
Seems some sheep lost or ill
No Mamma No Pappa No Uncle Sam
And the sheep dog does not give a Damn.

Isaac the huge once worked in this store full bore
Now struts as pleases barnyard rooster at Hen's front door
No Mamma No Pappa No Uncle Sam
Strutting rooster Damn.

Ashely a Mona Lisa with serenity that appeases
Kept by faith with certainty in Christy as pleases
No Mamma No Pappa No Uncle Sam
Mona Lisa does not give a Damn.

Dan the man hits the fan never eases
Tart and bitter yet full of sugar when unleashes
No Mamma No Pappa No Uncle Sam
Dan gives not a tinker's dam Damn.

Dan came to work as schedule pronounced
ASM pounced demanded renounce
No Mamma No Pappa No Uncle Sam
ASM and schedules don't give a Damn.

Dan left came again when Christy failed to come through door
Hell frozen over said he for standing in once more
No Mamma No Pappa and No Uncle Sam
Dan did give a Damn.

Ace has place where we should go
Helps store win big pile of dough
No Mamma No Pappa No Uncle Sam
Ace sold his give to make a Damn.

Working 8 to 8 on Sunday's plate Ace never leaves nor late
Filling three departments in this slate hopes ingratiates
No Mamma No Pappa No Uncle Sam
Ace ready to cry Uncle Damn.

Mason below line that bears name
Puts zing into work wins same
No Mamma No Pappa No Uncle Sam
This Mason jar gives a Damn.

Work caused Mason to leave this ring
Took another job ended Depot fling
No Mamma No Pappa No Uncle Sam
And 33rd degree does not give a Damn.

Rocky and Bullwinkle walk all through store
Balboa lies punched out on the floor
No Mamma No Pappa No Uncle Sam
Bullwinkle and Balboa do not give a Damn.

Rolling rolling rolling … keep those sales flowing Rawhide
Through dark and stormy weather Roland keeps us together
No Mamma No Pappa No Uncle Sam
Rawhide does not give a Damn.

Flooring struck by Red virus each day
Useless diapers and Alkie wipers did not keep away
No Mamma No Pappa No Uncle Sam
No one in flooring left to give a Damn.

Kevin the Red makes all things fit nice
Front end neat when listen to his advice
No Mamma No Pappa No Uncle Sam
Kevin unlike Erik the Red gives a Damn.

You can always trust Bob when on floor
He simply cares and does so much more
No Mamma No Pappa No Uncle Sam
Need I say Bob gives a Damn.

Close Garden at eight by locking gate
No coverage to nine customers doubt this great
No Mamma No Pappa No Uncle Sam
Close gate and don't give a Damn.

Paul in lumber cuts mighty fine timber
Drywall and concrete for customers unlimbered
No Mamma No Pappa No Uncle Sam
Paul like Bunyan gives a Damn

Chris the soldier jumped from planes without chute
Very good training for this ASM toot
No Mamma No Pappa No Uncle Sam
And Green Berets don't give a Damn.

Phyllis doubled over carried to car
Depot refused to file First Report memoir
No Mamma No Pappa No Uncle Sam
Refused to file First Report Damn.

Out for extended period unable to work
Had to work extra to pay medical bills perk
No Mamma No Pappa No Uncle Sam
Why have workers compensation then Damn.

Olive quit stay at HC with fractured foot
Agreed and seen that Phyllis kaput
No Mamma No Pappa No Uncle Sam
Broken Olive tried to give a Damn.

Phyllis bought the lie and took jab
Down in back off lying on a slab
No Mamma No Pappa No Uncle Sam
The jab does not give a Damn.

Signs on shelves confuse many
Arrows should point to skinny
No Mamma No Pappa No Uncle Sam
Arrow up arrow down Damn.

This Mary not the least contrary more like a goodly fairy
She is pretty petite and complete for customers very
No Mamma No Pappa No Uncle Sam
Innocents do give a Damn.

Omega seeks Alpha betwixt and between
Roughly provides service rarely seen
No Mamma No Pappa No Uncle Sam
Omega seeking Alpha gives a Damn.

Omega strickened by cancer determined to stay
Unable to eat at times an awful way so pray
No Mamma No Pappa No Uncle Sam
For this one give a Damn.

Savannah new to cashiers but manages through
Efficient and effective no invective too
No Mamma No Pappa No Uncle Sam
Savannah smiles does give a Damn.

Breasted in Egypt Wells Outline of History
At this store recipe for endless misery
No Mamma No Pappa No Uncle Sam
Breasted and Wells do not give a Damn.

Nick stands a priest at Mass offering thanks
When customers boiling never shoots blanks
No Mamma No Pappa No Uncle Sam
Priests at Mass cannot say Damn.

A bale of hay in play caused him to pop his back
Stooped as if by croup swoons unable to stack
No Mamma No Pappa No Uncle Sam
Nick at night can't give a Damn.

Home alone off clock called out
Nick no first report of injury for this bout
No Mamma No Pappa No Uncle Sam
No First Report just like Phyllis Damn.

Returned to work after a day or three stiffily
Glad to see even if but briefly
No Mamma No Pappa No Uncle Sam
Nick gives a Damn.

Few buggies in Garden at close on Friday
Means Saturday's party will not tidy
No Mamma No Pappa No Uncle Sam
Saturday's Garden will not give a Damn.

Open machines at SCO to see if receipt tapes OK
Pack rat left empty spools in way
No Mamma No Pappa No Uncle Sam
Christy's empty spools don't give a Damn.

Amber in Garden stranded and alone
Did not call for help on telephone
No Mamma No Pappa No Uncle Sam
Amber never had a chance Damn.

Blanca hides face behind eyelids and muck
Helps customers when not acting like a shmuck
No Mamma No Pappa No Uncle Sam
Winking lids of deceit do not give a Damn.

Silences Bard with face twisted in hate
Becoming and proper to her ingrate
No Mamma No Pappa No Uncle Sam
This ingrate gives not a Damn.

New employees drop like flies on no pest strip
Never seen on a trip few give a rip
No Mamma No Pappa No Uncle Sam
And spend shift getting acquainted Damn.

Depot at night when it gets crazy
For many more like time for lazy
No Mamma No Pappa No Uncle Sam
Lazy and crazy don't give a Damn.

Sylvia in PRO learned where customer pleases
Gum she chews brings peace from pieces
No Mamma No Pappa No Uncle Sam
A forest chewing gum Damn.

Sylvia passed by Self checkout
Said PRO needed Bard look out
No Mamma No Pappa No Uncle Sam
They won't let Bard touch PRO Damn.

A relentless limp thud on floor struggles Charley
Finds customers serves tartly and smartly
No Mamma No Pappa No Uncle Sam
Limps like Ahab and gives a Damn.

Alone covering Garden and customers via
Charlie made sure had their visas
No Mamma No Pappa No Uncle Sam
Charlie helped customers give a Damn.

On Aprils Fools April fooled through and through
Bought Christyoma treated by drinks and ginseng too
No Mamma No Pappa No Uncle Sam
April fools April but do give a Damn.

Cole may look like Queequeg in Moby Dick
Built like a rock but gentle as a lamb near French Lick
No Mamma No Pappa No Uncle Sam
French Lick does not give a Damn.

Amanda the brunette dyed never lied
Finds many ways to avoid work applied
No Mamma No Pappa No Uncle Sam
Flag wavers never give a Damn.

Tom Swift alive and well as Josh younger
His machines cause screams way out yonder
No Mamma No Pappa No Uncle Sam
Tom Swift and machines do not give a Damn.

Yo Yo in tizzy to do strip not easy
Wanted no more notes made dizzy
No Mamma No Pappa No Uncle Sam
Yo Yo does her strips Damn.

Swift rolled newest machine across floor
Able to make yellow tags and more
No Mamma No Pappa No Uncle Sam
This Swift machine scary Damn.

Denisovich life and day for bricks to lay
Home Depot sold bricks and mortar if today
No Mamma No Pappa No Uncle Sam
Solzhenitsyn does not give a Damn.

0884 rose to middle of pack from way back
Those sad sacks below real bad acts
No Mamma No Pappa No Uncle Sam
Bad acts and sad sacks do not give a Damn.

Another one bites dust
Much more like ashes and rust
No Mamma No Pappa No Uncle Sam
Dust or rust who gives a Damn

Missy rides lawnmowers hair flowing
Customers wish seen this mowing
No Mamma No Pappa No Uncle Sam
And Lady Godiva does not give a Damn.

Sackcloth and ashes order of the day
At Depot no one ever joins in this parade
No Mamma No Pappa No Uncle Sam
Sackcloth and ashes don't give a Damn.

Tim could lay out with his bout be ordinaire
Instead chooses to live life extraordinaire
No Mamma No Pappa No Uncle Sam
Tim says God bless us everyone Damn.

Housekeeping in disarray April something to say
Better learn to keep in a better way
No Mamma No Pappa No Uncle Sam
Pick up after yourself Damn.

Joyce lost husband to dreaded cancer thing
Moved to freight and built quite a team
No Mamma No Pappa No Uncle Sam
Best in freight Damn.

Captain Queeg rolled dice to raise Cain
Josh stacks toilet paper all the same
No Mamma No Pappa No Uncle Sam
Dice or toilet paper Damn.

Leave Garden nice and neat when store closes
Garden uses blowers dust then reposes
No Mamma No Pappa No Uncle Sam
Blowing dirt does not give a Damn.

Beans to count with abacus before
Josh never runs out of them to hoard
No Mamma No Pappa No Uncle Sam
Josh Bean Counter does not give a Damn.

Craig keeps list and manages to wink
Paper to ink into black avoid stink
No Mamma No Pappa No Uncle Sam
Wink and ink don't give a Damn.

Chris Wasco the bear almost never growls
Playful as a cub makes customers mild
No Mamma No Pappa No Uncle Sam
This Bear not Smokey does give a Damn.

Mandy a dandy in tools we all see as nice
Customers appreciate her advice
No Mamma No Pappa No Uncle Sam
Mandy a dandy and gives a Damn.

Samuel arrived for relief in cold Garden today
No coat aloof but made to stay
No Mamma No Pappa No Uncle Sam
Bard gave him his coat Damn.

Eclectic and eccentric Bard that sees
Owns job does what right in this endless sieve
No Mamma No Pappa No Uncle Sam
Writes for the condemned Damn.

Three Ps apply Present Prepared Perform
Store paid customer served inventory adorned
No Mamma No Pappa No Uncle Sam
Who else to give a Damn.

Chasmyn slender and nice not sugar nor spice
Lifts 80 pound bags engaging customers nice
No Mamma No Pappa No Uncle Sam
Wonder Woman does give a Damn.

Toro took leave without proper pay out Chasmyn's way
SKU failed to say nay mower rode away
No Mamma No Pappa No Uncle Sam
Toro does not give a Damn.

Sunday eve customer asked for four hundred paddles
No such number to sell nor way to win battle
No Mamma No Pappa No Uncle Sam
And no one can run forklift either Damn.

Steve great in paint no one can match his tint
Customers moved to tears may even faint
No Mamma No Pappa No Uncle Sam
Steve in paint gives a Damn.

Christian named Hollywood for sunglasses outdoors
Now inside does not need them anymore
No Mamma No Pappa No Uncle Sam
Christian great and gives a Damn.

Christian has sister Yoslyn working in freight
Pretty enough to make Moctezuma ache
No Mamma No Pappa No Uncle Sam
Just like a priestess before Kukulkan Damn.

Daniel like Boone hunted coon more likely than not
Made to leave lest go postal forgot
No Mamma No Pappa No Uncle Sam
This nice kid might go postal Damn.

Returned to visit and check without being mean
Daniel now employed as a wolverine
No Mamma No Pappa No Uncle Sam
Red Dawn does not give a Damn.

More lost than found in PRO mangled
Merchandise tangled and wrangled
No Mamma No Pappa No Uncle Sam
Tangled webs weaved do not give a Damn.

Orders partially filled next to returns spilled
Employees get to select their thrill
No Mamma No Pappa No Uncle Sam
Tie a yellow ribbon on returns Damn.

Bard covered his Sin by training ascend
Until trouble on floor forced rescind
No Mamma No Pappa No Uncle Sam
Sin never gives a Damn.

Shelf called for five varieties only had four
Display unfinished sprawled across aisle and floor
No Mamma No Pappa No Uncle Sam
Customers can trip over it Damn.

April calls seeking resolve to endless melee
Always on point acts as anointed referee
No Mamma No Pappa No Uncle Sam
Endless melee does not give a Damn.

Scheduling a ruse rarely used
April sees we never abused
No Mamma No Pappa No Uncle Sam
April does give a Damn.

Deemed essential in this government plot
Vital to sell Red Chinese trash from this spot
No Mamma No Pappa No Uncle Sam
Red Chinese trash essential Damn.

James a victim of vaccine autism does best
Carries cross empties lot with little rest
No Mamma No Pappa No Uncle Sam
This victim of jab still gives a Damn.

Home Depot encourages jab
Hope many will not end up on slabs
No Mamma No Pappa No Uncle Sam
Jab does not give a Damn.

Remember rules of gold for store
Payment received buyer served inventory restored
No Mamma No Pappa No Uncle Sam
And who appreciates this Damn.

Told management how to acquire endless cards desired
Responded by rejecting almost having Bard fired
No Mamma No Pappa No Uncle Sam
Work in credit does not give a Damn.

The Milky Way a galaxy of stars
Just candy for sale at Depot's bar
No Mamma No Pappa No Uncle Sam
Milky Way does not give a Damn.

Rarely receive tubes from back anymore
Keep them safe in vault cash lays on floor
No Mamma No Pappa No Uncle Sam
Tubes greater than cash Damn.

0884 three ring circus gone with the wind
This Wild West show has no end
No Mamma No Pappa No Uncle Sam
PT Barnum does not give a Damn.

Schedule split to offset spasm chasm and pain
No one remembers if this sane
No Mamma No Pappa No Uncle Sam
Spasm and chasm do not give a Damn.

Bard sees what is done writes for fun
Blasphemers may soon be on the run
No Mamma No Pappa No Uncle Sam
And memorialized Damn.

Home Depot cards great for consumers
Charge 26% interest and late fee bloomers
No Mamma No Pappa No Uncle Sam
Even the Mafia blushes Damn.

Custer Little Bighorn Sennacherib Jerusalem Napoleon Waterloo
Home Depot now has Tippecanoe and Tyler too
No Mamma No Pappa No Uncle Sam
None of these can ever give a Damn.

Defarge had knitting while sitting
Bard has pen for bidding while flitting
No Mamma No Pappa No Uncle Sam
The Guillotine does not give a Damn.

Inconvenient truth never in way
At Depot lies rule day
No Mamma No Pappa No Uncle Sam
Lies do not give a Damn.

Brought stuff to aisle this eve looked like modern art
Blocked aisle with carts left open for people not smart
No Mamma No Pappa No Uncle Sam
Modern art does not give a Damn.

Two women alone as cashiers ill at ease during eve
Bard came went came again to fill their need
No Mamma No Pappa No Uncle Sam
Bard split in two did give a Damn.

Placed markdowns on shelf for customers to view
Cashier back exposed not advised askew
No Mamma No Pappa No Uncle Sam
And a back turned robbed Damn.

Take what thieves want when choose
Employees cannot turn any screws
No Mamma No Pappa No Uncle Sam
Screws unturned don't give a Damn.

Garden opened but coverage not
Forgot to schedule in this slot
No Mamma No Pappa No Uncle Sam
Staffing never gives a Damn.

On the whole Fields rather here than Philadelphia
Fields never saw Depot such a nice fella
No Mamma No Pappa No Uncle Sam
WC Fields does not give a Damn.

More hours needed but they rather not
Wonder why store is in tough spot
No Mamma No Pappa No Uncle Sam
No hours no employees who gives a Damn.

They call and ask why training not complete
Seems forgot no monitors nor times on sheet
No Mamma No Pappa No Uncle Sam
Why should we give a Damn.

Phyllis had customer with damaged door
Asked to take off $50 almost fell to floor
No Mamma No Pappa No Uncle Sam
Called Bo Peep out of fear Damn.

Three Lot attendants took leave permanently
Ones remaining just scream interminably
No Mamma No Pappa No Uncle Sam
Who needs Lot attendants Damn.

Dan the man told Christy fix Garden register
Nothing done now an empty barrister
No Mamma No Pappa No Uncle Sam
Christy tried to fix Damn.

Management has monkeys on their back
They give them to us in big brown sacks
No Mamma No Pappa No Uncle Sam
These monkeys do not give a Damn.

A door to the store says exit proclaimed
Buggies there but nowhere near entrance exclaimed
No Mamma No Pappa No Uncle Sam
In out and out in who gives a Damn.

When Depot throws monkeys on the floor
Pound with sledgehammers drive out the door
No Mamma No Pappa No Uncle Sam
Don't give us your monkeys Damn.

Lot littered with nails bolts and screws fill car tire tubes
Lights very dim and grim hollow blackened rubes
No Mamma No Pappa No Uncle Sam
Flat tires in the dark do not give a Damn.

Part time scheduling makes them grow old
Three to five to two and one simply not bold
No Mamma No Pappa No Uncle Sam
Do they really have any idea how to schedule Damn.

Abandoned carts full thousand dollars in drawer unstripped
Lines of legion with no reason for PRO Sunday trip
No Mamma No Pappa No Uncle Sam
Strip or unstripped who gives a Damn

Buck in lumber a treat for customers in need
Always there to solve fix and load at full speed
No Mamma No Pappa No Uncle Sam
Uncle Buck gives a Damn.

Gail a tempest brew never ever quits crew
Customers love to sample her brew
No Mamma No Pappa No Uncle Sam
Gail makes a difference Damn.

Called for tubes when deplete none sent to complete
Two hours later tubes and strips remain beat
No Mamma No Pappa No Uncle Sam
Money unstripped does not give a Damn.

No managers in Home Depot alone moan and groan
Soon customers will cause fall of this Rome
No Mamma No Pappa No Uncle Sam
The Xth Legion did not give a Damn.

Dakota her name customer service explains
Quiet and shy gets by all the same
No Mamma No Pappa No Uncle Sam
This shy Dakota gives a Damn.

Grandeur to Greece and glory to Rome
Depot no grandeur nor glory at Home
No Mamma No Pappa No Uncle Sam
Glory and grandeur do not give a Damn.

Lumber like a bow seeking arrow
Perhaps used to hit a sparrow
No Mamma No Pappa No Uncle Sam
Lumber not culled does not give a Damn.

Associate teams compete against each other
Sport may sort but only business matters brother
No Mamma No Pappa No Uncle Sam
And jocks and jockettes do not give a Damn.

Lysol kills Red Virus CDC people say
Home Depot too cheap to use this spray
No Mamma No Pappa No Uncle Sam
And as usual they don't give a Damn.

A customer old and in a bad way
Bob came through helped save day
No Mamma No Pappa No Uncle Sam
Bob came through Damn.

Phyllis stayed an extra thirty to play
Everyone in management thought OK
No Mamma No Pappa No Uncle Sam
Thirty minutes more they don't give a Damn.

Worked almost seven with hardly a break
At the end more than full of ache
No Mamma No Pappa No Uncle Sam
Helping for seven is hard Damn.

Training remains only instead we get named
Hard to explain but they sure place blame
No Mamma No Pappa No Uncle Sam
Blame or shame who gives a Damn.

Caesar his Rubicon did cross
At Depot probably another loss
No Mamma No Pappa No Uncle Sam
Caesar does not give a Damn.

We scan what we can if not customer must stand
Inventory uber alles in these stupendous follies
No Mamma No Pappa No Uncle Sam
And soon these customers won't give a Damn.

Yellow SKU askewed causes disaster
The line behind rises to rafter
No Mamma No Pappa No Uncle Sam
A disaster is but a disaster Damn.

April faced a never-ending riddle
Manage and supervise while rest fiddle
No Mamma No Pappa No Uncle Sam
April dealing with this Damn.

The scan gun fails we wail
Pin pad quits the card we bail
No Mamma No Pappa No Uncle Sam
Pin pads and scan guns do not give a Damn.

Phone numbers not answered not one Apron in sight
Close Garden gate lock up this blight goodnight
No Mamma No Pappa No Uncle Sam
Lock Garden and they will give a Damn.

Roberson his Titan did see and write
What awaits Home Depot's leased ship contrite
No Mamma No Pappa No Uncle Sam
Remember the Titans Damn.

Veni Vidi Vici to Senate did write Caesar
At Depot more likely causes swamp fever
No Mamma No Pappa No Uncle Sam
SPQR does not give a Damn.

Garden parched and dry no water there
Roaches die on pale birds flew elsewhere
No Mamma No Pappa No Uncle Sam
Parched Gardens do not give a Damn.

Associate reached for help told never to ask for same
Helping customer a practice reserved for insane
No Mamma No Pappa No Uncle Sam
Insane or inane they do not give a Damn.

Manage morning after caused great laughter
Brilliant at hindsight using endless chatter
No Mamma No Pappa No Uncle Sam
Monday morning quarterbacks Damn.

No one would answer a call for help in loading
John appeared to keep customer from exploding
No Mamma No Pappa No Uncle Sam
John gives a Damn.

Drywall delivered today piled outside
Took a while to decide bring inside
No Mamma No Pappa No Uncle Sam
And drywall wet is not worth a Damn.

Cashier at station panicked unable to sign on
No one told to update barcode and play on
No Mamma No Pappa No Uncle Sam
They don't train worth a Damn.

GET Greet Engage and Thank customer at store 0884
Means GIT Grab Interrogate and Terrorize even more
No Mamma No Pappa No Uncle Sam
GET to GIT Damn.

They tell us to be CEOs over the fifty
Demand why used for customer swiftly
No Mamma No Pappa No Uncle Sam
And these CEOs over the 50 don't give a Damn.

Smile at customer behind mask
This seems to be no small task
No Mamma No Pappa No Uncle Sam
See-thru masks might give a Damn.

We are empowered they say waiting for hay
They have power embalmed this way
No Mamma No Pappa No Uncle Sam
The embalmed do not give a Damn.

They blocked lumber every which way
Told customers to wait and not stray
No Mamma No Pappa No Uncle Sam
Blocked lumber does not give a Damn.

Congratulate and articulate heavy work nuts
Refuse to pay more much less trust us
No Mamma No Pappa No Uncle Sam
Work before us does not give a Damn.

Running store we they say
Until time for pay then nay
No Mamma No Pappa No Uncle Sam
Who runs the store Damn.

Seven dollar check brought disaster in Garden
Shut down register for twenty minutes hardened
No Mamma No Pappa No Uncle Sam
Register quit and left cashier adrift Damn.

Helen of Troy stood in Agamemnon's way
Home Depot had absolutely nothing to say
No Mamma No Pappa No Uncle Sam
Helen of Troy does not give a Damn.

Trojan Horse opened for Argive waves
Home Depot a spigot for Red China today
No Mamma No Pappa No Uncle Sam
This Red Trojan Horse does not give a Damn.

Christy inside cylinder of orange light through roof
Bard humbled by this awe and reproof
No Mamma No Pappa No Uncle Sam
Surrounded by orange glory Damn.

Best in retail they exclaim to us unwashed
Paid like pigs dripping in slop totally sloshed
No Mamma No Pappa No Uncle Sam
The unwashed don't give a Damn.

Exit proclaimed on PRO's sliding door
Completely ignored means nothing anymore
No Mamma No Pappa No Uncle Sam
Who cares what is written on the door Damn.

What are we working for
Could it be the next big box store
No Mamma No Pappa No Uncle Sam
And next stop not Vietnam Damn.

One cashier in store all alone
Certainly had no time to be on phone
No Mamma No Pappa No Uncle Sam
And no one said thanks Damn.

Say thank you hope they buy more looty
Management kicks booty when moody
No Mamma No Pappa No Uncle Sam
Moody management does not give a Damn.

Out of service tags for use in store
No one knows where kept anymore
No Mamma No Pappa No Uncle Sam
Yellow tags do not give a Damn.

Buggy caused racket when tire broke away
Customer declined offer to switch and behave
No Mamma No Pappa No Uncle Sam
This buggy does not give a Damn.

Lowes uses blue because that to customers they do
Depot likes orange we crush ours too
No Mamma No Pappa No Uncle Sam
Blue or orange who gives a Damn.

Clint the skint sold two electric carts to another store
Now we have none that work anymore
No Mamma No Pappa No Uncle Sam
Past store manager Clint made bonus Damn.

Empty aisles can't say hi to customers on this stage
Silent cash registers moot to say hey or ease rage
No Mamma No Pappa No Uncle Sam
And say hey to Willie Mays Damn.

Brothers Grimm wrote tales galore
Grinning idiots make store bad sore
No Mamma No Pappa No Uncle Sam
Grimm does not give a Damn.

G means to greet after customers GOT
Engage and **Thank** to make them GIT
No Mamma No Pappa No Uncle Sam
GOT to GET then GIT Damn.

Bard called in when storms begin
Everyone called out in fear at their spin
No Mamma No Pappa No Uncle Sam
Storms do not give a Damn.

Sav in Garden loads customers then humors
Survivor of surgery for brain tumors
No Mamma No Pappa No Uncle Sam
Tumors and humors Damn.

Homer Fund fun for employees in need
When dollar match far from greed
No Mamma No Pappa No Uncle Sam
Dollar matches in Homer Fund give a Damn.

Amazing for worker bees to see Management that won't
Explain how to do what they have never done and don't
No Mamma No Pappa No Uncle Sam
Don't and won't do not give a Damn.

When a shooter comes act as band on the run
Hide and seek then fight as if this game for fun
No Mamma No Pappa No Uncle Sam
Paul McCartney does not give a Damn.

No turkey ever soars with an eagle
Home Depot prefers vultures and beagles
No Mamma No Pappa No Uncle Sam
Vultures never give a Damn.

Home Depot rarely rebuilds unlike Walmart
Dividends rise instead of buildings their art
No Mamma No Pappa No Uncle Sam
Stewart Saunders did same to N&W Damn.

PRO left for lunch declined to return on a hunch
Leaving Bob and one to manage PRO crunch
No Mamma No Pappa No Uncle Sam
PRO crunch does not give a Damn.

Criminal Disease Center run by Red Sinos and pharma
Stanford says engage in very bad mask karma
No Pappa No Mamma No Pappa No Uncle Sam
Masks bad says Stanford Damn.

Electric carts whisked out door
Fled to nearby store by customers bored
No Mamma No Pappa No Uncle Sam
Carts in nearby store do not give a Damn.

Keep April OK lest a return to Christy's way
Vertical at store versus horizontal at home all day
No Mamma No Pappa No Uncle Sam
And Self interest gives a Damn.

Customers come and go like Michelangelo
Hope like us more than big orange jello
No Mamma No Pappa No Uncle Sam
Michelangelo does not give a Damn.

Only two electric carts left for store
Neither hold charge much anymore
No Mamma No Pappa No Uncle Sam
Two or four who gives a Damn

Home Depot a consuming monster goon
Swept under rug with a big broom
No Mamma No Pappa No Uncle Sam
Monsters do not give a Damn.

Yellow SKU afflicted means Customer must wait
This of course way leighs and makes them late
No Mamma No Pappa No Uncle Sam
Way leighed do not give a Damn.

Customers filled Garden a spending orgy
Pending storms bought more for Porgy
No Mamma No Pappa No Uncle Sam
Porgy and Bess do not give a Damn.

Life goes on but does it matter
Mad hatters never end mindless chatter
No Mamma No Pappa No Uncle Sam
And this tea party does not give a Damn.

Hollowed by temper strawed by strife into flame
No past present nor future endless bits of same
No Mamma No Pappa and No Uncle Sam
T. S. Eliot does not give a Damn.

Fans on in Garden and YoYo frozen
Thawed when off and shelf broken
No Mamma No Pappa No Uncle Sam
Icicles make poor cashiers Damn.

They may say thank you but shall remember not
Better to have been given slop from chamber pot
No Mamma No Pappa No Uncle Sam
Who wants slop from a chamber pot Damn.

The snow fell and we were deplete
They brought us pizza so we could eat
No Mamma No Pappa and No Uncle Sam
And pizza caused us to give a Damn.

Amber blue and windblown in Garden cold
Lips bruised face red teeth chattering behold
No Mamma No Pappa No Uncle Sam
Amber too cold to give a Damn.

Savannah came to stay in front end
Works too provides fresh blend
No Mamma No Pappa No Uncle Sam
Savannah smiles and gives a Damn.

Sohrab and Ruston joined their saber stroke
Employee at work most always broke
No Pappa No Mamma No Pappa No Uncle Sam
Sohrab and Ruston don't give a Damn.

Joust and spar make happy through day
Customers like recognition in every play
No Mamma No Pappa No Uncle Sam
And you can help them give a Damn.

They circle like Musk Ox in heat
Wait their turn to speak
No Mamma No Pappa No Uncle Sam
And you think Musk Ox give a Damn.

Big Blue Lowes parked truck in Depot Lot
Confused customers about who was what
No Mamma No Pappa No Uncle Sam
Confused don't give a Damn.

We say Big Blue great store for trade
Customers snort do not make grade
No Mamma No Pappa No Uncle Sam
Even customers don't like Big Blue Damn.

Customer yelled at Christy for middle open
Given blessed day sent on way fully spoken
No Mamma No Pappa No Uncle Sam
Condescension does not give a Damn.

Pet friendly not always pretty
Spray waste and leave gritty
No Mamma no Pappa no Uncle Sam
Dogs and cats do not give a Damn

Fertilizer bag opened dripped over store
Long time to sweep mess off floor
No Mamma no Pappa No Uncle Sam
No one said thanks Damn.

Brought paint to pay today
Top fell away floored crimson way
No Mamma No Pappa No Uncle Sam
Crimson found clover on floor Damn.

0884 old and small against Lowes standing tall
They do two we do one for this reason Y'all
No Mamma No Pappa No Uncle Sam
Y'all give us a store and w'all win Damn.

All along the watchtower walked women too
Won't find that at this Depot zoo
No Mamma No Pappa No Uncle Sam
Hendrix does not give a Damn.

Three riders approached store
Wind began to howl opened door
No Mamma No Pappa No Uncle Sam
They definitely don't give a Damn.

Store dirt and gristle in lumber end
Carts froze up unable to spin
No Mamma No Pappa No Uncle Sam
Fewer carts less sales Damn.

Three sons of Japheth from Occident came
Why Home Depot has name and fame
No Mamma No Pappa No Uncle Sam
Japheth does not give a Damn.

The register freezes beyond reprieve grieve
Customer so mad could just heave
No Mamma No Pappa No Uncle Sam
This customer obscene did say Damn.

Washington Battle of Trenton came and went
Trent almost in splint because spent
No Mamma No Pappa No Uncle Sam
Washington does not give a Damn.

Overnight freight brought wood and drywall for more
Rather than stack or stockpiled on the floor
No Mamma No Pappa No Uncle Sam
Inventory abandoned does not give a Damn.

Returned from stay of his daughter's birth
Trent gave notice left Depot's berth
No Mamma No Pappa No Uncle Sam
Trent no longer gives a Damn.

Home Depot a wolf in lamb's clothing
No end to their wool or self loathing
No Mamma No Pappa No Uncle Sam
Wolves don't give a Damn.

Alex at station a fixture sensation
Who dares interrupt ear pod fascination
No Mamma No Pappa No Uncle Sam
Ear pods don't give a Damn.

Phyllis wonders and ponders across store wanders
When gone returns dazed to take ease maunder
No Mamma No Pappa No Uncle Sam
And they made her full time Damn.

Hunter the butterball rolls across floor
Works very well much adored
No Mamma No Pappa No Uncle Sam
This butterball gives a Damn.

Hunter comes to work no more
Left to find butter for his ball an endless chore
No Mamma No Pappa No Uncle Sam
Butterball turkeys frozen don't give a Damn.

Butterball and Christy did not make good history
Tried to cook on rotisserie
No Mamma No Pappa No Uncle Sam
And we lost a good employee Damn.

Graham more than cracker and milk
Training more likely G Man's ilk
No Mamma No Pappa No Uncle Sam
J Edgar does not give a Damn.

G Man gone far away from Depot stay
Army ordered play soldier their way
No Mamma No Pappa No Uncle Sam
Graham crackers and milk Damn.

G Man with crackers away returned to stay
Placed in receiving heaving hooray
No Mamma No Pappa No Uncle Sam
Great to see G Man back again Damn.

Dropping like flies encased in spray
Employees leaving every day
No Mamma No Pappa No Uncle Sam
Flies don't give a Damn.

Donna makes improvements to like
Dutch boy finger poked firmly in dike
No Mamma No Pappa No Uncle Sam
Donna finger stuck in dike Damn.

Cashier at attention like military detention
Customers wonder if need special attention
No Mamma No Pappa No Uncle Sam
Attention and detention don't give a Damn.

Three strips an hour in PRO shift
Home Depot appreciates newfound thrift
No Mamma No Pappa No Uncle Sam
And three strips who gives a Damn.

Sprinklers in Garden all set to proceed
One knocked in head must precede
No Mamma No Pappa No Uncle Sam
This head knocked does not give a Damn.

Associate in pain offered chair for bane
Orange flag on pole tin cup in hand shame
No Mamma No Pappa No Uncle Sam
Never gives a Damn.

Pennies matter more than math
No one can count their succotash
No Mamma No Pappa No Uncle Sam
Succotash does not give a Damn.

Customer service orders unfulfilled
No one in lumber enjoyed this drill
No Mamma No Pappa No Uncle Sam
Unfulfilled don't give a Damn.

Yellow tag declined to scan number concrete
Make customer wait for repeat this defeat
No Mamma No Pappa No Uncle Sam
Concrete and customer do not give a Damn.

Offer Card yellow tag HVAC service Crayola and survey
Customer crazed dazed hazed traumatized with scurvy
No Mamma No Pappa No Uncle Sam
Pity the customer Damn

Crayola colors encrypt receipt
Color and marks make romper room complete
No Mamma No Pappa No Uncle Sam
And you think Crayolas give a Damn

They call us in when games begin we slim
PRO overrun whole day to reclaim trim
No Mamma No Pappa No Uncle Sam
Slim does not give a Damn.

Brianna helped Garden in very fine way
Customers glad stayed to help their day
No Mamma No Pappa No Uncle Sam
Brianna gives a Damn.

Called needing more flat cars in Garden
Lot said too busy but had time to stew regarding
No Mamma No Pappa No Uncle Sam
Time to say you don't give a Damn.

Flowers made Christy happy today
Whole department smiled she walked away
No Mamma No Pappa No Uncle Sam
Department smiling does not give a Damn.

She moved to Paint and Flooring
You could hear their roar adoring
No Mamma No Pappa No Uncle Sam
Christy in Flooring may give a Damn.

Called ASM asked for some carts our way
Agreed but said too busy not today
No Mamma No Pappa No Uncle Sam
ASM and carts don't give a Damn.

Space heater placed on Orange Life bucket
Gee hangman's loop also above us
No Mamma No Pappa No Uncle Sam
Looks like they have a plan Damn.

When Ace had flooring always visible
Toted sales to front indivisible
No Mamma No Pappa No Uncle Sam
Ace raised the floor Damn.

Josh a Wolverine fan in land of the Tide
I am sure must feel he has died
No Mamma No Pappa No Uncle Sam
And the Buckeyes do not give a Damn.

Christy not following Ace's lead to succeed
Remains very much in Flooring need
No Mamma No Pappa No Uncle Sam
Christy needs to learn from Ace Damn.

Shylock and usury abound in store
Just use orange card on floor
No Mamma No Pappa No Uncle Sam
Shylock in Venice does not give a Damn.

Home Depot card commend as planned
Late fees and interest not banned
No Mamma No Pappa No Uncle Sam
Usury for free does not give a Damn.

Geeks and freaks along way
Home Depot horror show here to stay
No Mamma No Pappa No Uncle Sam
Freaks don't give a Damn.

Never ask why at Home Depot's show
If you do they teach not to know
No Mamma No Pappa No Uncle Sam
Depot does not give a Damn.

Strips not burlesque at good ole store 0884
Tubes tied but rarely used for cash anymore
No Mamma No Pappa No Uncle Sam
Burlesque does not give a Damn.

$1400 in cash drawer hardly hold more
50 twenties registered on Saturday floor
No Mamma No Pappa No Uncle Sam
No one gives a Damn.

No flat cars less buggies anywhere around Garden spot
How does customer carry their plants and pots
No Mamma No Pappa No Uncle Sam
No buggies no flat cars Damn.

No training for returns exchanges nor sales at other stores
Customer Service struggles when must do all and more
No Mamma No Pappa No Uncle Sam
And train cashiers to help Damn.

Asked for Tubes four times today received endless delay
Three hours later registers full no tubes great dismay
No Mamma No Pappa No Uncle Sam
Registers full and don't give a Damn.

Customer paid 50 twenties register filled a riddle
No tubes available carried cash from SCO to middle
No Mamma No Pappa No Uncle Sam
Tubes spend more time in vault than cash Damn.

Christy responded to Paint after a while
Excuses and blame made hostile
No Mamma No Pappa No Uncle Sam
Hostile does not give a Damn.

Home Depot pushes values a self-righteous clan
Please ignore avarice and greed behind scam
No Mamma No Pappa No Uncle Sam
Self righteous do not give a Damn.

Dan the man promised to break four hour stay
No way it happened closed Garden our way
No Mamma No Pappa No Uncle Sam
And they did not give a Damn.

Emily Bo Peep mashed schedule balloon face marooned
Switch in time place refined more attuned
No Mamma No Pappa No Uncle Sam
Marooned or attuned who gives a Damn

Creed easy to see when you think
Yours mine what is mine is mine do not blink
No Mamma No Pappa No Uncle Sam
Orange Life a Dead Sea scroll Damn.

Bard called in by Ashley to make ends meet
Autism in Lot Garden pot PRO slot incomplete
No Mamma No Pappa No Uncle Sam
Who gives a Damn.

How to fix store they sometimes want to say
Bulldozers employed might first be the way
No Mamma No Pappa No Uncle Sam
Start over and then maybe give a Damn.

Curtain torn very sad ruined Temple's day
At Home Depot more material for pay
No Mamma No Pappa No Uncle Sam
Curtain torn not worn Damn.

Josh demands we train humiliates names in posting
No schedule hosted only marshmallows roasting
No Mamma No Pappa No Uncle Sam
Roasted marshmallows do not give a Damn.

Orders not taken because customer mistaken on carriage and bolly
Forced Home Dept to make room for remains of their folly
No Mamma No Pappa No Uncle Sam
These customers simply don't give a Damn.

Area 51 quit today refused work for no reason
Need to execute an exorcism on this treason
No Mamma No Pappa No Uncle Sam
Area 51 does not give a Damn.

Area 51 made cash go away 52 followed soon
Three days before repairs can fix boom
No Mamma No Pappa No Uncle Sam
ET does not give a Damn.

Donna brings pad and paper for shifts more
Need jobs and shifts filled all over store
No Mamma No Pappa No Uncle Sam
What is happening in this store Damn.

Chance had little stayed to finish
Four already by schedule burned and blemished
No Mamma No Pappa No Uncle Sam
They burn them like candles at both ends Damn.

Bard and Olive only cashiers this night
Appears all others took flight
No Mamma No Pappa No Uncle Sam
As usual no one else gives a Damn.

Our lights dim because don't
Light off at register won't
No Mamma No Pappa No Uncle Sam
No one to bring us light Damn.

Andrea yet another cashier newbie
Showed thing or two register beauty
No Mamma No Pappa No Uncle Sam
Coverage thin she at SCO Damn.

At this store stand around
Seek nickel that fell to ground
No Mamma No Pappa No Uncle Sam
Wooden nickels do not give a Damn.

Josh did not let Ashley have interview or say
Associate deserves even when no way
No Mamma No Pappa No Uncle Sam
Josh tells employees pound sand Damn.

Leg in cramp called in to help toe line
Scrunched in pain worked did not feel fine
No Mamma No Pappa No Uncle Sam
Cramped and swollen leg does not give a Damn.

A haughty spirit before a fall pride to destruction
Store 0884 ready for approaching humiliation
No Mamma No Pappa No Uncle Sam
After destruction who will give a Damn.

1984 had tele on forced to view
Home Depot attended this school too
No Mamma No Pappa No Uncle Sam
And Orwell knew of Depot too Damn.

Store more call-outs than drop-ins
No quorum close store or catch bends
No Mamma No Pappa No Uncle Sam
No quorum says they don't give a Damn.

Sylvia blue as sea in storm made her stun
Bob leaving has left all training undone
No Mamma No Pappa No Uncle Sam
Bob left and does not give a Damn.

Ashley came to interview but Josh said no
Happy Birthday Ashley feel free to go
No Mamma No Pappa No Uncle Sam
Once again they do not give a Damn.

Christy told Bard no longer in play
Paint and Flooring headed her way
No Mamma No Pappa No Uncle Sam
Paint and Flooring getting Christy Damn.

Promoted from FES after missing 14 straight
Told Josh had to go through swinging gate
No Mamma No Pappa No Uncle Sam
Promote them for not coming to work Damn.

Ugly false rumors about Josh and Christy tales
No one can see through fog nor read entrails
No Mamma No Pappa No Uncle Sam
Tales squashed rightly so Damn.

Christy returned to Decatur from Florence
Denied disability from injury assigned torrents
No Mamma No Pappa No Uncle Sam
Christy lost position as ASM Damn.

Failed to return protect ASM position
Did not go back there even in remission
No Mamma No Pappa No Uncle Sam
Christy surrendered hard-earned position Damn.

Corporate sent Josh to Decatur not because succeeding
More like bleeding or possibly just career receding
No Mamma No Pappa No Uncle Sam
And you think anyone gives a Damn.

Josh to Decatur again over Christy
Hope both exist wistfully
No Mamma No Pappa No Uncle Sam
Just a job to do Damn.

0884 a graveyard for management types
Where sent when fail or get yipes
No Mamma No Pappa No Uncle Sam
Exit means exit and does not give a Damn.

Who knows what happened today much less then
All may be but vapors and whim
No Mamma No Pappa No Uncle Sam
Vapors and whims who gives a Damn.

Two hired then three fired in Lot
No wonder it has gone to pot
No Mamma No Pappa No Uncle Sam
Corral rodeos are not worth a Damn.

Lot a sea of pillage and plunder
Victim of more scheduling blunders
No Mamma No Pappa No Uncle Sam
Lot fled Sodom Damned.

Blanca moved near flooring Christy not adoring
Now maybe will walk plank mooring
No Mamma No Pappa No Uncle Sam
Blanca moved to rear Damn.

Stocking merchandise art rarely perfected
Customers ignore until half empty selected
No Mamma No Pappa No Uncle Sam
If shelf full customer does not give a Damn.

Please Mr. Custer I don't wanna go muster
At this store more like fall of Usher
No Mamma No Pappa No Uncle Sam
Custer does not give a Damn.

Christy's son never in store seen
Hard to know what means
No Mamma No Pappa No Uncle Sam
Family rarely comes to store for anyone Damn.

Thanksgiving for Depot at least
Preludes Black Friday greedy feast
No Mamma No Pappa No Uncle Sam
Greed never says thanks Damn.

Donna muses to Amber Christy reached climax
Fire or move her adopted Imax
No Mamma No Pappa No Uncle Sam
Imax does not give a Damn.

Sunday shift left April astray
No one wanted to come in for pay
No Mamma No Pappa No Uncle Sam
Sunday and no one gives a Damn.

Rube Goldberg in Garden seeking no pardon
Wired lawnmower with register really no bargain
No Mamma No Pappa No Uncle Sam
Rube does not give a Damn.

Eighty year old strayed across parking lot
Hit by car flown away nearly funeral pot
No Mamma No Pappa No Uncle Sam
And profit before safety Damn.

Concern over Alex being stalked
Sent another to Garden she balked
No Mamma No Pappa No Uncle Sam
Alex wanted to be alone Damn.

Little Christy clapped like a seal in heat
When learned of Christy's final retreat
No Mamma No Pappa No Uncle Sam
Even trained seals do not give a Damn.

Christy leaving a relief to front end
Flooring and Paint next to watch ascend
No Mamma No Pappa No Uncle Sam
Ascend or descend who gives a Damn.

Saturday schedule changed with another
Rain and storm coming oh brother
No Mamma No Pappa No Uncle Sam
And we will need snorkels in Garden Damn.

Lights in Garden on at dark or at least supposed to
Very hard to see light in this shift through
No Mamma No Pappa No Uncle Sam
Lighting does not give a Damn.

On Sunday day opened register in PRO
$2,000 and more unguarded had go
No Mamma No Pappa No Uncle Sam
No Tubes no strips and no one gives a Damn.

New lighting overhead winks and blinks
Robbers know who where on brink
No Mamma No Pappa No Uncle Sam
And lowers power bill Damn.

Jim skins 'em says let 'em go
Christy go became woe we all know
No Mamma No Pappa No Uncle Sam
Jim Skinner and Ford do not give a Damn.

Bob met Lisa after Lana and Mitch served Ham with Mac
Who would want to invite this group back
No Mamma No Pappa No Uncle Sam
Bob Carol Ted and Alice do not live in this store Damn.

Hire new cashiers dump on April
No training no prep throw on floor make fatal
No Mamma No Pappa No Uncle Sam
Push them out and bring them in Damn.

Cashier in middle backed up not enjoying fate
Why not reduce line by opening SCO gate
No Mamma No Pappa No Uncle Sam
And process customer as needed Damn.

Customer in heat hard to sweeten
Get them gone before beaten
No Mamma No Pappa No Uncle Sam
Some customers slam because they can Damn.

Christmas season comes once a year
Home Depot must close did you hear
No Mamma No Pappa No Uncle Sam
And forget Hanukkah Damn.

Hindenburg at Elmhurst met fate
Another missed sale for Depot too late
No Mamma No Pappa No Uncle Sam
Hindenburg does not give a Damn.

Keeping store closing to 9 a perfect time
In Decatur roll up sidewalks into a dime
No Mamma No Pappa No Uncle Sam
And no one is out at 9 Damn.

Home Depot never wastes disaster
Great way to increase profit thereafter
No Mamma No Pappa No Uncle Sam
Home Depot makes sure disasters give a Damn.

A goat entered finding new wonders explore
Head butts and kicks followed through store
No Mamma No Pappa No Uncle Sam
Goats may Billy but never give a Damn.

Inventory has story to tell
Charge up write off ring bell
No Mamma No Pappa No Uncle Sam
Charged off inventory does not give a Damn.

Dog entered walked over floor then exited
Looking for cat to act as second
No Mamma No Pappa No Uncle Sam
This dog knew how to give a Damn.

PA announces customers must wear mask
Since when did store have authority for such task
No Mamma No Pappa No Uncle Sam
PA does not give a Damn.

Asked for cash for match in Homer Fund
No checks nor cards less than $500 max no fun
No Mamma No Pappa No Uncle Sam
And you cannot help an associate Damn.

Store may expand to ten from nine
Rubber band broken left behind
No Mamma No Pappa No Uncle Sam
Empty store does not give a Damn.

Other stores open to ten what a mess
For us stay at nine best
No Mamma No Pappa No Uncle Sam
Decatur closed Damn.

Bard a gun retired for when things unwired
Bring in extinguish fire
No Mamma No Pappa No Uncle Sam
Fire extinguished Damn.

Training ever ongoing must pass outgoing
When system fails remain unknowing
No Mamma No Pappa No Uncle Sam
Outgoing unknowing ongoing who gives a Damn.

Double training cut sites in half
Complain not acting in their behalf
No Mamma No Pappa No Uncle Sam
Training does not give a Damn.

Plastic bags all in a row simply for show
Thinner than nylons split half in two oh no
No Mamma No Pappa No Uncle Sam
Kroger bags work and do give a Damn.

They don't come to work when weather bad
They won't come to work when weather good
No Mamma No Pappa No Uncle Sam
The Good Bad and Ugly do not give a Damn.

Two thieves store closed did not leave
Home Depot gave them reprieve
No Mamma No Pappa No Uncle Sam
Thieves surrounded don't give a Damn.

Propane exchange empty for thee
Remainder under strict lock and key
No Mamma No Pappa No Uncle Sam
Gas hisses and passes but gives no Damn.

Batteries and cokes for folks handily
It seems neither stocked steadily
No Mamma No Pappa No Uncle Sam
Blokes and cokes don't give a Damn.

Customers follow Bard through store to register
Always provides good cheer cerebral hemisphere
No Mamma No Pappa No Uncle Sam
Cerebral Hemisphere may give a Damn.

Vendors block Garden all through day
Why not come in eve then stay
No Mamma No Pappa No Uncle Sam
Vendors unloading in eve would give a Damn.

Chips and candy too rarely seen
Boaz for Ruth leaves little to glean
No Mamma No Pappa No Uncle Sam
Boaz and Ruth do not give a Damn.

Six days on the road gonna make it home tonight
Long hours on floor tests all one's might
No Mamma No Pappa No Uncle Sam
Feeling alright but don't give a Damn.

Drums keep pounding rhythm to make us leap
Registers take in more and more as we reap
No Mamma No Pappa No Uncle Sam
Sony and Cher do not give a Damn.

Management throws bones for customers to chew
Associates bones thrown seen through
No Mamma No Pappa No Uncle Sam
And these bones do not give a Damn.

Snafu the accomplished way in this zoo
Managed so well all now cuckoo
No Mamma No Pappa No Uncle Sam
Cuckoos don't give a Damn.

Stimulus checks sure bet
Depot competes with Starbucks no regret
No Mamma No Pappa No Uncle Sam
Starbucks does not give a Damn.

Wheelbarrows chained never free
Manager usually has lost key
No Mamma No Pappa No Uncle Sam
Wheelbarrows don't give a Damn.

Easter eve no reprieve
Open Easter morn gentile ease
No Mamma No Pappa No Uncle Sam
Money changers don't give a Damn.

Milwaukee tool sale and banner for all to see
Unable to ring up cover with placard glee
No Mamma No Pappa No Uncle Sam
Placard and glee do not give a Damn.

Many on Easter did not come in
On Monday we took it on shin
No Mamma No Pappa No Uncle Sam
The road to Emmaus does not give a Damn.

Scheduled three days they want three more
Schedule two because they do voyeur
No Mamma No Pappa No Uncle Sam
Two three or four who gives a Damn

Woman run over flown to hospital not neo natal
Operating table brain bleeding not stable
No Mamma No Pappa No Uncle Sam
Skull removed who gives a Damn.

Crime scene tape from accident lined garbage today
Relatives appeared wanted video replay
No Mamma No Pappa No Uncle Sam
And now they give a Damn.

This Home Depot rot for customer slop
Housekeeping and cleaning have gone to pot
No Mamma No Pappa No Uncle Sam
Slop and pot may rot but do not give a Damn.

Clean store when area managers wander in
Slop orange lipstick on pig for them
No Mamma No Pappa No Uncle Sam
Who wants to kiss this pig Damn.

Area Manager today Christy stayed away
No role to play for visit all day
No Mamma No Pappa No Uncle Sam
And who in these gives a Damn

Red Virus name Depot loves to say
Ever increasing sales and profit this way
No Mamma No Pappa No Uncle Sam
These lies do not give a Damn.

Called awesome by Ashley during shift
Thanked for making sure do not drift
No Mamma No Pappa No Uncle Sam
Ashley appreciates and gives a Damn.

Front end of old 0884 owns a record none dare repeat
No functioning FSE three years straight complete
No Mamma No Pappa No Uncle Sam
No functioning FSE and they don't give a Damn.

April pitched fit over Garden slum
Those that leave in mess beaten like a drum
No Mamma No Pappa No Uncle Sam
Clean up Garden and give a Damn.

Housekeeping practice rarely seen anymore
Whoever looks at mess on floor
No Mamma No Pappa No Uncle Sam
A pigsty barn and no one gives a Damn.

Employee Lot vacant means few in store
No quorum found anywhere on floor
No Mamma No Pappa No Uncle Sam
No quorum no service and who gives a Damn.

Christy to Garden from Flooring for Bard a break
Nothing to say treated him as lint to flake
No Mamma No Pappa No Uncle Sam
Thanks for the memories Christy Damn.

Sunday morn managers take warn at eve take leave
Leaving others to audit money received
No Mamma No Pappa No Uncle Sam
Morn and eve don't give a Damn.

Home Depot rich young ruler
Unwilling to study under sage or tutor
No Mamma No Pappa No Uncle Sam
Alexander and Aristotle do not give a Damn.

Something this way wicked comes
At Home Depot beat drums twist thumbs
No Mamma No Pappa No Uncle Sam
Wicked does not give a Damn.

Emily Bo Peep in a great way today
Helps entire store to make hay
No Mamma No Pappa No Uncle Sam
Great to have Bo Peep happy Damn.

Byzantine maze endless paralysis
No one thinks or acts zealous
No Mamma No Pappa No Uncle Sam
Byzantium does not give a Damn.

Customers to Associates ceaselessly swore
Police called to escort them out the door
No Mamma No Pappa No Uncle Sam
And police on floor did give a Damn.

They make us empty SCO machines
Force them to spill all their beans
No Mamma No Pappa No Uncle Sam
Spilt beans don't give a Damn.

Shields in Garden broken as jagged glass crashed
Unsafe for eight months before cashed
No Mamma No Pappa No Uncle Sam
Crashed glass does not give a Damn.

Chris Sullins liked the interview
Appreciated answers gave an interlude
No Mamma No Pappa No Uncle Sam
This interview gives a Damn.

Sullins later accosted for statement
Threatened to be sent to basement
No Mamma No Pappa No Uncle Sam
Chris had to protect his job and family Damn.

Marcus in Lot worked to clean mess from the day
Customers helped corrals cleaned flat cars back in play
No Mamma No Pappa No Uncle Sam
This Marcus gives a Damn.

Marcus walked into Lot and stayed in truck
Home Depot never to pay him another buck
No Mamma No Pappa No Uncle Sam
This Marcus no Aurelius gone Damn.

Entered store no one in paint SCO or middle
Called manager asked to answer riddle
No Mamma No Pappa No Uncle Sam
Shrinkage out the door wide open Damn.

Middle and SCO abandoned no one in Paint to see
Customer approached unaproned Bard to leave
No Mamma No Pappa No Uncle Sam
Apron on apron off who gives a Damn

Self-esteem usuallyabsent in this store
Employees need much much more
No Mamma No Pappa No Uncle Sam
Low self-esteem employees don't give a Damn.

Walmart provides same-day service and product delivery
Home Depot stores wonder what is in truck livery
No Mamma No Pappa No Uncle Sam
Walmart delivers and Home Depot does not give a Damn.

Called manager about safety with forklift
Told to take over cliff
No Mamma No Pappa No Uncle Sam
And you think safety gives a Damn.

Christy in Paint this Saturday slamming lids much to say
Some flooring out door helped make pay
No Mamma No Pappa No Uncle Sam
Christy liked mixing paint Damn

Area 51 on SCO floor rules over 52 and more
Halts front end moor blocks door
No Mamma No Pappa No Uncle Sam
Area 51 rules because it can wham!

Christy corralled by Flooring all through day
Cornered Associate family pics made him pay
No Mamma No Pappa No Uncle Sam
This cornered Associate does not give a Damn.

Knock knock knock on Heaven's Door for Christy Paint
Customers know must act like saints
No Mamma No Pappa No Uncle Sam
Bob Dylan does not give a Damn.

Mouse ran across Locker room floor
Ran under fridge like it a door
No Mamma No Pappa No Uncle Sam
Of mice and men who gives a Damn

Convinced customer to use check
System made pain in neck
No Mamma No Pappa No Uncle Sam
And it was only a check Damn.

Eight dead in Indianapolis Fed Ex shooting
Unarmed unprotected next for looting
No Mamma No Pappa No Uncle Sam
Disarmed and don't give a Damn.

Barcodes missing or astray in various ways
Cashier must find new ballets for pay
No Mamma No Pappa No Uncle Sam
Cashiers not ballerinas Damn.

Health plan for employees not a rave more like a grave
High deductibles and copays make them slaves
No Mamma No Pappa No Uncle Sam
This health plan does not give a Damn.

Store 0884 like a chocolate chip cookie
Control the chip and rest Ka bookie
No Mamma No Pappa No Uncle Sam
We dropped our cookie oh Damn.

Time clock snarled would not unlock
Reset waving a Bloch
No Mamma No Pappa No Uncle Sam
Bloch made timeclock hold up hands Damn.

Customer had yellow SKU that said $9.92
Sign said a penny would do
No Mamma No Pappa No Uncle Sam
This hotrod Lincoln does not give a Damn.

No coverage in lumber PRO Millwork and more
Gee does anyone really work in this abandoned store
No Mamma No Pappa No Uncle Sam
Abandoned does not give a Damn.

Catch-22 run amok leave nothing lots of luck
No budget no change Yassarian better duck
No Mamma No Pappa No Uncle Sam
Catch-22 does not give a Damn.

Call for aid reached Bean Counter
Demanded what three already bantered
No Mamma No Pappa No Uncle Sam
Who in this wasteland gives a Damn.

Span of control does not exist in this store
When doors open customers pour onto floor
No Mamma No Pappa No Uncle Sam
Victor Charlie overruns ARVIN Damn.

Two cashiers dismayed called Bard for help
Solved problem without a yelp
No Mamma No Pappa No Uncle Sam
For them Bard gives a Damn.

Dan asked Bard to work two only took one
Explained to Roland why not present when done
No Mamma No Pappa No Uncle Sam
Work one and don't give a Damn.

Dan left Bard in Garden during frozen sun
Wanted Bard to relish all the fun
No Mamma No Pappa No Uncle Sam
Frozen sun not fun Dan Damn.

Wind blew hard from north through tunnel in Garden
Nature had in mind to not give a pardon
No Mamma No Pappa No Uncle Sam
And plants frozen do not give a Damn.

Customer sought tool chest up high on shelf
Tried to climb and scale using self help
No Mamma No Pappa No Uncle Sam
Climbers do not give a Damn.

Ace in flooring sat out front and bargained
Christy needs to sharpen or face another Argand
No Mamma No Pappa No Uncle Sam
Christy needs to be in that seat Damn.

Blanca sent from customer service restoring
Christy said no way John took her outpouring
No Mamma No Pappa No Uncle Sam
Christy knows Blanca all too well Damn.

Congratulated before John for move to new mooring
Startled and flinched looked pinched not adoring
No Mamma No Pappa No Uncle Sam
And win Blanca with kindness Damn.

New lights in Garden much brighter in bargain
No longer ask for customer pardon
No Mamma No Pappa No Uncle Sam
We can sell those coal lamps now Damn.

Called in by Isaac on Saturday Eve
Asked to take leave he agreed relieved
No Mamma No Pappa No Uncle Sam
Isaac gave a Damn.

No HC on floor when cashiers arrive
Phyllis attempted to keep hive alive
No Mamma No Pappa No Uncle Sam
Queen bee required or hive dies Damn.

Stood on drywall pallet to view timber way above reach
Avoided both injury and welt no Associate to screech
No Mamma No Pappa No Uncle Sam
No one there to give a Damn.

Cashier on phone wanting to discount damaged cement
Bard helped overcome this terrible lament
No Mamma No Pappa No Uncle Sam
This cashier learned to give a Damn.

When store hot and hard to breathe
Customers seek cooler reprieve
No Mamma No Pappa No Uncle Sam
No air conditioning and contempt Damn.

Brought in buggies while not on clock
Thanked for all that you do around the block
No Mamma No Pappa No Uncle Sam
At least they noticed Damn.

Phyllis made cashier of the month not to demean
Melanin age and gender make almost obscene
No Mamma No Pappa No Uncle Sam
You can't make this up Damn.

Wasco tried to help in Garden with register
Did not last long fled non-sequitur
No Mamma No Pappa No Uncle Sam
Wasco learned what lines mean Damn.

Cashier stuck in mud customer rubbed
Void and give to one that does not flub
No Mamma No Pappa No Uncle Sam
Stay out of the mud Damn.

One cold day sent to Garden for pay
Irrigation leaked flooded the way
No Mamma No Pappa No Uncle Sam
Space heater in water's way Damn.

Management and half the store had Red virus
Wear those masks stay apart in this crisis
No Mamma No Pappa No Uncle Sam
Red Chinese virus does not give a Damn.

James moved carts helped customers relieve
Moved garbage from front to back receive
No Mamma No Pappa No Uncle Sam
And the autistic do give a Damn.

Brought buggies to Garden when asked one day
Grabbed customer unheeded made his play
No Mamma No Pappa No Uncle Sam
James gives a Damn.

Rug used to wipe feet position Lot enjoyed
Cashier gum on foot of management deployed
No Mamma No Pappa No Uncle Sam
Rugs and gum do not give a Damn.

Barcodes covered with stickers
Freight loves to snicker
No Mamma No Pappa No Uncle Sam
Barcodes covered do not give a Damn.

Transparency light onto truth beyond reproof
At Depot little more than fiddler on roof
No Mamma No Pappa No Uncle Sam
Fiddler on the Roof does not give a Damn.

No one in paint today number not working
Called Christy asked for help no lurking
No Mamma No Pappa No Uncle Sam
Stop the excuses Christy who cares Damn.

Too many in building full of why not
Lack any semblance of want or hot shot
No Mamma No Pappa No Uncle Sam
Why not does not give a Damn.

Garden closed with more customers entering gate
Simply did not have coverage to wait
No Mamma No Pappa No Uncle Sam
No coverage and don't give a Damn.

Bids fly into store with ease
Like to nest and rest as may please
No Mamma No Pappa No Uncle Sam
Birds of a feather do not give a Damn.

There is no me in team they say
Forgot the M&E or so believed
No Mamma No Pappa No Uncle Sam
M&E do not give a Damn.

Want three cashiers in Garden to process customers
Three lines create more problems for others
No Mamma No Pappa No Uncle Sam
Three lines in Garden create risk Damn.

Rains came ending drought string
Pots flew in wind without much strain
No Mamma No Pappa No Uncle Sam
Rain and wind do not give a Damn.

Sprinkler system never activated
Best hope no smoke nor fire agitated
No Mamma No Pappa No Uncle Sam
Fire next time and insurance says Damn.

Bathrooms in Red China not very nice
At Home Depot similarly suffice
No Mamma No Pappa No Uncle Sam
Third world bathrooms who gives a Damn.

Bags and goods from Red China in rush
Uyghurs on harvest row make stuff now hush
No Mamma No Pappa No Uncle Sam
Slave labor and Home Depot do not give a Damn.

Asked to change Sunday schedule to quell rebels
Increased from four to six without becoming disheveled
No Mamma No Pappa No Uncle Sam
April said awesome Damn.

Red China's flag red and yellow
Home Depot mixes to make orange be mellow
No Mamma No Pappa No Uncle Sam
Red orange and yellow who gives a Damn.

Voice of Associate dismayed stilted wick with pox
Not one shot at truth from twisted vox
No Mamma No Pappa No Uncle Sam
VOA does not give Damn.

Depot has brown in color scheme
Do not get obscene about this meme
No Mamma No Pappa No Uncle Sam
You think brown gives a Damn.

Red virus attacks obese leaving very few for work feast
Home office says go health department says no not in least
No Mamma No Pappa No Uncle Sam
Obese on meds do not give a Damn.

Customer cursed over treatment and billing
We had to do a lot of back filling
No Mamma No Pappa No Uncle Sam
Own it and give a Damn.

Feedback loops rarely used at this Depot store
Nor chain of command deaf dumb blind and more
No Mamma No Pappa No Uncle Sam
Three Blind Mice do not give a Damn.

Garden written off like Black hole of Calcutta
No manager dares go there Siberia in Russia
No Mamma No Pappa No Uncle Sam
Black hole does not give a Damn.

Birds fly in again and again all over store
One perched over register stared at floor
No Mamma No Pappa No Uncle Sam
Alfred Hitchcock and feathered friends do not give a Damn.

Park where they do because they choose
Often rude and crude when they do
No Mamma No Pappa No Uncle Sam
These customers do not give a Damn.

Depot often treats employees like serfs
Customers ask why on earth do we have no worth
No Mamma No Pappa No Uncle Sam
Serfs do not give a Damn.

Customers and grace have much in common
Depot and employees rarely awesome
No Mamma No Pappa No Uncle Sam
And they don't give a Damn.

Bard came in to do his training
Called back again because raining
No Mamma No Pappa No Uncle Sam
And Bard delivers the mail Damn.

Spigots broke in Garden house main no hose end
Associates cannot even begin to bring water in
No Mamma No Pappa No Uncle Sam
No water no judgment and don't give a Damn.

Olive spied customer at closing did not grieve
Gave help so he could leave
No Mamma No Pappa No Uncle Sam
Olive Oil looking for Popeye gives a Damn.

A three bus week for store hire more
Most flee before end spring war
No Mamma No Pappa No Uncle Sam
Raw recruits not trained and who gives a Damn.

Phyllis spied by Olive acting insane
Reported told to ignore same
No Mamma No Pappa No Uncle Sam
Phyllis full-time insane Damn.

Customers broke and phones died
No one available to help turn tide
No Mamma No Pappa No Uncle Sam
And riptide does not give a Damn.

Homer Fund for employees in need
Wages reduced by corporate greed
No Mamma No Pappa No Uncle Sam
Homer Fund would like to give a Damn.

They tried displays for store to go fore with more
Finished blemish looked more like a sore
No Mamma No Pappa No Uncle Sam
Sore displays do not give a Damn.

They say love and relate
Why then hate and replace
No Mamma No Pappa No Uncle Sam
Hate and replace do not give a Damn.

Customer run over in lot no one answered call
Christy not believe Management dropped ball
No Mamma No Pappa No Uncle Sam
Fumble fumble fumble stumble don't give a Damn.

Pallets of drywall laid across way
Aisles blocked by stay entire day
No Mamma No Pappa No Uncle Sam
Drywall does not give a Damn.

Jaundice everywhere even on yellow tags seen
Hollowed and gaunt almost obscene
No Mamma No Pappa No Uncle Sam
Jaundice does not give a Damn.

Bounty mutiny cursed by many
Home Depot keeps with skinny
No Mamma No Pappa No Uncle Sam
Nordhoff Bounty does not give a Damn.

Safety priority when marketable
Doing what right only when profitable
No Mamma No Pappa No Uncle Sam
Mammon does not give a Damn.

Hose turned on in Garden during day
Sav jumped into puddle to play
No Mamma No Pappa No Uncle Sam
Grown kids playing in puddles Damn.

They share success orange green yellow and blue
Disease Famine Pestilence and Death ride too
No Mamma No Pappa No Uncle Sam
Four Horsemen don't give a Damn.

Donna passes through looking for many
Store wants to relocate all over plenty
No Mamma No Pappa No Uncle Sam
Why moving all over store Damn.

Clock strikes nine almost through
Time to tell customers shoo
No Mamma No Pappa No Uncle Sam
They had fifteen hours Damn.

Inventory a subject of scorn and wrath
Items gone numbers wrong do math
No Mamma No Pappa No Uncle Sam
Ghostly inventory does not give a Damn.

A friend and son came to Phyllis creating huge chore
Asked to discount damaged door apply for card more
No Mamma No Pappa No Uncle Sam
Phyllis flipped out but Emily fixed Damn.

A magician with tricks Christy keying locks
Almost matches dread red hair shlock
No Mamma No Pappa No Uncle Sam
And who is in Paint or Flooring Damn.

Forklift abandoned along lumber way
Customers climb over to get bays
No Mamma No Pappa No Uncle Sam
Abandoned forklifts don't give a Damn.

Bard bounced from Orange E system
Truth really would not listen
No Mamma No Pappa No Uncle Sam
Fired or hired Damn.

Management pumps front end higher
Hard to fix this flat tire
No Mamma No Pappa No Uncle Sam
And like a soufflé fallen this tire Damn.

OSB board placed outside no place inside
Thieves may come after hours to reside
No Mamma No Pappa No Uncle Sam
OSB made easy to steal Damn.

Provided cookies for day shift today
Walmart marked down to give away
No Mamma No Pappa No Uncle Sam
Cheap cookies do not give a Damn.

In lot Drugs or women bought and sold
Drunk asleep in shed like horse and foal
No Mamma No Pappa No Uncle Sam
Home Depot card not accepted on this lot Damn.

Spider alarm remover gone from PRO
No way to make these webs go
No Mamma No Pappa No Uncle Sam
And again who gives a Damn.

Amber came to whine not relieve nor release
No one will listen except Bard to please
No Mamma No Pappa No Uncle Sam
Whine does not give a Damn.

Pipes in plumbing fittings in Garden
Hard to explain beg customer pardon
No Mamma No Pappa No Uncle Sam
Pipes and fixtures don't give a Damn.

Fired two today for their behavior
Stayed in car to talk to their tailor
No Mamma No Pappa No Uncle Sam
They did not give a Damn.

Two in Garden on display in play
One alone in PRO found way
No Mamma No Pappa No Uncle Sam
Pro and Garden don't give a Damn.

Overhead wailed for load help in Garden
No one gave farthing to harken
No Mamma No Pappa No Uncle Sam
Overhead speakers are worthless Damn.

Little Christy cashier sight to behold
An English teapot at teatime she goes
No Mamma No Pappa No Uncle Sam
And this spewing teapot gives a Damn.

Home Alone movie way back in day
At Home Depot another burden in way
No Mamma No Pappa No Uncle Sam
Home Depot Alone does not give a Damn.

Lights dim at end do not extend
Customers know to go woe to end
No Mamma No Pappa No Uncle Sam
Closing time does not give a Damn.

No god but Mammon Depot contrived
Makes hard for employee to stay alive
No Mamma No Pappa No Uncle Sam
Don't kneel before Mammon Damn.

Shazam Shazam Shazam Gomer Pyle did say
At Depot never managed this way
No Mamma No Pappa No Uncle Sam
Shazam does not give a Damn.

Two cashiers on display in Garden way
No Garden support vendors abort customer stay
No Mamma No Pappa No Uncle Sam
Customers waiting in Garden Damn.

Seven for Garden to cover customer needs
Removed all customers grieve
No Mamma No Pappa No Uncle Sam
No Garden support and no one gives a Damn.

Melanie HR squared grabbed register in Garden
No one else around made less spartan
No Mamma No Pappa No Uncle Sam
One alone did give a Damn.

April and Bard discussed Garden snafu
Agreed there to see it through
No Mamma No Pappa No Uncle Sam
And at least one in Garden will give a Damn.

Customers wait endlessly because Depot acts stupidly
Depot no coverage to process Garden repeatedly
No Mamma No Pappa No Uncle Sam
Stupid does not give a Damn.

Let's go places Toyota says in auto spaces
Took Bob away credit spacious
No Mamma No Pappa No Uncle Sam
Bob left for Toyota Damn.

April stressed fighting battles for service one way
Bard suggested step away use as prey
No Mamma No Pappa No Uncle Sam
Bard not watching April stress and fail Damn.

Call two numbers no one home put ASM on phone
Lot called out number kaput alone
No Mamma No Pappa No Uncle Sam
Communicate coordinate who gives a Damn.

When in Garden test numbers find aprons that roam
No coverage no numbers lock gate go home
No Mamma No Pappa No Uncle Sam
A locked gate is not great Damn.

A hump trips unwary cashier oh dear
Two mats masking tape make unclear
No Mamma No Pappa No Uncle Sam
Mats and tape do not give a Damn.

Interviewed for part-time HC to help April
Need to support never ungrateful
No Mamma No Pappa No Uncle Sam
Bard wants tools to support April Damn.

Register in Garden had no money
Customers really thought a bit funny
No Mamma No Pappa No Uncle Sam
No money in the drawer and no one gives a Damn.

Retired newbie in hardware looking for more
Close then opened learned dread said no more
No Mamma No Pappa No Uncle Sam
Close then open who gives a Damn.

Associates employees with names to hear
To management nothing but numbers to smear
No Mamma No Pappa No Uncle Sam
Humans as numbers do not give a Damn.

Depot believes employees but numbers
Inventory with blood encumbers
No Mamma No Pappa No Uncle Sam
People inventory Damn.

They reward us with green yellow and blue
Most simply no clue working in this zoo
No Mamma No Pappa No Uncle Sam
And their reward does not give a Damn.

Green for success yellow for spending blue all too true
Orange left why we are code blue
No Mamma No Pappa No Uncle Sam
Success sharing hardly worth a Damn.

Phyllis frenzied over break forgotten and late lunch
Declined to divulge schedule when asked by a bunch
No Mamma No Pappa No Uncle Sam
Phyllis pre-Alzheimer's and no one gives a Damn.

Olive agreed Phyllis' act insane
When reported and witnessed again shamed
No Mamma No Pappa No Uncle Sam
And again Phyllis full-time Damn.

Management execution favored by many
Cannot manage Cokes in coolers any
No Mamma No Pappa No Uncle Sam
No Cokes in coolers Damn.

During Spring rush one cashier moved to freight
No one to replace our fate isn't great
No Mamma No Pappa No Uncle Sam
Freight does not give a Damn.

Two cashiers in Garden make a mind-boggling jam clogging
Customers stuck orders unpulled vendors carts blogging
No Mamma No Pappa No Uncle Sam
Garden gridlocked and no one gives a Damn.

They leave stakes at Garden front door
Customer free to trip and impale on floor
No Mamma No Pappa No Uncle Sam
Stake through the heart Damn.

Told April about Garden concerns and meeting
Did not want boss to have any loss greeting
No Mamma No Pappa No Uncle Sam
And just give a Damn.

Scanner will not pass through warranty screen
Makes cashier leery customers scream
No Mamma No Pappa No Uncle Sam
More garbage that delays from Atlanta Damn.

Cashier brings in twenty-five carts
Far more remain on lot so have a heart
No Mamma No Pappa No Uncle Sam
Carts in lot do not give a Damn.

Cheap geld in Orange Land
More important than making brand
No Mamma No Pappa No Uncle Sam
Cheap is cheap not a brand Damn.

A tornado hit Lumber today mess in every way
Jetsam and flotsam with no one to say
No Mamma No Pappa No Uncle Sam
Jetsam flotsam who gives a Damn.

Olive wanted Bard to have break but only two
No one to help either until shift through
No Mamma No Pappa No Uncle Sam
At least Olive gave a Damn.

Days on end many decline to come and join in
Miss their role in fun and games that never end
No Mamma No Pappa No Uncle Sam
And for this alone the Bard comes in Damn.

On cue no Hardware nor Lot for evening time slot
Thanks a Lot for scheduling gone to pot
No Mamma No Pappa No Uncle Sam
No Lot no Hardware Damn.

Pin pad in Garden stopped party
Left customers much less hearty
No Mamma No Pappa No Uncle Sam
Pin pad does not give a Damn.

Red tool chest very best bought
No one available to help wrought
No Mamma No Pappa No Uncle Sam
And a guest with chest Damn.

Customers in PRO helped through stay
Enjoyed practicing honesty all day
No Mamma No Pappa No Uncle Sam
Customers too good for this store Damn.

Make it up or be disparaged when you don't
No answer applies to store that won't
No Mamma No Pappa No Uncle Sam
Don't and won't do not give a Damn.

Garden party place to please
Customers mostly at ease in this breeze
No Mamma No Pappa No Uncle Sam
Garden Party is the place to be Damn.

Four cashiers on floor inside too much and more
Time for Bard to exit through front door
No Mamma No Pappa No Uncle Sam
Count to three then skidoo Damn.

Joyce ordered pizza in freight
Bard paid tip to get pizza there mate
No Mamma No Pappa No Uncle Sam
Joyce said thanks Damn.

Store zapped on Sunday
No one called Michael Faraday
No Mamma No Pappa No Uncle Sam
Michael Faraday does not give a Damn.

Candy bought for child today
Made hay for parents hooray
No Mamma No Pappa No Uncle Sam
Buying candy for child Damn.

Customer run over by his truck today
Called 911 they brought a bouquet
No Mamma No Pappa No Uncle Sam
And this unbelievable Damn.

Called five numbers about run over customer
Police arrived before MOD hustler
No Mamma No Pappa No Uncle Sam
Wish MOD answered phone Damn.

Corporate changed schedule with two day notice
Ashley called as if on hypnosis
No Mamma no Pappa No Uncle Sam
Jerked around by corporate who gives a Damn.

Depot does it backwards pays for time off
Should instead pay for time on engulf
No Mamma No Pappa No Uncle Sam
Pay them to not come in Damn.

Stand like sacrificial priests in temple
Orange life requires devotion made simple
No Mamma No Pappa No Uncle Sam
These temple priests do not give a Damn.

Ordered receipt tapes received that don't
Automation at Depot largely a won't
No Mamma No Pappa No Uncle Sam
Automation at Depot strictly Looney Damn.

Win one for Gipper keeps Irish in luck
Orange Crushed lacks all kinds of pluck
No Mamma No Pappa No Uncle Sam
Orange Crushed does not give a Damn.

Emily Bo Peep caught by concrete monster
Full-time now no plan to conquer
No Mamma No Pappa No Uncle Sam
She will be another Christy Damn.

Stephen quit today missed vacation pay
Just one more day needed to stay
No Mamma No Pappa No Uncle Sam
Stephen learned to count Damn.

'Thanks' a word rarely employed at Depot store
Simply do not want that sound anymore
No Mamma No Pappa No Uncle Sam
No thanks and don't give a Damn.

April ordered bags and tapes three weeks ago
No bags arrived tapes strictly no-go
No Mamma No Pappa No Uncle Sam
And they can't even fill orders Damn.

Thanks for offer but don't participate
Causes much agitation need to berate
No Mamma No Pappa No Uncle Sam
Bait and switch don't give a Damn.

Customer a run-in with Amber
Wanted service had none slammed her
No Mamma No Pappa No Uncle Sam
Amber without help in Garden Damn.

New bags arrived from another store 0884 had no more
Stick together rip in two what a Red Chinese bore
No Mamma No Pappa No Uncle Sam
You cannot even burn them Damn.

Met Josh over Garden registers an idea
Use one not three a second to free panacea
No Mamma No Pappa No Uncle Sam
Keep the customers safe Damn.

Cars loading in annex next to customer gate
Makes for a very dangerous fate
No Mamma No Pappa No Uncle Sam
Open both gates and give a Damn.

Wanted money for one in need matched to $500 not more
Cash on the barrel only at risk from bank to store
No Mamma No Pappa No Uncle Sam
Carry cash and don't give a Damn.

Dan the man slammed Mandy in hardware
Wants to go there or be nowhere
No Mamma No Pappa No Uncle Sam
Mandy will push him to flooring and Christy Damn.

Many stores make binders to show how to do
Home Depot none to help work through
No Mamma No Pappa No Uncle Sam
No binders Damn.

Employees **Greet Engage Thank** customers for this
For employees **Ridicule Interrogate** and **Dismiss**
No Mamma No Pappa No Uncle Sam
GET RID does not give a Damn.

Ace moved from Plumbing and Electric rules roost
All merchandise on floor now to boost
No Mamma No Pappa No Uncle Sam
Ace now runs stuff on floor Damn.

Yellow Roses for Christy exiting position
This Yellow Rose of Texas suffers from attrition
No Mamma No Pappa No Uncle Sam
Rose Marie and Clementine do not give a Damn.

Amber hair red as Christy's locks
Looks like both may have chicken pox
No Mamma No Pappa No Uncle Sam
These Wendy lookalikes do give a Damn.

Christy appeared to Amber from flooring way
Told looked like her in red hair display
No Mamma No Pappa No Uncle Sam
Amber never meant this Damn.

Silos to grain Depot's endless mane
Moves numbers from one to another no pain
No Mamma No Pappa and No Uncle Sam
No turnaround in a silo Damn.

Roses used to send Christy away
Made happy caused her to wave
No Mamma No Pappa No Uncle Sam
Christy never knew truth Damn.

Customers now know Bard by name and exclaim
Want to be sure and remember his name
No Mamma No Pappa No Uncle Sam
Customers remember to give a Damn.

Schedule well during day because they choose
Late afternoons remain Looney Tunes lose
No Mamma No Pappa No Uncle Sam
Looney Tunes cartoons do not give a Damn.

Garden overrun and twenty-five deep
Asked inside to ring up mulch to keep
No Mamma No Pappa No Uncle Sam
Garden in meltdown and no one gives a Damn.

Called Manager for help for Amber in Garden
No cashiers available Manager none to bargain
No Mamma No Pappa No Uncle Sam
Bean Counter Josh Damn.

Customer patient in line Bard explained delay
Bard said no way if he a customer so delayed
No Mamma No Pappa No Uncle Sam
And thanks for this customer Damn.

Humpty Dumpty sat on his wall took a big fall
Depot sold bricks and mortar replaced wall
No Mamma No Pappa No Uncle Sam
Depot did not put Humpty Dumpty together Damn.

April failing and ill in back
Still refuse to cut her slack
No Mamma No Pappa No Uncle Sam
No training no coverage and no one gives a Damn.

Chris in Garden to pick up Homer check
Said Friday night fever coverage wreck
No Mamma No Pappa No Uncle Sam
Friday night fever who gives a Damn.

April saw no coverage for PRO and Garden
Suggested call ASM and strike a bargain
No Mamma No Pappa No Uncle Sam
Five slots three cashiers Damn.

A customer danced shoes missed floor
Back stood slack moved some more
No Mamma No Pappa No Uncle Sam
And the embarrassed Damn.

Home office engages in job security
Creating misery source of this fury
No Mamma No Pappa No Uncle Sam
Home Office does not give a Damn.

Prepared Garden for storms coming
Keep it open or store will take a drumming
No Mamma No Pappa No Uncle Sam
And a wet store not worth a Damn.

Some companies have Mission statement ingrained
Home Depot no mission nor statement ashamed
No Mamma No Pappa No Uncle Sam
No mission no statement who gives a Damn.

Welcome to Depot after dark barked
Customers say pot called stark
No Mamma No Pappa No Uncle Sam
Depot after dark does not give a Damn.

Strength of schedule in college views
Home Depot hourly allocations are PU
No Mamma No Pappa No Uncle Sam
PU stinks and does not give a Damn.

Phones for Garden stuck on busy
Caused cashier great tizzy
No Mamma No Pappa No Uncle Sam
Garden phones busy do not give a Damn.

Irrigation system fixed in rain
Now have very wet stain
No Mamma No Pappa No Uncle Sam
Wet is wet who gives a Damn

Customers class in this morass
Expectations nil met with impasse
No Mamma No Pappa No Uncle Sam
Customers expect nothing Damn.

Easy to see how to please customers in view
Employees don't receive from management crew
No Mamma No Pappa No Uncle Sam
Employees treated this way won't give a Damn.

Three feet high and rising song did say
Ignore and hit floor Depot way
No Mamma No Pappa No Uncle Sam
Three feet high and rising who gives a Damn.

Sign on Bard must have said vent
Customers and employees could rent
No Mamma No Pappa No Uncle Sam
Customers venting do give a Damn.

Ave Imperator morituri te salutant
At Home Depot for the repentant
No Mamma No Pappa No Uncle Sam
Who gives a Damn about Latin Damn.

Depot wage and hour with government that sues
Forgot to apply rules rude very Snafu
No Mamma No Pappa No Uncle Sam
Government does not give a Damn.

PRO and Lumber reorganized almost clean
Wow really an impressive sheen
No Mamma No Pappa No Uncle Sam
PRO and Lumber now give a Damn.

Baseball cap on head Christy walking spread
No longer full of dread looking good instead
No Mamma No Pappa No Uncle Sam
She does give a Damn.

Nine came and went one had to stay
Head Cashier had no other way
No Mamma No Pappa No Uncle Sam
And stay to give a Damn.

Load shelves up to ceiling without sealing
Do not block adjacent aisle where customer reeling
No Mamma No Pappa No Uncle Sam
Loaders do not give a Damn.

Hey hey LBJ how many did you kill today once said
Hey hey how much money did you make today instead
No Mamma No Pappa No Uncle Sam
Landslide Lindy does not give a Damn.

Customers at store no buggies by entrance door
No buggies around much less found inside store
No Mamma No Pappa No Uncle Sam
Carry and drag but don't give a Damn.

Bonus paid lunch provided not rotten
Red Virus all but forgotten
No Mamma No Pappa No Uncle Sam
Bonus or lunch who gives a Damn.

Monopoly game played each shift by sane
Dial departments check cash order tubes same
No Mamma No Pappa No Uncle Sam
Monopoly game does not give a Damn.

Garbage cans hide sanitation station
Three days to empty in this crazy nation
No Mamma No Pappa No Uncle Sam
And who gives a Damn about garbage cans

Bard finds it hard to function amidst chaotic malfunction
Ribs sore from laughter endless business dysfunction
No Mamma No Pappa No Uncle Sam
Malfunction dysfunction who gives a Damn.

April to again cut five and take five
No overtime allowed in this dive
No Mamma No Pappa No Uncle Sam
April said no Damn.

PRO closed on Saturday but not forgotten
Contractors with sales and returns think rotten
No Mamma No Pappa No Uncle Sam
And no one gives a Damn.

Ship of Fools from Plato's pen did sail
Practiced and perfected in Home Depot's fail
No Mamma No Pappa No Uncle Sam
Plato does not give a Damn.

Audit night Emily assumed Bard in play
Agreed no way right ASM held sway
No Mamma No Pappa No Uncle Sam
Bo Peep's hook released this sheep Damn.

Walmart took order and delivered that day
Home Depot says no way
No Mamma No Pappa No Uncle Sam
No way does not give a Damn.

Gurneys astray in aisles over Garden way
Seems no one wanted to pray end their stay
No Mamma No Pappa No Uncle Sam
Gurneys abandoned do not give a Damn.

Flat cars abound in Lumber and lot
Nowhere seen in Flooring Plumbing or Garden spot
No Mamma No Pappa No Uncle Sam
These flat cars do not give a Damn.

Candy and junk moved behind cashier
Shelf blocked by gurneys carts funeral biers
No Mamma No Pappa No Uncle Sam
Walking through biers behind cashiers Damn.

At this store turnover and turnstiles rule day
Need a scorecard to see who in play
No Mamma No Pappa No Uncle Sam
And come to leave because they do Damn.

Bard put in Garden but could not stay
Wind driven cold retreat away
No Mamma No Pappa No Uncle Sam
Ashley came and gave a Damn.

Home Depot animal friendly a zoo that pets
Those that don't have no right to fret
No Mamma No Pappa No Uncle Sam
Humans mean less than pets at this store Damn.

Describing red to a blindman
Like working on Home Depot's Saipan
No Mamma No Pappa No Uncle Sam
Saipans do not give a Damn.

The beat goes on and cars keep getting faster
Home Depot swamped endless mirth and laughter
No Mamma No Pappa No Uncle Sam
And the mirth and laughter go on and on … Damn.

Brianna and Mom came to Garden to buy this cold day
A forgotten card made Mom pay Bri blushed all stay
No Mamma No Pappa No Uncle Sam
Brianna blushing gives a Damn.

Orange last color seen before blindness and dark
Why Home Depot chose this as their mark
No Mamma No Pappa No Uncle Sam
Orange to black who gives a Damn.

Pallet of tile on aisle 19 customer in to claim
Called over store to find and avoid blame
No Mamma No Pappa No Uncle Sam
And no one wanted to help his claim Damn.

Lights in lot like candles aglow
Darker than coal mine canary below
No Mamma No Pappa No Uncle Sam
These parking lot lights dim Damn.

Inventory real until not then squat
Customers often found in victim's spot
No Mamma No Pappa No Uncle Sam
Ghost inventory does not give a Damn.

SKU from lumber yard cut in two
Cannot scan or enter no report to yard nor crew
No Mamma No Pappa No Uncle Sam
Yard and crew who gives a Damn.

Gurneys missing from PRO today
Moved all over store and far away
No Mamma No Pappa No Uncle Sam
Gurneys missing don't give a Damn.

Corporate once had an idea or so rumored
Many treatments finally removed tumor
No Mamma No Pappa No Uncle Sam
Ideas like tumors do not give a Damn.

Home Depot finds initiative to target
Manage and crush oligarchic
No Mamma No Pappa No Uncle Sam
Oligarchs do not give a Damn.

Jesus His Cross impaled in Roman tale
At Home Depot more nails and wood for sale
No Mamma No Pappa No Uncle Sam
And you think Home Depot gives a Damn

Young Chris in lumber sought work to do
Saw woman with child struggling helped them through
No Mamma No Pappa No Uncle Sam
Wok generation does give a Damn.

Melisha tall and dark smart with customers never bark
A postal worker she works on a lark always hits mark
No Mamma No Pappa No Uncle Sam
Rain or shine this Melisha delivers mail Damn.

Money changers in temple never flirt
At this store merely more sales to skirt
No Mamma No Pappa No Uncle Sam
Money changers and dirt don't give a Damn.

Attempt reason in house of insanity
Learn quickly insanity reasons inanity
No Mamma No Pappa No Uncle Sam
Insanity and inanity do not give a Damn.

Greenbaum his Spirit in sky
Depot brings tears we know why
No Mamma No Pappa No Uncle Sam
Norman Greenbaum does not give a Damn.

April new FES set to bring her best
First time in years FES will function meet test
No Mamma No Pappa No Uncle Sam
A functioning FES time to give a Damn.

Vendors in Garden bring plants and flowers in
Then leave residue filling trash bins
No Mamma No Pappa No Uncle Sam
And you think vendors give a Damn.

Door to loading in Garden unlocked
Cashier alone found this and clocked
No Mamma No Pappa No Uncle Sam
This cashier did give a Damn.

Ding dong witch dead wicked witch of dread
A goodly witch transformed bringing joy instead
No Mamma No Pappa No Uncle Sam
Munchkin City does not give a Damn.

Dan playing his one-man band
Declined to help Garden make stand
No Mamma No Pappa No Uncle Sam
No help from Dan Damn.

Diogenes lamp finds Odysseus left blind
Neither lamp nor blind store entwine
No Mamma No Pappa No Uncle Sam
Diogenes does not give a Damn.

Christy on Black Friday wonder to behold
Filled with glee offering sympathy in fold
No Mamma No Pappa No Uncle Sam
Will miss this Christy Damn.

Macomber's wife used Mannlicher on lion that day
Husband in way Home Depot encouraged stay
No Mamma No Pappa No Uncle Sam
Macomber and Mannlicher do not give a Damn.

Serling and Bradbury wrote fiction to view
Designed Home Depot's computers too
No Mamma No Pappa No Uncle Sam
All Martians now and do not give a Damn.

Easter Saturday manager stood on his hoof
Lines overrun merchandise undone piles toilet paper to roof
No Mamma No Pappa No Uncle Sam
Toilet paper what needs to be done right Damn.

Discovered that license on accounts no longer matter
Reported dismissed with disparaging chatter
No Mamma No Pappa No Uncle Sam
License and social security do not give a Damn.

Josh told Christy to fix Garden overrun
Bard stepped into made run fun
No Mamma No Pappa No Uncle Sam
Bard made Garden party run Damn.

Christy needed Bard in both Garden and PRO
The choice meant Bard no go or oh no
No Mamma No Pappa No Uncle Sam
Wanted to split Bard in two Damn.

Call-outs have function in store
Guard ghost inventory ever more
No Mamma No Pappa No Uncle Sam
Ghosts do not give a Damn.

Nora Roberts read by Christy out the door
Does she then drive or stop to explore
No Mamma No Pappa No Uncle Sam
Nora Roberts does not give a Damn.

Christy's blonde mane stained dark crimson
Much like Queen of Babylon risen
No Mamma No Pappa No Uncle Sam
Queen of Babylon does not give a Damn.

Store 0884 like a big bad baboon
Unable to manage drink machines dragoon
No Mamma No Pappa No Uncle Sam
Baboons do not give a Damn.

Today Christy called in to Paint and Flooring an extra day
Calls out caused come in and cover both for pay
No Mamma No Pappa No Uncle Sam
Christy in Flooring and Paint gives a Damn.

They draw them in from church's holy bin
Help them to sin while spend
No Mamma No Pappa No Uncle Sam
Open on Sunday who gives a Damn.

Space heaters work in calm spaces
Never for windblown Garden places
No Mamma No Pappa No Uncle Sam
Space heaters do not give a Damn.

Customers cold in Garden wind tunnel
Explained wrong in Beau Brummell Chunnel
No Mamma No Pappa No Uncle Sam
Beau Brummell does not give a Damn.

Fingers like frozen ice sealed to scan gun on floor
Unable to move past warranty blocked screen door
No Mamma No Pappa No Uncle Sam
Fingers frozen and warranty screen don't give a Damn

Store opened Easter Sunday not too late
Between tomb opening and sundown tempting fate
No Mamma No Pappa No Uncle Sam
Count money before Sun goes down Damn.

Allstate warranty promises offered
McKinsey chisels when claims proffered
No Mamma No Pappa No Uncle Sam
Allstate and McKinsey don't give a Damn.

Discovered a broom and pan for use in middle
April swept floor made place look like a fiddle
No Mamma No Pappa No Uncle Sam
April cleaning up Damn.

Returns formerly stacked left forlorn
Now bundled and processed reborn
No Mamma No Pappa No Uncle Sam
And front end beginning to function Damn.

Four customers with orders to fill in Garden
Chasmyn said could handle bargain
No Mamma No Pappa No Uncle Sam
Chasmyn stood alone and gave a Damn.

John for Generac in Tennessee and Kentucky domain
Home Depot disparaged quality and name
No Mamma No Pappa No Uncle Sam
Depot wants cheap not good Damn.

Dr. Seuss is Loose in Depot offering green eggs and ham
The Cat I Am I Am better scram
No Mamma No Pappa No Uncle Sam
Dr. Seuss and Cat don't give a Damn.

Drink machines empty Deja vu all over again
Bill Murray and Groundhog Day understand remand
No Mamma No Pappa No Uncle Sam
Punxsutawney Phil does not give a Damn.

Brianna and Adam talking smack
Thought freight great to avoid customer attack
No Mamma No Pappa No Uncle Sam
Talking smack does not give a Damn.

Garden vendors an independent group take all spots
Bring in flowers and block other merchandise slots
No Mamma No Pappa No Uncle Sam
Vendors don't give a Damn.

Orders to fill come stand at PRO end
Customers left alone find in bin
No Mamma No Pappa No Uncle Sam
Neither Customer Service nor PRO give a Damn.

No drinks to display in coolers
Distributor made this a fooler
No Mamma No Pappa No Uncle Sam
This distributor does not give a Damn.

Emily left SCO for dinner and play
Customers wanted to make their way
No Mamma No Pappa No Uncle Sam
Dinner and play don't give a Damn.

Pinocchio found tail on Pleasure Island
Home Depot Leviathan swims to Hyland
No Mamma No Pappa No Uncle Sam
The Beast does not give a Damn.

Home Depot a 2D object in 3D world
Their empty sound and fury like whorls
No Mamma No Pappa No Uncle Sam
Whorls do not give a Damn.

No one helps close oh woe
Stay late and finish before go
No Mamma No Pappa No Uncle Sam
They don't give a Damn.

Olive saw Bard worked seven straight but a single break
Made sure he left when store closed make no mistake
No Mamma No Pappa No Uncle Sam
And Olive took care of Bard Damn.

Drinks look slim and grim
Dirty grimy no sign of a whim
No Mamma No Pappa No Uncle Sam
And slim and grim do not give a Damn.

Coolers dirty and worn not bright nor gay
Distributor wants them to look like Bombay
No Mamma No Pappa No Uncle Sam
Bombay does not give a Damn.

Cabinet in Garden uncovered for rain
Monitor and pin pad hardly stand strain
No Mamma No Pappa No Uncle Sam
Monitors and pin pads so arraigned oh Damn.

Lock in Garden warehouse gate left unsecured
Anyone that locks should be revered
No Mamma No Pappa No Uncle Sam
Unlocked car gates don't give a Damn.

Christy to PRO at close saw customer in Uriah's Heep
Offered to get help but this promise could not keep
No Mamma No Pappa No Uncle Sam
Uriah Heep does not give a Damn.

Accounting magic may make store stand
How else could win and withstand
No Mamma No Pappa No Uncle Sam
Stand and withstand but do not give a Damn.

Carts jammed in way down PRO's stay
Another Saturday no one all day
No Mamma No Pappa No Uncle Sam
Nobody at work does not give a Damn.

Vendor in Garden working tardy on Easter day
Cut corner smashed display in her way
No Mamma No Pappa No Uncle Sam
And do not stand in her way Damn.

Closed store with Bard outside
Customer with wood spilled needed bromide
No Mamma No Pappa No Uncle Sam
And this spy did not come in from the cold Damn.

Adam looks like Hitler Youth forsooth
Always great with customers never uncouth
No Mamma No Pappa No Uncle Sam
And this Aryan gives a Damn.

Depot endless scream about lead in paint
Why then sell Roundup with no complaint
No Mamma No Pappa No Uncle Sam
Concern only when enlarges profit Damn.

Another new Mary joined front end
Autism took for spin she managed to win
No Mamma No Pappa No Uncle Sam
This Mary no Magdalene must give a Damn.

Management and many crossed River Styx
Leaving rest in Black Friday eve fix
No Mamma No Pappa No Uncle Sam
River Styx does not give a Damn.

Treat paint on floor an environmental sore
Bags used fill landfills much adored
No Mamma No Pappa No Uncle Sam
Hypocrisy Depot enduring value Damn.

One-eyed king in this land of blind
This store always playing from behind
No Mamma No Pappa No Uncle Sam
One-eyed do not give a Damn.

Rub dirt in keep playing coach did scream
Still alive and well in store's daily scheme
No Mamma No Pappa No Uncle Sam
They don't give a Damn.

Received success share two cents on dollar
Hardly made joyful or want to holler
No Mamma No Pappa No Uncle Sam
Two cents worth who gives a Damn

Register turned on no Washingtons in drawer
HC explains none to keep score
No Mamma No Pappa No Uncle Sam
Who cares about change in the drawer Damn.

Door ringer cams found way up in bay
Forgotten and never in place to sell anyway
No Mamma No Pappa No Uncle Sam
When inventory is but storage who gives a Damn.

Christy locked out of her phone
Had to shout like a megaphone
No Mamma No Pappa No Uncle Sam
No phone and they don't give a Damn.

This golden age gold why wars waged
At Home Depot today greed why they rage
No Mamma No Pappa No Uncle Sam
Bono and U2 do not give a Damn.

Sell Frito-Lay to customers that pay
For Associates order Walmart cheap way
No Mamma No Pappa No Uncle Sam
Home Depot cheap does not give a Damn.

Home Depot says home improvements store
Why contractors walk through PRO door
No Mamma No Pappa No Uncle Sam
And this house divided can stand

Displays very high along way
Block view to PRO to this very day
No Mamma No Pappa No Uncle Sam
A blocked view does not give a Damn.

10 to 2 changed to 9 to 1 on whim
Makes no difference in this crazy gym
No Mamma No Pappa No Uncle Sam
Four is four on floor who gives a Damn

Dial numbers when no one answers you threw
Loads not pulled goods not sold sounds of silence blue
No Mamma No Pappa No Uncle Sam
Simon and Garfunkel do not give a Damn.

Customers from inside store to Garden for checkout
Sought Garden party to empower walk out
No Mamma No Pappa No Uncle Sam
No waiting in Garden store does not give a Damn.

Two kids offered candy today by Apron
Parents thought more than thoughtful patron
No Mamma No Pappa No Uncle Sam
Parents like when stores give a Damn

A compliment from profaned delivered
Line backlog cleaned in minutes not considered
No Mamma No Pappa No Uncle Sam
The profaned noticed we did give a Damn.

Do as they say when they do but never say what they do
Not the least like eating great cordon bleu
No Mamma No Pappa No Uncle Sam
Say or do or do and say who gives a Damn.

You can do this for Home Depot tag ended run
Now how doers get more done this not fun
No Mamma No Pappa No Uncle Sam
Do and done do not give a Damn.

On Easter eve Bard cleaned up PRO Garden and SCO
Worked like a Nor'easter striking blow
No Mamma No Pappa No Uncle Sam
Nor'easter does not give a Damn.

Yo Yo in PRO suffered near cardiac arrest
Bard cleaned mess gave her rest
No Mamma No Pappa No Uncle Sam
Yo Yo knows Bard has her back Damn.

David Bathsheba made him swoon
At Home Depot this most inopportune
No Mamma No Pappa No Uncle Sam
Did Home Depot sell the bathtub Damn.

Abandoned in Garden one cold eve
Locked gate walked away to warmth and ease
No Mamma No Pappa No Uncle Sam
Lock gate and don't give a Damn.

Alex to lunch did go per schedule
Amber angry she left red bull
No Mamma No Pappa No Uncle Sam
Angry red bulls don't give a Damn.

Home Depot and government much in common
Both empower bondage not Rahman
No Mamma No Pappa No Uncle Sam
Rahman does not give a Damn.

Reform from top or revolution below
St. Petersburg breadlines started woe
No Mamma No Pappa No Uncle Sam
Czar Nicholas did not give a Damn.

Samuel in Garden swamped by ruin
Unable to control left like a bruin
No Mamma No Pappa No Uncle Sam
Bruin does not give a Damn.

Phyllis provided break today for another
Fifteen minutes later line backed suffer
No Mamma No Pappa No Uncle Sam
You call this a break Damn.

Down to two at close on Easter eve
No reason so be peeved
No Mamma No Pappa No Uncle Sam
Closing with one plus Christy very risky Damn.

Saturday afternoon beaten and sweaty
Stress and duress ready for settee
No Mamma No Pappa No Uncle Sam
Settee does not give a Damn.

Went to Garden party but rather drive a truck
Rather than deal with memories of this shucks
No Mamma No Pappa No Uncle Sam
Ricky Nelson does not give a Damn.

Two lines in Garden no coverage for loads
Here come vendors melt down woes
No Mamma No Pappa No Uncle Sam
No coverage two lines and vendors Damn.

Christy a cart full of flooring sold
Turned to help Bard on register consoled
No Mamma No Pappa No Uncle Sam
Christy just had to give a Damn.

JC no Sunshine Band in plumbing aisle
Treats all customers well never vile
No Mamma No Pappa No Uncle Sam
This one-man band gives a Damn.

When Area manager is in ASMs walk floor
Check for plaster or more at PRO front door
No Mamma No Pappa No Uncle Sam
ASMs need map to walk floor Damn.

Bard in PRO all Sunday eve no relief
Garden and middle flowed beyond belief
No Mamma No Pappa No Uncle Sam
Customers seek out Bard Damn.

Schedule changed put in system
April lost unable to decipher new wisdom
No Mamma No Pappa No Uncle Sam
And the system does give a Damn.

Home Depot an orange family they say
Then why treat in such brutal ways
No Mamma No Pappa No Uncle Sam
This kind of family does not give a Damn.

Josh took tag off electric cart not in play
Felt endless loud beep screech more than okay
No Mamma No Pappa No Uncle Sam
Electric cart bleeps and does not give a Damn.

Charlie spied this cart took it away
Not charged customer found out hard way
No Mamma No Pappa No Uncle Sam
Cart uncharged does not give a Damn.

Mandy and Christy had plan for Dan
Not to meet the boys in band
No Mamma No Pappa No Uncle Sam
Women scorned have great fury Dan Damn.

April gave accuracy test to Bard today
Employed separate cart to pass and make hay
No Mamma No Pappa No Uncle Sam
How beat the accuracy test Damn.

Bard took accuracy receipt from another's test
Printed copy but April druthered stop being a pest
No Mamma No Pappa No Uncle Sam
Bard found a new way Damn.

Stock at three hundred buybacks ablaze
Maintenance unfunded by this silly malaise
No Mamma No Pappa No Uncle Sam
Don't need no stinking maintenance Damn.

Alex in Garden fought for sale quite a lot
Price had to match plant in pot
No Mamma No Pappa No Uncle Sam
Alex the Great before Darius Damn.

Wasco assailed over plant charges and SKUs
Poor man had no clue quickly skidooed
No Mamma No Pappa No Uncle Sam
Wasco too smart to give a Damn.

Gee Lee colorful dreadlocks flowing to feet
Works smart and hard always complete
No Mamma No Pappa No Uncle Sam
Who cares if she gives a Damn.

Kimme a singer with great voice and eyes
Appearance and looks leave many surprised
No Mamma No Pappa No Uncle Sam
This wild one gives a Damn.

Tripped and wrenched over rug tied in a cinch
Ripped and removed without a flinch
No Mamma No Pappa No Uncle Sam
Wrenched knee or not give a Damn.

A little rain must fall in every life they say
At Depot more like a flood driven tidal wave
No Mamma No Pappa No Uncle Sam
Depot has no gopher wood Damn.

Contractors bring Missy Sylvia and Angela donuts
Drives their weight watching nuts
No Mamma No Pappa No Uncle Sam
Weight Watchers do not give a Damn.

They say make hay for store we ought
Why then no hay to sell or be bought
No Mamma No Pappa No Uncle Sam
Aught and bought don't give a Damn.

Cashiers must process when customers abound
Few know how to do on these grounds
No Mamma No Pappa No Uncle Sam
Send in clowns and don't give a Damn.

Two cashiers scheduled in Garden increase flow
Take Garden employees away now slow
No Mamma No Pappa No Uncle Sam
No Garden support and don't give a Damn.

Street with no name U2 sang for all to hear
Home Depot brings lots of fearful tears
No Mamma No Pappa No Uncle Sam
These tears do not give a Damn.

Air conditioners piled like mile-high pie
A leaning tower of Pisa that is no lie
No Mamma No Pappa No Uncle Sam
Leaning Tower of Pisa does not give a Damn.

Brad worked Lot his way made pay
Manager no way Brad ended stay
No Mamma No Pappa No Uncle Sam
Brad learned not to give a Damn.

Ten cashiers in store today all on display
Forced one to end stay and go away
No Mamma No Pappa No Uncle Sam
Ten cashiers at once don't give a Damn.

Chance wrestled mower onto pallet
Reminded him not to hurt his mallet
No Mamma No Pappa No Uncle Sam
Mallets and pallets don't give a Damn.

Rachel in PRO for hours health plan and dough
Told Bard not worth that job a long time ago
No Mamma No Pappa No Uncle Sam
Rachel left a waste of plans and dough Damn.

Bard offered thirty in PRO to fill hole
Told he not right for role
No Mamma No Pappa No Uncle Sam
Why should Bard give a Damn

Store on Saturday no carts gurneys lumber carts nor flats
No Customer nor employee had clue where at
No Mamma No Pappa No Uncle Sam
Merchandise dragged across floor who gives a Damn.

Order delivered to job site only half complete
Two to deliver on Saturday no small feat
No Mamma No Pappa No Uncle Sam
Can't fill much less deliver orders Damn.

Customer asked for extended warranty for drill
Allstate claim service would make ill
No Mamma No Pappa No Uncle Sam
Allstate not good hands Damn.

April thanked for vote of confidence in renaissance
Making a difference each and every day with response
No Mamma No Pappa No Uncle Sam
Renaissance and response give a Damn.

Crowds hold sway Garden way each day
Register broke another work no hope for pay
No Mamma No Pappa No Uncle Sam
Customers come out to checkout Damn.

Shave and a haircut two bits
At Home Depot a great big fit
No Mamma No Pappa No Uncle Sam
Two bits do not give a Damn.

Unfixed Garden fixture exposed to rain
Hope electricity does not cause pain
No Mamma No Pappa No Uncle Sam
Exposed fixtures in water who gives a Damn.

Dump truck driver backed under shingles his way
Missy had hissy told him to stop or go away
No Mamma No Pappa No Uncle Sam
Missy more than said Damn.

30 days in the hole at this store often with no reason
Like four hours straight no break Garden cold season
No Mamma No Pappa No Uncle Sam
The HC left us to freeze and did not give a Damn.

When no Lot store has jamboree
Employees not attend few free
No Mamma No Pappa No Uncle Sam
This jamboree not attended Damn.

Lightning threatened to end Garden array
Management just looked other way
No Mamma No Pappa No Uncle Sam
Lightning does not give a Damn.

Offered to purchase choice of candy
Two young children raced to pick their dandy
No Mamma No Pappa No Uncle Sam
These parents know this store gives a Damn.

When no reason every fool has season
Motley a fool but at least had reason
No Mamma No Pappa No Uncle Sam
Motley fools do not give a Damn.

New cashiers thrown on floor with no training
No wonder their heads soon spinning
No Mamma No Pappa No Uncle Sam
Untrained and who gives a Damn.

Depot demands employees wear face diapers
Customers do not see Associates hyper
No Mamma No Pappa No Uncle Sam
The incontinent do not give a Damn.

Garden depraved left to rot anyway
Even customers must find a new way
No Mamma No Pappa No Uncle Sam
Who gives a Damn.

Amber agreed April by store in awful fix
Suggested pull together help pickup stix
No Mamma No Pappa No Uncle Sam
Or don't give a Damn.

Exhausted by seven straight Bard could not move carts in PRO
Twenty-five backed up in Garden could not stay and make go
No Mamma No Pappa No Uncle Sam
Low blood sugar does not give a Damn.

Fourteen days in a row still they call Bard in
Never an end to this skin's sin
No Mamma No Pappa No Uncle Sam
This story has no end Damn.

No buggies no flat cars customers stuck in Garden jam
Called Lot but they brought nothing to ease this slam
No Mamma No Pappa No Uncle Sam
Customers in Garden Damn.

Customer brought U-Haul truck to Garden gate
Really had to scrinch to get in mate
No Mamma No Pappa No Uncle Sam
Thank goodness the mirrors collapsed Damn.

Home Depot embraces sin not sinner
Almost always leads to bad ender
No Mamma No Pappa No Uncle Sam
Embrace sin and do not give a Damn.

Donna came over and said thanks a lot
Came for cover while cramping fix spot
No Mamma No Pappa No Uncle Sam
A cramping leg does not give a Damn.

Buck ended shift with book in hand
About werewolves tearing up land
No Mamma No Pappa No Uncle Sam
Werewolves do not give a Damn.

Management mouths evil and deceit
Probably how Depot best competes
No Mamma No Pappa No Uncle Sam
Deceit is deceit Damn.

Alex in locker room on break
Seems to have most awfully sad face
No Mamma No Pappa No Uncle Sam
Alex too young to be this sad Damn.

Gina Martini came to Garden after Tractor Supply fling
Management abusive joined the Orange team
No Mamma No Pappa No Uncle Sam
Martini and Rossi may give a Damn.

Saturday afternoon before Mom's Day a quiet gloom
No customer could fund this room
No Mamma No Pappa No Uncle Sam
On this Saturday PRO a ghost Damn.

New lights overhead lighten way
Customers now see what seek and pay
No Mamma No Pappa No Uncle Sam
Blue light that hurts eyes does not give a Damn.

No buggies at door for Saturday's roar
Wasco agreed had to even score
No Mamma No Pappa No Uncle Sam
How can customers buy Damn.

Cheap good and available pick any two
At Home Depot good almost always through
No Mamma No Pappa No Uncle Sam
Cheap and available don't give a Damn.

Placed buggies at rest where customers find
Gone quicker than gold from mine
No Mamma No Pappa No Uncle Sam
Buggies gold in Garden Damn.

Seed to harvest quoted as best
Depot has neither seed nor harvest in Spring fest
No Mamma No Pappa No Uncle Sam
Eat your seed and don't give a Damn.

When alone left a buggy with three returns at PRO
Next eve full no one moved or made it go
No Mamma No Pappa No Uncle Sam
Cashiers don't do returns Damn.

Fighting men from sky had green berets
Associates on floor have Homer orange craze
No Mamma No Pappa No Uncle Sam
Homers do not give a Damn.

Sink the Bismarck world depends on them
At Home Depot chances really slim
No Mamma No Pappa No Uncle Sam
Bismarck does not give a Damn.

Deming red bead parable and process to manage
Home Depot no beads and savages ravage
No Mamma No Pappa No Uncle Sam
Deming does not give a Damn.

Covey his seven habits on display
Home Depot will never behave this way
No Mamma No Pappa No Uncle Sam
Steven Covey does not give a Damn.

Pasteurize and homogenize may work on milk
At Home Depot more often just plain ilk
No Mamma No Pappa No Uncle Sam
Pasteurized homogenized who gives a Damn.

Garbage not emptied in three days
Piles left this way for an extended stay
No Mamma No Pappa No Uncle Sam
Garbage unemptied stinks Damn.

Strobe lights illuminate store
Like a Broadway show galore
No Mamma No Pappa No Uncle Sam
This show strictly off Broadway Damn.

Let's go and Wild Bunch did
How to blow Home Depot's lid
No Mamma No Pappa No Uncle Sam
Let's go does not give a Damn.

Fall in behind the Major and did with Dundee
Neither Major nor Dundee in Depot's Bungee
No Mamma No Pappa No Uncle Sam
Sierra Charriba does not give a Damn.

Working to master another Saturday disaster at PRO
Customers concerned requested Bard go slow
No Mamma No Pappa No Uncle Sam
Customers like and give a Damn.

Carts blocked way to candy and chips
Kids climbed over lost their grips
No Mamma No Pappa No Uncle Sam
And no one gives a Damn.

Daniel visited store to catch up
Still at Wolverine working a young pup
No Mamma No Pappa No Uncle Sam
This Wolverine does not give a Damn.

Amber had first moment as HC then fled away
Olive arrived and finished the day
No Mamma No Pappa No Uncle Sam
Amber learning Damn.

One problem at this store endless excuses
No one has results only reasons and recluses
No Mamma No Pappa No Uncle Sam
Excuses don't give a Damn.

Dan hung up on Mandy
She thought this pretty namby pamby
No Mamma No Pappa No Uncle Sam
A hang-updoes not give a Damn.

Three lines in Garden increase parking lot flow
Registers filled more targets to hit you know
No Mamma No Pappa No Uncle Sam
Ring registers and don't give a Damn.

Rule of management at Depot evermore
Do everything but and lose score
No Mamma No Pappa No Uncle Sam
Score lost does not give a Damn.

Customer left saw at checkout bay
Managed to catch him not too far away
No Mamma No Pappa No Uncle Sam
This customer said thanks for giving a Damn.

Terrier jumped out of car and ran away
Three aprons chased he too smart to stay
No Mamma No Pappa No Uncle Sam
Terriers don't give a Damn.

Sylvia concerned that Bard bought candy for child today
Believed corporate might say nay
No Mamma No Pappa No Uncle Sam
You can't buy candy for a child Damn.

Silver to bullet Bard to register at this store
Simply makes so much more while on floor
No Mamma No Pappa No Uncle Sam
Use your silver bullet Damn.

April in tizzy growing dizzy
Back pain inflamed admin makes fizzy
No Mamma No Pappa No Uncle Sam
April no tin Lizzy Damn.

Paul's friend took Red virus shot
Rotted gut doctor said lots of luck
No Mamma No Pappa No Uncle Sam
Now we can all go to pot Damn.

Help customers in line get on their way
Ask them to have in hand means to pay
No Mamma No Pappa No Uncle Sam
They don't think Damn.

Put in for HC to meet need
Thought might improve speed
No Mamma No Pappa No Uncle Sam
A bit of catalyst might make a Damn.

YoYo stymied by customer in PRO
Bard took register and made it go
No Mamma No Pappa No Uncle Sam
YoYo muttered and sputtered Damn.

YoYo a statue at PRO could hardly breathe anyway
Pollen and asthma took breath another had to stay
No Mamma No Pappa No Uncle Sam
Asthma and pollen don't give a Damn.

Bard arrived for YoYo to leave Waddenzee
Poor girl turned on gleeful frenzy
No Mamma No Pappa No Uncle Sam
YoYo ready to leave Damn.

Lot in this store a black hole
Anyone worked never paroled
No Mamma No Pappa No Uncle Sam
Lot a black hole to the end Damn.

Ace in the hole wins in poker
In this store more like joker
No Mamma No Pappa No Uncle Sam
Waste the Ace when two will do Damn.

Return to sender a song in the day by Elvis Presley
Put in hand won't understand like Wesley
No Mamma No Pappa No Uncle Sam
Elvis does not give a Damn.

Depot hates intelligence and initiative
Runs counter to collectivist derivative
No Mamma No Pappa No Uncle Sam
They don't want us to give a Damn.

Garbage unemptied for days mice happy to stay
Stench may wrench no clinch for delay
No Mamma No Pappa No Uncle Sam
These mice do not give a Damn.

Five minutes to close and two customers inside door
Spent $650 cash did not ask for anything more
No Mamma No Pappa No Uncle Sam
Bard has them trained Damn.

Why ask why at this store whatever
It has been this way forever
No Mamma No Pappa No Uncle Sam
Forever does not give a Damn.

Lowes buys Stainmaster carpet for profit and sales
Depot buys back stock to trim sails
No Mamma No Pappa No Uncle Sam
Lowes is growing and gives a Damn.

Store 0884 more like Lusitania than Titanic
No iceberg only torpedo to make frantic
No Mamma No Pappa No Uncle Sam
Sultana did not give a Damn.

Little Christy called out tonight causing a bit of spot
Somebody forgot to put water in her steam pot
No Mamma No Pappa No Uncle Sam
Another call-out Damn.

Three HCs said Bard awesome and great
Appreciate work and not being late
No Mamma No Pappa No Uncle Sam
They do notice and give a Damn.

Interviewed for HC not disaster
Sullins said great Josh said no wait
No Mamma No Pappa No Uncle Sam
Bean Counter does not give a Damn.

Assigned another to HC today
Told Bard did not think he could play
No Mamma No Pappa No Uncle Sam
Bard told to pound sand Damn.

Told another interviewed better by management team
April eating dinner did not attend scene
No Mamma No Pappa No Uncle Sam
Management team does not give a Damn.

Discrimination by age major thrust
Bard told to stay out and just go bust
No Mamma No Pappa No Uncle Sam
They lie and don't give a Damn.

Met with management team to bury Caesar not to praise
Interred trust relations for verification validation purple haze
No Mamma No Pappa No Uncle Sam
Excuse while sky kissed Damn.

Reminded they lied wanted Bard to go away and die
Why couldn't they just have been honest cast die
No Mamma No Pappa No Uncle Sam
The die really cast Damn.

Applied for HC part-time to help HCs and April with pokes
Told applying for position really nothing but a joke
No Mamma No Pappa No Uncle Sam
Pokes and jokes no fun Damn.

Another selected for HC based on age
Bard did not give into rage
No Mamma No Pappa No Uncle Sam
Age does not give a Damn.

Bard wanted to help others by offering more to many
Instead treated like a silly ninny
No Mamma No Pappa No Uncle Sam
Even ninnies give a Damn.

Failure to promote not very nice note
Management appears to like approach rote
No Mamma No Pappa No Uncle Sam
Failure to promote Damn.

April mad Bard did not stop for tea when liability did see
Made sure people at risk must cross Tappan Zee
No Mamma No Pappa No Uncle Sam
And a bridge to nowhere does not give a Damn.

No more call-ins extra work no longer a perk
Do job described don't be a jerk
No Mamma No Pappa No Uncle Sam
Jerks don't give a Damn.

I got your back old order of day
I don't care do job new preferred way
No Mamma No Pappa No Uncle Sam
I don't care means don't give a Damn.

Josh told Bard too irregular in High and Lo
Claimed did not make Home Depot go
No Mamma No Pappa No Uncle Sam
Hi Ho Hi Ho off to work we go Damn.

Josh called Bard in to claim unprofessional and a thief
Turned out just causing mischief and grief
No Mamma No Pappa No Uncle Sam
Josh does like to Damn.

John declined to send key to unlock wheelbarrows
Sent customer inside looking for straight arrow
No Mamma No Pappa No Uncle Sam
Wheelbarrows don't give a Damn.

Five cashiers plus two asked April if could go away
Had to call management who said yes in every way
No Mamma No Pappa No Uncle Sam
Management agreed Bard gave a Damn.

John stopped Bard to speak while leaving
Asked if call deceiving no not grieving
No Mamma No Pappa No Uncle Sam
John nice to give a Damn.

Management and supervisors giving cold shoulder
Fear and guilt make them faint grow much older
No Mamma No Pappa No Uncle Sam
They are afraid Damn.

Like kids caught with hand in cookie jar
Now Management acts really bizarre
No Mamma No Pappa No Uncle Sam
Bizarre does not give a Damn.

Truth and trust are like red to blind
Not the time to be kind
No Mamma No Pappa No Uncle Sam
Truth and trust no longer give a Damn.

Decisions lead to consequences and collateral damage
Great employee lost by senseless Mammon Ramage
No Mamma No Pappa No Uncle Sam
A great employee lost does not give a Damn.

Battle ax buried in shoulders no reason nor rhyme
Should really view as a great crime
No Mamma No Pappa No Uncle Sam
Management buried the ax Damn.

Hate to say but losers rule the day not merry
Trust made extinct honesty and ethics contrary
No Mamma No Pappa No Uncle Sam
Losers do not give a Damn.

Invisible man wrote Ellison then
For Bard today deeper than skin
No Mamma No Pappa No Uncle Sam
Discrimination does not give a Damn.

Schedule released no change and hours assigned in new week
Have they fired and not let leak
No Mamma No Pappa No Uncle Sam
Does this mean Bard should scram Damn.

Amber despondent as new HC to Garden in pall
Managers told to put Bard on Do Not Call
No Mamma No Pappa No Uncle Sam
The wall of silence does not give a Damn.

Amber not want to hear Bard all over floor
Did she want to be around Bard anymore
No Mamma No Pappa No Uncle Sam
Now they pile on Damn.

Bard separates work from rest
Unlike others in management expressed
No Mamma No Pappa No Uncle Sam
Bard has job to do Damn.

Not good enough says Josh of HC job blend
Not good enough for call-ins or HC job function spins
No Mamma No Pappa No Uncle Sam
Call new HC not Bard's problem Damn.

Bard frozen out for speaking truth
These managers remind him of Baby Ruth
No Mamma No Pappa No Uncle Sam
Baby Ruth does not give a Damn.

Sullins hushed for speaking truth about interview
Made to retract or face really bad job news
No Mamma No Pappa No Uncle Sam
Sullins is the victim Damn.

Christy did not want to hear about this din
Afraid might have to take it on chin
No Mamma No Pappa No Uncle Sam
Fear does not give a Damn.

Came to work on a beautiful day
Weather changed and a terrible storm came our way
No Mamma No Pappa No Uncle Sam
Weather does not give a Damn.

During storm helped old woman with two bags of concrete
Wind blew hard made it bleak to raise bags discrete
No Mamma No Pappa No Uncle Sam
The little old lady from Pasadena does not give a Damn.

Called Roland before storm rolled in April at din din
Cashier at risk and equipment exposed for hit on chin
No Mamma No Pappa No Uncle Sam
I guess we had to wait on dinner Damn.

Bard helped cashier with problem galore
April wanted to know what for
No Mamma No Pappa No Uncle Sam
April mad because Bard handled Damn.

Joyce came to store from vacation
Glad missed Bard's five-page incantation
No Mamma No Pappa No Uncle Sam
Encyclicals do not give a Damn.

Removed all numbers of Management from phone
Did not want them to have one stoned
No Mamma No Pappa No Uncle Sam
No numbers no phone and no one gives a Damn.

Employees and wrenches are same to Depot all the more
One sold other paid but only one blood in their core
No Mamma No Pappa No Uncle Sam
Wrenches like employees do not give a Damn.

Rocky has reason to celebrate
Moving to Electrical and Plumbing exculpate
No Mamma No Pappa No Uncle Sam
Ace replaced by a Rock Damn.

Bryan now in PRO a weekly role
Told Bard to pick up his stuff and go
No Mamma No Pappa No Uncle Sam
Again Bard cast aside Damn.

April brought cashiers some sweets to eat
Including Bard so to speak kind of neat
No Mamma No Pappa No Uncle Sam
Hemlock does not give a Damn.

Phyllis appeared down PRO way
As usual little to do but much to say
No Mamma No Pappa No Uncle Sam
Turn the orange light on Damn.

Dan the man in locker room holding court
Said Bard retired trophy from this sport
No Mamma No Pappa No Uncle Sam
You bet that trophy is retired Damn.

Dan said there is no free lunch
His profile recovering from paunch
No Mamma No Pappa No Uncle Sam
Free lunch does not give a Damn.

I shall return MacArthur from PT Boat promised
Returns at Home Depot more Psalmist
No Mamma No Pappa No Uncle Sam
PT Boats not made of Depot lumber Damn.

Register in PRO developed fatal error
Neither Bard nor April could lift scarab
No Mamma No Pappa No Uncle Sam
This register is fatal Damn.

Good cop bad cop prescription in this drone
Bet have fun throwing stones
No Mamma No Pappa No Uncle Sam
Coppers don't give a Damn.

Josh and team organizing in PRO scheme
None really wanted to make this scene
No Mamma No Pappa No Uncle Sam
Bard does not give a Damn.

Caesar looking for Brutus in lot
Bard explained role in this plot
No Mamma No Pappa No Uncle Sam
Caesar does give a Damn.

Flatcars and lumber carts parked by PRO register
Customers can't reach candy nor drinks at divestiture
No Mamma No Pappa No Uncle Sam
These do not give a Damn.

Sylvia upset at returns in buggy
Acted as if this made druggie
No Mamma No Pappa No Uncle Sam
Returns don't give a Damn.

Ladies in the night rarely bright
At Home Depot never a knight
No Mamma No Pappa No Uncle Sam
These ladies and knights do not give a Damn.

Hell is for heroes once said in fear
At Depot no heroes Hell still near
No Mamma No Pappa No Uncle Sam
Hell is for heroes Damn.

Trust no one care less run fast
Best way to survive Depot cast
No Mamma No Pappa No Uncle Sam
These never give a Damn.

Oh say can you see the anthem did read
If you do at Depot end in the Red Sea
No Mamma No Pappa No Uncle Sam
Pharoah's troops did not give a Damn.

Closing time you can't stay here
So says the Home Depot cheer
No Mamma No Pappa No Uncle Sam
Places you will be from don't give a Damn.

Customer returned three times in four
The merchandise just kept becoming more
No Mamma No Pappa No Uncle Sam
Three trips in four hours Damn.

Bury my heart at Wounded Knee
More reason to come to Depot you see
No Mamma No Pappa No Uncle Sam
Wounded Knee does not give a Damn.

Lightning crashes puts glory out from hide
At Home Depot you never see this side
No Mamma No Pappa No Uncle Sam
Lightning crashing does not give a Damn.

Martell smashed Moorish horde at Tours one day
Home Depot would never see it that way
No Mamma No Pappa No Uncle Sam
And this Hammer not sold Damn.

Management believes they conjure ghost of Caesar
Anytime they need him for their geezer
No Mamma No Pappa No Uncle Sam
Caesar not resurrected Damn.

Tape ran five feet long ringing up purchase
Customer enjoyed wait like burgess
No Mamma No Pappa No Uncle Sam
Made a great unit count Damn.

Customer had $1,135 on bill but only $500 to spend
Declined card invite left kind of thin
No Mamma No Pappa No Uncle Sam
Customer did return with funds Damn.

Calley a problem in My Lai 22 no longer alive
Depot provides similar lies to survive
No Mamma No Pappa No Uncle Sam
Thank you for your service Calley Damn.

Volunteering at Depot never right nor lark
No good unpunished no bad unrewarded that smarts
No Mamma No Pappa No Uncle Sam
Think military and never volunteer Damn.

Missy hurled apron at Bard in PRO
Later returned did burn Bard made it go
No Mamma No Pappa No Uncle Sam
Why hurl her fifteen pound weighted apron Damn.

Customer approached with flat car looking for buggy lost
Caesar claimed salad rediscovered this sauce
No Mamma No Pappa No Uncle Sam
Three hundred items in buggy Damn.

Pallet placed in front of candy and snacks
Asked management to pick up slack
No Mamma No Pappa No Uncle Sam
This vendor knows they cannot manage worth a Damn.

Pleasant day at home on Sunday on Do Not Call
They really did Bard a favor with this Y'all
No Mamma No Pappa No Uncle Sam
Bard likes DNC much more than call-ins Damn.

From the Halls of Montezuma to shores of Tripoli
From desk of paint to wall at far end officially
No Mamma No Pappa No Uncle Sam
No one is in who gives a Damn.

Donna promised pallet moved
Still sits there not wanting to be rude
No Mamma No Pappa No Uncle Sam
This pallet is not rude Damn.

Mickey his Mantle Roger his Maris
At Home Depot rather just scare us
No Mamma No Pappa No Uncle Sam
Mickey and Roger don't give a Damn.

ASM came by and said hey
Told Bard not wanting to play
No Mamma No Pappa No Uncle Sam
Hay and play don't give a Damn.

Stench and wrench may lead to clench
Strong stomach required or throw in wrench
No Mamma No Pappa No Uncle Sam
Wrench clenched does not give a Damn.

Red Ball express moved supplies through war's mess
At Depot they could not care less
No Mamma No Pappa No Uncle Sam
Red Ball express does not give a Damn.

The battle ax placed between blades hurts
Depot works this way in spurts
No Mamma No Pappa No Uncle Sam
Spurts and hurts do not feel a Damn.

Treat as we say management mantra
Never receive treatment offered employees ultra
No Mamma No Pappa No Uncle Sam
This mantra does not give a Damn.

Contractor with huge return directed to Customer Service
Declined repeat to manager became nervous
No Mamma No Pappa No Uncle Sam
Keep PRO closed and don't give a Damn.

Bard same for customers and those that work
For management think he but a twerp
No Mamma No Pappa No Uncle Sam
Twerps don't give a Damn.

Employees at rest have weight distress
Simply pre-eaten ahead much less
No Mamma No Pappa No Uncle Sam
And the obese don't give a Damn.

Dan the HC on Mother's Day eve looking to leave
Determined to close before becomes diseased
No Mamma No Pappa No Uncle Sam
Dan the man wants out Damn.

Called HC no coverage they say
Dan said try to get manager in play
No Mamma No Pappa No Uncle Sam
No coverage on to Customer Service Damn.

Give em Hell Harry he did too
At Home Depot know you are through
No Mamma No Pappa No Uncle Sam
Truman does not give a Damn.

Struggling to fight through six-hour shift
Management prefers to sink us like drift
No Mamma No Pappa No Uncle Sam
A drift does not give a Damn.

Lied to abused now be kind and use
Management plays this good and bad ruse
No Mamma No Pappa No Uncle Sam
Good cop bad cop neither give a Damn.

Part-time employees full-time customers too
Management never understands how rude
No Mamma No Pappa No Uncle Sam
You can bet part-times don't give a Damn.

Management wants Caesar to return
Then maybe store will no longer burn
No Mamma No Pappa No Uncle Sam
Caesar's ghost does not give a Damn.

What to do as cashier when employees few
Call HC send to Customer Service say adieu
No Mamma No Pappa No Uncle Sam
Adieu is French for not giving a Damn.

The Way We Were not things that will ever be
At Depot were and be never add up you see
No Mamma No Pappa No Uncle Sam
Were and be won't give a Damn.

Employees that won't receive mark of Cain
Once refused usually wane or become insane
No Mamma No Pappa No Uncle Sam
And beware the Mark of Cain Damn.

Road not taken ceases to exist
The chosen hard to resist so enlist
No Mamma No Pappa No Uncle Sam
Robert Frost does not give a Damn.

Collin alone in Lot Marcus does not do much
Complained to Isaac his Dutch means do not touch
No Mamma No Pappa No Uncle Sam
The Dutch do not give a Damn.

Stutters when asked to speak his thoughts
Reminded Bo Jackson connects these dots
No Mamma No Pappa No Uncle Sam
Collin is really great in his own way Damn.

Stuttered once too often Collin left for land of cotton
Replaced by others but never forgotten
No Mamma No Pappa No Uncle Sam
Collin did work when he worked Damn.

Ice cubes in winter and solar lamps in Summer
Merchandising simply gets dumber and dumber
No Mamma No Pappa No Uncle Sam
Merchandising does not give a Damn.

Rain and flood came to Cherrapunji
Not at all looney in Depot Koizumi
No Mamma No Pappa No Uncle Sam
Indian monsoons do not give a Damn.

No HC no FSM sent to Garden without end
Four hours in cold called forgotten dead end
No Mamma No Pappa No Uncle Sam
Left alone and forgotten in Garden cold Damn

Olive returned as HC after working a nine-hour shift
Discussed the mess and decided to uplift
No Mamma No Pappa No Uncle Sam
Nine hours then four more you think they give a Damn.

Told Olive been cold for four enough
No break provided leave store rebuff
No Mamma No Pappa No Uncle Sam
Olive said go for it Damn.

Hostile workplace almost always in play each day
They never run out of ways to make Bard pay
No Mamma No Pappa No Uncle Sam
Hostile work environment does not give a Damn.

April ill and left store with Dakota on cue
Bard wanted HC for these times to view
No Mamma No Pappa No Uncle Sam
They told Bard to pound sand Damn.

Earlier today they had eight cashiers a HC and FES in line
Later left one in Garden for four hours straight not so fine
No Mamma No Pappa No Uncle Sam
Too many too few who gives a Damn.

A Behr loose in Lot really cleans and removes
Hunts like a Grizzly for anything that moves
No Mamma No Pappa No Uncle Sam
This Behr gives a Damn.

Chase not the bank makes deposits in work
No Overdrawn nor closed accounts lurk
No Mamma No Pappa No Uncle Sam
Chase Bank does not give a Damn.

Ashley at Customer Service no one in paint nor SCO
Bard took up position to make sure this might go
No Mamma No Pappa No Uncle Sam
Noon and all seemed swooned Damn.

Brittany in Customer Service plans to stay day after day
Rather be here than resting on sandy shore this way
No Mamma No Pappa No Uncle Sam
Brittany needs therapy Damn.

Missy and Bean Counter at desk in PRO
Making Paul look after entire show
No Mamma No Pappa No Uncle Sam
Making work for Paul not giving a Damn.

Customer with Steeler mask talking trash about them Boys
Bradshaw moment door reversed to Customer Service annoyed
No Mamma No Pappa No Uncle Sam
And the Raiders still say Harris trapped the ball Damn.

Pipeline not worth a Continental
Manually driven by two smoking oriental
No Mamma No Pappa No Uncle Sam
No gas no customers and who gives a Damn.

Jesse a young woman in front end
Home Depot has made her blend
No Mamma No Pappa No Uncle Sam
This Jesse not for Rick Springfield Damn.

Gee Lee in Customer Service asked about no-shows
Replied this normal not to worry they pros
No Mamma No Pappa No Uncle Sam
Gee Lee really a pro Damn.

April in swoon and Christy in room
Might have to stand in and resume this position soon
No Mamma No Pappa No Uncle Sam
Christy over front end again will not give a Damn.

EEOC contacted about wrong committed
Decided to try and cause it to be requitted
No Mamma No Pappa No Uncle Sam
EEOC gives a Damn.

Age discrimination a major rift
Attorneys may decide to create a tiff
No Mamma No Pappa No Uncle Sam
Plaintiff attorneys and money give a Damn.

Attorney said case not a way despite Bard flayed
Standard to meet for age replete did not make grade
No Mamma No Pappa No Uncle Sam
And there is no case Damn.

April swooned went home to be horizontal
Stress and guilt with Bard tout ensemble
No Mamma No Pappa No Uncle Sam
April misses Bard having her back Damn.

Pickett at Gettysburg charged into guns
Sold at Home Depot before day begun
No Mamma No Pappa No Uncle Sam
These pickets never charge Damn.

Purgatory for Christy simply this and no more
Make ASM with Phyllis as FES direct report keep score
No Mamma No Pappa No Uncle Sam
Two for one and who gives a Damn.

Seen in paint mixing colors employee watched in dismay
Colors and things instead of Flooring people her way
No Mamma No Pappa No Uncle Sam
Christy likes finger painting Damn.

Keying locks into doors down in PRO
Christy making mechanical devices go
No Mamma No Pappa No Uncle Sam
Christy and lock keying amazing Damn.

Brian in PRO a new fixture that plays
Bard and he work as one these days
No Mamma No Pappa No Uncle Sam
Bryan has what he wants Damn.

Sylvia left for lunch and returned two hours late
Brian asked why missed her date
No Mamma No Pappa No Uncle Sam
PRO Desk vacant for two hours Damn.

Paul has diesel Volkswagen
Gets great mileage but wheezes like weasel
No Mamma No Pappa No Uncle Sam
Check engine light shuts down the car Damn.

Ashley came to Bard said her piece
There to do her job smiled at peace
No Mamma No Pappa No Uncle Sam
Bard and Ashley do their jobs Damn.

Pallets block candy shelf view
Makes everything a bit skewed
No Mamma No Pappa No Uncle Sam
Can't manage drop zones or candy Damn.

Managers like large roster they can posture
Roster rarely works resembles imposter
No Mamma No Pappa No Uncle Sam
Management but roosters right Damn.

Customer has need call numbers that apply indeed
If not call HC then to Customer Service believe
No Mamma No Pappa No Uncle Sam
Never call a manager again Damn.

Greeted Christy in store by saying hi
Jumped and reacted as if could just die
No Mamma No Pappa No Uncle Sam
Hi does not give a Damn.

Josh left early to find gas for beast
Colonial Pipeline must have been his release
No Mamma No Pappa No Uncle Sam
Josh cannot manage gas for truck Damn.

Explained to Steve in paint buy gas before Thursday
Asked how I knew true and convey
No Mamma No Pappa No Uncle Sam
Steve ignores Bard Damn.

Thursday came and pipeline dry
Not Russians but Sun caused to go awry
No Mamma No Pappa No Uncle Sam
CME centered over pipeline does not give a Damn

Spring flowers bloom birds nest and sing
At Depot new employees green as gourds bring
No Mamma No Pappa No Uncle Sam
No experience and no one gives a Damn.

Labor market very tough hard to find right stuff
Fog a mirror no arrest warrants no drugs more than enough
No Mamma No Pappa No Uncle Sam
A fogged mirror does not give a Damn.

Joey on vacation sliced arm blood poisoned
Proffered prosthetic to lower cost health plan reasoned
No Mamma No Pappa No Uncle Sam
After three weeks cut it off and get to work Damn.

Today was call Mandy in Hardware
Never swerved or went elsewhere
No Mamma No Pappa No Uncle Sam
A great job Mandy Damn.

Store by managers who fail tip scales
Never understand leads to sales fails
No Mamma No Pappa No Uncle Sam
Scales measure but do not give a Damn.

Josh not in building because he wins
Much more likely sent because of sins
No Mamma No Pappa No Uncle Sam
Purgatory not Heaven Josh Damn.

Dan found clots all over body
Placed in ICU to try and stop embody
No Mamma No Pappa No Uncle Sam
Dan in ICU Damn.

Management wants Bard to leave feel relieved
Guilt and anger badly deceived
No Mamma No Pappa No Uncle Sam
Bard not leaving Damn.

Mene mene tekel upharsin
At Depot like Greek to a parson
No Mamma No Pappa No Uncle Sam
Writing on the wall does not give a Damn.

Depot put jerry cans for sale in aisle
Customers wanted fuel in them meanwhile
No Mamma No Pappa No Uncle Sam
These Jerries don't give a Damn.

The colonials made victorious gas flows
Home Depot full of jerry cans feels woe
No Mamma No Pappa No Uncle Sam
Put gas in those cans Damn.

Whenever Sun erupts and comes to Earth
Expect Home Depot to profit and laugh with mirth
No Mamma No Pappa No Uncle Sam
CMEs don't give a Damn.

Brought returns to Customer service
Most cashiers do not their druthers
No Mamma No Pappa No Uncle Sam
They don't manage returns Damn.

Mary acted quite contrary did not show for work
Left rest feeling like helpless desk clerks
No Mamma No Pappa No Uncle Sam
At least call out Mary Damn.

Wood too valuable to waste or burn
A national disgrace they never learn
No Mamma No Pappa No Uncle Sam
Scarcity great for Depot Damn.

Fence paddles arrive by truck load
Sold in pallets almost before unload
No Mamma No Pappa No Uncle Sam
Keep ten percent double price Damn.

Failure to promote EEOC files complaint
Expect Home Depot to lose all restraint
No Mamma No Pappa No Uncle Sam
Revenge of the nerd at hand Damn.

Oh Say can you see when EEOC arrives
May cause some to take a deep dive
No Mamma No Pappa No Uncle Sam
Colors still streaming don't give a Damn.

Josh said no way and vented animus
EEOC may ask to be more magnanimous
No Mamma No Pappa No Uncle Sam
Josh not magnanimous Damn.

He will wail and vituperatively be nailed
Especially when told to let Bard set sail
No Mamma No Pappa No Uncle Sam
Payback time and no one gives a Damn.

April wheezing and seizing while running shift
Does not look good going forward in this shrift
No Mamma No Pappa No Uncle Sam
Wheezing and seizing do not give a Damn.

Alex fled from cashier reign sought to begin
Full-time Garden duty became new din
No Mamma No Pappa No Uncle Sam
And Alex fled from her register Damn.

When Eagle's notice comes they will squall
Depot management will claim not fair at all
No Mamma No Pappa No Uncle Sam
Don't mess with this Eagle Damn.

Caesar conquered Vercingetorix in Gaul
At Home Depot this may well mark their fall
No Mamma No Pappa No Uncle Sam
Gaul does not give a Damn.

April may find all this stimulus and stress too much to bear
Collapse and realize way too much wear much less dare
No Mamma No Pappa No Uncle Sam
Should have been there April Damn.

Home Depot employs cost benefit paralysis
Do cheap not right their analysis
No Mamma No Pappa No Uncle Sam
Doing what is right not their scheme Damn.

Pittsburgh paint declined scan or accept numbers entered
Somehow this paint from system censored
No Mamma No Pappa No Uncle Sam
Customers tried this in SCO Damn.

Coy Tennessee fan discussed plan
Hope new coach huge hit with fans
No Mamma No Pappa No Uncle Sam
A loyal fan this daughter of UT Damn.

Dan the man suffered from blood clots
Not sure what was up with this cheap shot
No Mamma No Pappa No Uncle Sam
Oh Damn.

Sent to ICU Dan tried to breeze through
Discovered tumor more trouble brew
No Mamma No Pappa No Uncle Sam
Dan in ICU Damn.

Surgery tried to keep Dan alive
Coded red did not survive
No Mamma No Pappa No Uncle Sam
Dan dead Damn.

Dan gone now that not fun
Musk Ox decreased by one undone
No Mamma No Pappa No Uncle Sam
Gone and undone Damn.

Conference room wall lined with them all
Told news wanted us to bawl
No Mamma No Pappa No Uncle Sam
Another reason to hate Satan Damn.

Called told then back on floor
A leaden weight feeling shift a great chore
No Mamma No Pappa No Uncle Sam
Life goes on even when wonder why Damn.

Offered opportunity to attend his funeral hymn
David wrote not come but go to child then
No Mamma No Pappa No Uncle Sam
Wash up dress and eat Damn.

Let dead bury dead He did proclaim
Dan neither don't be lame nor ashamed
No Mamma No Pappa No Uncle Sam
Thanks Dan for being you Damn

Torn by stress liquor family and weight
Combined to end this man's fate
No Mamma No Pappa No Uncle Sam
You know he really did give a Damn.

Dan an onery cuss always ready to make a scene
No longer can we see him release steam
No Mamma No Pappa No Uncle Sam
The cuss has left Damn.

Always ready to punch foes real and imagined
Now nothing more than a part of legend
No Mamma No Pappa No Uncle Sam
A legend Dan Damn.

Roared like a grizzly missing meat
Inside nothing but a heart that beat
No Mamma No Pappa No Uncle Sam
When comes another Dan Damn.

No Christy no Dan few stories to thrill
Work going to be a much tougher drill
No Mamma No Pappa No Uncle Sam
Never again to see Dan Damn.

Christy called Dan a jerk when at work
No longer will have this perk
No Mamma No Pappa No Uncle Sam
And who is the jerk now Christy Damn.

Customer asked how day going
Explained Dan no longer rowing
No Mamma No Pappa No Uncle Sam
This customer gave a Damn.

Why does Bard care about them in play
Like a knight simply built this way
No Mamma No Pappa No Uncle Sam
Knights do give a Damn.

Know when to play them when to fold them
Time enough for counting when done chum
No Mamma No Pappa No Uncle Sam
Kenny Rogers does not give a Damn.

John Barleycorn must die that no lie
Dan used it to spit in their eye
No Mamma No Pappa No Uncle Sam
Here is to you John Barleycorn Damn.

April brought Dan some shine of the moon
He thought it great to drink and groom
No Mamma No Pappa No Uncle Sam
No more Thunder Road for Dan Damn.

Man's search for meaning tested by Dan's death
What does it mean after his last breath
No Mamma No Pappa No Uncle Sam
And you think Frankl gives a Damn.

Izvestia has no news nor Pravda truth
At Home Depot these spins long in tooth
No Mamma No Pappa No Uncle Sam
Truth and news don't give a Damn.

Management bone stuck in throat
Employees bone between two dogs rote
No Mamma No Pappa No Uncle Sam
Dogs and bones don't give a Damn.

Christy at work in Flooring does bidding
Little more than personal rigging
No Mamma No Pappa No Uncle Sam
Christy is Christy when comes another Damn.

Bo Peep and Amber out for stroll
Much more to life so pay your toll
No Mamma No Pappa No Uncle Sam
Go to college Damn.

Lumber not in good place
Employees have quit race
No Mamma No Pappa No Uncle Sam
Lumber is but dead wood Damn.

Lot has coverage and men at work
Really ends need for smirk
No Mamma No Pappa No Uncle Sam
Lot fixed Damn.

Fear glues them to store with little lament
Bard wants to free them from this awful cement
No Mamma No Pappa No Uncle Sam
Fear does not give a Damn.

Christy a poster child for what Home Depot will do
Why don't the young see and eschew
No Mamma No Pappa No Uncle Sam
Better wake up Damn.

Told what seen many not believe
Home Depot too good to deceive
No Mamma No Pappa No Uncle Sam
And you think Pollyanna gives a Damn.

Milwaukee tool rep a real beauty to behold
Knows her stuff keeps all tools cold
No Mamma No Pappa No Uncle Sam
Milwaukee more than beer Damn.

Phone usually rings busy not answered when rung
Major problem for cashier customer no fun
No Mamma No Pappa No Uncle Sam
Busy or unanswered who gives a Damn.

Managers avoid Bard like plague
Told to stay away let April find way
No Mamma No Pappa No Uncle Sam
All up to April Damn.

Vendors in Garden work hard to make nice
Well arranged with color in good taste precise
No Mamma No Pappa No Uncle Sam
These vendors give a Damn.

Customer asked for wood sliced
Three times no one came no dice
No Mamma No Pappa No Uncle Sam
No one will cut wood Damn.

Did Dan take so called vaccination
Caused blood clot perturbation
No Mamma No Pappa No Uncle Sam
Bard begged you Dan Damn.

Rocky stood on lift to reach wayward sign in rafter
Brought down with a bang causing great laughter
No Mamma No Pappa No Uncle Sam
Laughter does not give a Damn.

No more masks if you take jab and risk to die
Over one million adverse reactions that no lie
No Mamma No Pappa No Uncle Sam
Super breeders roam free Damn.

OSHA says if Employers insist on jab sue
Forcing masks on healthy very rude
No Mamma No Pappa No Uncle Sam
Burn your mask Damn.

Joey returned to work today with arm of gangrene
Crippled like Kaiser and black obscene
No Mamma No Pappa No Uncle Sam
Joey one tough man Damn.

Dan portrait surrounded by candles and Apron in middle today
Add Myrrh and Frankincense then shrine complete charade
No Mamma No Pappa No Uncle Sam
Work around this shrine Damn.

Dan a flower flourished in field and store
Wind blew gone place remembered no more
No Mamma No Pappa No Uncle Sam
Flowers in field don't give a Damn.

Bo Peep given suggestions for help in front
Take credit if surfaced them with grunt
No Mamma No Pappa No Uncle Sam
When nice oh Damn.

Paul a veteran of two other stores
Likes Melanie much much more
No Mamma No Pappa No Uncle Sam
Different strokes for different folks Damn.

Young lady with paint and stuff in buggy
Ran short of funds Bard prevented ugly
No Mamma No Pappa No Uncle Sam
She said it meant a lot Damn.

Dan complained about Mandy to Home Office
Now moot dismissed with prejudice
No Mamma No Pappa No Uncle Sam
Just as well Damn.

Assailed for making light of tragedy
Many considered this more than blasphemy
No Mamma No Pappa No Uncle Sam
Get over it Damn.

For the young this grief very new and unexpected
Learning their way into adulthood now affected
No Mamma No Pappa No Uncle Sam
Time promised to no man Damn.

Life goes on with who what when and where
Why much tougher to answer they swear
No Mamma No Pappa No Uncle Sam
Life gives a Damn.

Truck did not arrive in Lumber causing Paul awry
Needed to unload before home could drive
No Mamma No Pappa No Uncle Sam
Trucks need to deliver on time Damn.

Something brewing no one knows exactly what
Management and supervision not naughty but nice klutz
No Mamma No Pappa No Uncle Sam
Klutz does not give a Damn.

Eagle has processed launched in flight to deliver
EEOC compliant soon to put chunk in yogurt now shiver
No Mamma No Pappa No Uncle Sam
And they may soon say Damn.

Customer arrived with two carts of things
Checkout took twenty tape a large ball of string
No Mamma No Pappa No Uncle Sam
Five hundred items on receipt tape Damn.

Bo Peep came to watch this incredible haul
Seemed plenty to cause pure awe
No Mamma No Pappa No Uncle Sam
This unit count does not give a Damn.

Store closes disconnect screens pull scanners off the switch
Next day plug scanners connect screen see them twitch
No Mamma No Pappa No Uncle Sam
Reboot and catch updates Damn.

Has Eagle landed Bard can't say
Management quiet keeping out of way
No Mamma No Pappa No Uncle Sam
Has the Eagle landed Damn.

Rebooted register at station three receipt printer not alive
Bo Peep arrived with cleaner spray and revived
No Mamma No Pappa No Uncle Sam
Use spray when rebooting Damn.

Dan took jab now we know
Caused clots laid him low
No Mamma No Pappa No Uncle Sam
Moderna fixed him permanently Damn.

Company in tizzy over relaxed mask frenzy if injected
If not Star of David selected
No Mamma No Pappa No Uncle Sam
Nazis at Nuremberg understand.

Posted an inscription on Dan's memorial apron deceased
This stillness created no peace not in the least
No Mamma No Pappa No Uncle Sam
Damn Dan Damn.

Call-outs go to managers but front never learns
Suggest call HC before they burn
No Mamma No Pappa No Uncle Sam
Management does not communicate Damn.

Booked my four and left a bit early
Way too many cashiers HC surly
No Mamma No Pappa No Uncle Sam
Surly does not give a Damn.

Andrea a newbie quite the beauty for all to see
Quiet as a mouse and sweeter than tea she
No Mamma No Pappa No Uncle Sam
At age 19 easy to give a Damn.

Something bad this way coming
Not sure why management succumbing
No Mamma No Pappa No Uncle Sam
The Coming Storm does not give a Damn.

Behr came and I don't mean paint
Looking for work found none to acquaint
No Mamma No Pappa No Uncle Sam
Fighting over buggies to work Damn.

John Henry made fifteen feet steam drill but nine
Chris and John played shaker drilled on time
No Mamma No Pappa No Uncle Sam
John Henry broke heart and does not give a Damn.

Christy stared at Bard today through a very heavy mask
Eyes flashed as he passed did not why to ask
No Mamma No Pappa No Uncle Sam
Christy's eye flash does not give a Damn.

Bo Peep a Christy in twenty and Amber in ten
Is there anyone that might make them see this trend
No Mamma No Pappa No Uncle Sam
They want to be the next Christy Damn.

Carly Simon sang anticipation over catsup
Bard waits for opportunity to know what's up
No Mamma No Pappa No Uncle Sam
Carly Simon does not give a Damn.

Mandy and Amber compared new tattoos for fun
Amber has one that says Da kummt die Sonne
No Mamma No Pappa No Uncle Sam
George Harrison does not give a Damn.

New schedule out on time with four days
Looks like Home Depot plays Purple Haze
No Mamma No Pappa No Uncle Sam
Purple haze does not give a Damn.

Business slow in PRO all afternoon
Clock stopped work swooned
No Mamma No Pappa No Uncle Sam
One customer paid with 12 Ben Franklins Damn.

Yo Yo came to PRO no register available
Begged pardon moved less debatable
No Mamma No Pappa No Uncle Sam
Finished shift in middle who gives a Damn.

Brian unable to get credit approved asked Bard to phone
Spoke with Sullins request gone to parts unknown
No Mamma No Pappa No Uncle Sam
Parts unknown does not give a Damn.

Mandy a delight to customers causing them purchase
Enjoys fray makes sure have great service
No Mamma No Pappa No Uncle Sam
Mandy on a friendly roll Damn.

Christy like the federal government here to help
Packs pelt provides a belt very svelte
No Mamma No Pappa No Uncle Sam
Federal government does not give a Damn.

Rocky packing pipe in Plumbing
Not about to take a drumming
No Mamma No Pappa No Uncle Sam
Rocky fully engaged Damn.

Rebooted number three so it might run free
Instead printer receipt decided to give third degree
No Mamma No Pappa No Uncle Sam
Printer receipt is making it tough Damn.

Five gallon paint on metal seat arrived at register
Checked who in paint returned to that character
No Mamma No Pappa No Uncle Sam
Jasmine in paint said thanks Damn.

Jasmine had Christy in flames working at paint
Not sure why Christy acting like this not a saint
No Mamma No Pappa No Uncle Sam
Jasmine knows paint Christy Damn.

Bo Peep arrived to work on three see what she might
Tried everything then cleaned it with all her might
No Mamma No Pappa No Uncle Sam
Used the shepherd's staff Damn.

Amber in charge as front end HC
Mistaken on assignments and time you see
No Mamma No Pappa No Uncle Sam
Corrected problem and gives a Damn.

Booked four and left floor to go
Amber did not grieve nor feel woe
No Mamma No Pappa No Uncle Sam
Do your time and leave Damn.

Who would believe what often seen
Theater of Absurd greatly amuses then
No Mamma No Pappa No Uncle Sam
Theater of Absurd Damn.

For purchases men prefer Bardot to Depot
Charge card or purchase with real dough
No Mamma No Pappa No Uncle Sam
Bridget does not give a Damn.

Jonathan new to store and Lot wants to impress
Says less and works more never repressed
No Mamma No Pappa No Uncle Sam
Jonathan in Lot gives a Damn.

Lumber futures hit skids plunged off cliff
Hope prices follow and set Depot adrift
No Mamma No Pappa No Uncle Sam
Lumber needs to collapse Damn.

Depot stock inflated beyond reason
Need to split introduce new season
No Mamma No Pappa No Uncle Sam
Split before collapse Damn.

Slow day down PRO way today
No customers wanted to come in and play
No Mamma No Pappa No Uncle Sam
Today customers don't give a Damn.

Sylvia looking to set sail with more sales
Returns in buggy caused to feel blackmailed
No Mamma No Pappa No Uncle Sam
Sylvia hates returns in buggy Damn.

Depot wants workout by employees performed
Katergozomai activity not their norm
No Mamma No Pappa No Uncle Sam
Workouts don't give a Damn.

Paul in Lumber trains Lot newbies no shame
Wants them to learn avoid later blame
No Mamma No Pappa No Uncle Sam
At least Paul teaches Damn.

Nothing new with EEOC
Waiting for management to say what they see
No Mamma No Pappa No Uncle Sam
Dawn's early light Damn.

Christy wrapping a pallet nothing to say
Left a message for us to checkout her way
No Mamma No Pappa No Uncle Sam
Enough with messages Damn.

Explained why price on blinds changed by Christy
Quit with excuses put on price not risky
No Mamma No Pappa No Uncle Sam
And a cashier only cares about price Damn.

Bo Peep never lost a sheep knows not how to weep
Experiencing death of one so close not sweet
No Mamma No Pappa No Uncle Sam
Welcome to adulthood Bo Peep Damn.

Nice to eschew useless mask and breathe again
Keep off except for customers raising Cain
No Mamma No Pappa No Uncle Sam
Raising Cain does not give a Damn.

Customers seek service in meek and mild terms
Shocked when provided by anyone in this firm
No Mamma No Pappa No Uncle Sam
Easy to exceed customer beliefs Damn.

Pine straw out for weeks
Plant burned made hay into freaks
No Mamma No Pappa No Uncle Sam
And a hot time in that barn tonight Damn.

OCR Online Cash register lacks reason in lumber
Fence posts not found 2 x 10s unnumbered
No Mamma No Pappa No Uncle Sam
OCR does not give a Damn.

JC afraid for his lung that may have Big C
Scheduled look-see followed by biopsy
No Mamma No Pappa No Uncle Sam
First Dan now JC Damn.

Hot Summer day in Garden with Jesse holding sway
Collected customers helped get on their way
No Mamma no Pappa No Uncle Sam
Jesse gives a Damn.

April in Garden because of call-outs
Wish Bard could agree to fall into this bout
No Mamma No Pappa No Uncle Sam
April misses Bard taking it on chin Damn.

Customers crushed Bard and April in Garden
Have payment handy speed up the bargain
No Mamma No Pappa No Uncle Sam
April took notes of payment statement Damn.

Bard asked April to call for coverage buggies and carts
Unable to reach management or help not a good start
No Mamma No Pappa No Uncle Sam
Raise the roof April and make management respond Damn.

Six hours in Garden today hot
Managed to keep stirring customer plot
No Mamma No Pappa No Uncle Sam
Four hours in with no break Damn.

Garden exit and road not safe at any speed indeed
Barricade street place pylons along annex accede
No Mamma No Pappa No Uncle Sam
Increase safety and profits Damn.

Bard asked April to take idea as own
Block road with guardrail no one will moan
No Mamma No Pappa No Uncle Sam
Block road and make it safe Damn.

Potting soil and mulch on sale caused large travail
Cars lined up like drive through along annex trail
No Mamma No Pappa No Uncle Sam
Lined up for mulch and soil who gives a Damn.

Across street at Tractor Supply people almost die
Shots fired window smashed in blink of an eye
No Mamma No Pappa No Uncle Sam
Bullets flying and who gives a Damn.

Jesse admitted does not handle heat
Under fan in shade Bard took Sun beat
No Mamma No Pappa No Uncle Sam
Jesse knows he has her back Damn.

Nice to reason that because of their battle ax treason
Bard will receive no call-in after this six-hour season
No Mamma No Pappa No Uncle Sam
And the battle ax may not be so bad Damn.

April needed people to come and help schedule
Have manager call and test Christy's mettle
No Mamma No Pappa No Uncle Sam
And let manager make Christy give a Damn.

Janet came to Garden towards end
Helped cover for Bard like a twin
No Mamma No Pappa No Uncle Sam
Covered Garden like dew Damn.

Developed new plan for store to restore
Move entrance to middle middle to entrance galore
No Mamma No Pappa No Uncle Sam
Entrance to middle and vice versa Damn.

Women with hair covering store
Red streaks or white icing in black hair s'more
No Mamma No Pappa No Uncle Sam
S'mores don't give a Damn.

Railroad ties not in Garden but Lumber
Must walk across store to find that number
No Mamma No Pappa No Uncle Sam
Makes no sense and who gives a Damn.

Sun came out from under metal roof
Timely haze prevented reproof
No Mamma No Pappa No Uncle Sam
This haze did give a Damn.

Nick appeared to run tow motor for orders of mulch
Filled truck then moved lawnmowers in clutch
No Mamma No Pappa No Uncle Sam
Why is Nick always inside Damn.

Wasco over Garden this is true
When ruling stays inside where cool
No Mamma No Pappa No Uncle Sam
Garden inside does not give a Damn.

Ran out of buggies and flatcars Behr replenished
There was no finish to this endless skirmish
No Mamma No Pappa No Uncle Sam
Thanks Behr for helping Damn.

Bard no longer moves buggies into Garden line
Now left outside customers must find
No Mamma No Pappa No Uncle Sam
No buggies in line they don't give a Damn.

Garden keeps buggy for returns for plants not bought
Customers empty take right on dot
No Mamma No Pappa No Uncle Sam
Customers miss buggies in line Damn.

Customer front end becoming nervous
After calls send them there for service
No Mamma No Pappa No Uncle Sam
Customer Service must give a Damn.

Flatcars absent without any pardon
Customer has no way to gather in Garden
No Mamma No Pappa No Uncle Sam
First buggies now flatcars who gives a Damn.

Logan alone covering Garden rest fled indoors
Filled needs of all customers as if corps
No Mamma No Pappa No Uncle Sam
At least Logan gives a Damn.

PRO and Customer Service joined as one
Everyone served on weekends what fun
No Mamma No Pappa No Uncle Sam
All in one great Damn.

Teleprompter offered employee stock option
One percent of pay most can auction
No Mamma No Pappa No Uncle Sam
One third of a share Damn.

Told vendors barcodes broke
Ran amok had stroke
No Mamma No Pappa No Uncle Sam
Just makes checkout a sham Damn.

Garden Party continued as sun declined
New people arrived to shine endless grind
No Mamma No Pappa No Uncle Sam
And we all shine on who gives a Damn.

New employees all around like surround sound
Reminds of being in lost and found
No Mamma No Pappa No Uncle Sam
Will anyone show them anything Damn.

Move Flooring close to Lumber another plan
One complements the other like rattan
No Mamma No Pappa No Uncle Sam
And put Christy closer to Lumber and locks Damn.

No increase for coins and dollars
Use the next size up be sure and holler
No Mamma No Pappa No Uncle Sam
Fail to replenish and don't give a Damn.

April brought gift today for what customer did say
Bragged on Bard thanked this way
No Mamma No Pappa No Uncle Sam
April knows Bard gives a Damn.

Bo Peep needed some sheep to complete sweep
Required Bard and Christy to earn their keep
No Mamma No Pappa No Uncle Sam
Bo Peep needs sheep Damn.

When Garden closed at eight Bard tried for the gate
Bo Peep needed to nine Bard swallowed the bait
No Mamma No Pappa No Uncle Sam
Bo Peep and her shepherd's staff Damn.

Bo Peep talked of Dan this eve stories did weave
Explained many times kidded and deceived
No Mamma No Pappa No Uncle Sam
Dan and his stories remembered Damn.

Funeral set for Friday two weeks after
This one will definitely be no Laffer
No Mamma No Pappa No Uncle Sam
Funerals and Dan Damn.

Bringing in staff from other stores for coverage in general
Many going to exit and be at Dan's funeral
No Mamma No Pappa No Uncle Sam
Dan not at this funeral Damn.

Vendor in Garden offered plants for free
Give them away never discount see
No Mamma No Pappa No Uncle Sam
Lost sales and they don't give a Damn.

Joey back in hospital with arm turning black
Treatments failing poison cutting no slack
No Mamma No Pappa No Uncle Sam
Joey needs prayer Damn.

Returned from UAH hospital given reprieve
Don't trust local doctors even with fleas
Mo Mamma No Pappa No Uncle Sam
Joey recovering and at work Monday Damn.

Ace and Sullins passed by self-checkout tonight
Said hi to Bard and smiled real bright
No Mamma No Pappa No Uncle Sam
When management smiles duck Damn.

MacArthur said old soldiers fade away
It did not happen to Dan this way
No Mamma No Pappa No Uncle Sam
Old soldiers don't give a Damn.

Customer left car unlocked engine running
Joyrider took car went gunning
No Mamma No Pappa No Uncle Sam
Car unlocked engine running Damn.

Fire alarm screamed at three did not relent
Customers fled left stuff with no lament
No Mamma No Pappa No Uncle Sam
Sprinklers do not give a Damn.

Drained system to seek reason for malfunction
Discovered water bled to floor unction
No Mamma No Pappa No Uncle Sam
Unction and malfunction don't give a Damn.

Dan lived to drink and drinked to live
Bring a keg to funeral he might imbibe
No Mamma No Pappa No Uncle Sam
This one is for you Dan Damn.

Tried to break bread with Dan one day
Did not want that to happen his way
No Mamma No Pappa No Uncle Sam
Wish he had said yes Damn.

Dan's wife visited store received some gifts
Smiled a lot when saw life insurance grift
No Mamma No Pappa No Uncle Sam
Life insurance does not give a Damn.

Oh the drunken Ira Hayes won't answer anymore
Dan not that whiskey drinking Indian chore
No Mamma No Pappa No Uncle Sam
And Old Crow did not give a Damn.

Very old lady bought two bags of soil
I think I can like the engine that could in toil
No Mamma No Pappa No Uncle Sam
This customer really impressive Damn.

Three straight in line tonight Mexico Red China and Russia
Thought in Decatur Alabama and America crusher
No Mamma No Pappa No Uncle Sam
And a nation of occupants no nation at all Damn.

Paul appeared old and grey in lumber badly torn
Left store previous eve no one replaced called back next morn
No Mamma No Pappa No Uncle Sam
Paul only in Lumber twenty-four hours Damn.

Yoslyn told Bard unmarried with child
Christian's sister will not be reviled
No Mamma No Pappa No Uncle Sam
Yoslyn and Christian are good people Damn.

JC and his knee are gimp
Waiting for biopsy hope for lung's glint
No Mamma No Pappa No Uncle Sam
JC worried Damn.

Yoslyn told Bard moving from freight
Going to be a cashier before too late
No Mamma No Pappa No Uncle Sam
Hope Bard can help Damn.

She the employee of the month in Freight
Seems like a long time ago due to weight
No Mamma No Pappa No Uncle Sam
Yoslyn staying the course Damn.

More yellow skews put in register pews
Do not scan why not tested causing blues
No Mamma No Pappa No Uncle Sam
Yellow SKU not tested not worth a Damn.

Dorothy not in Kansas anymore
Depot employees when on store's floor
No Mamma No Pappa No Uncle Sam
The Wizard of Oz does not give a Damn.

Tomorrow Dan put in ground
Many people will be gathered all around
No Mamma No Pappa No Uncle Sam
Dan in the ground not so Damn.

PRO door blocked and cancelled by buggies in way
James walks around them nothing to say
No Mamma No Pappa No Uncle Sam
Business as usual with buggies Damn.

Buggies blocking door in PRO
Four people there but none make them go
No Mamma No Pappa No Uncle Sam
Who needs to enter PRO right Damn.

Swing low sweet chariot coming home
Home Depot wants to sell your money's dome
No Mamma No Pappa No Uncle Sam
Swing lo sweet Chariot not in Depot Damn.

St. Peter don't you call them they can't go
They owe their soul to Depot card's woe
No Mamma No Pappa No Uncle Sam
St. Peter can't help them Damn.

April provided Depot tagged gift thought great
Made by slave labor don't be an ingrate
No Mamma No Pappa No Uncle Sam
They divided His garments too Damn.

Dan died but many more perishing
Tragic much more than discouraging
No Mamma No Pappa No Uncle Sam
The perishing don't give a Damn.

Store 0884 to Home Depot chain
Like a farmers market to Publix insane
No Mamma No Pappa No Uncle Sam
Not to give a bad name to a farmers market Damn.

Brad visited store to buy nuts and bolts with tool surmise
Asked if could exchange all looked surprise
No Mamma No Pappa No Uncle Sam
And they don't know the answer Damn.

Suggestions and ideas to Home Depot
What lead balloons to leido
No Mamma No Pappa No Uncle Sam
Lead balloons don't give a Damn.

Home Depot straight out of Dr. Seuss
Run stores here to there no excuse
No Mamma No Pappa No Uncle Sam
And Geisel laughs but does not give a Damn.

Union War Dead Day approaches sales notices
No true Southerner ever offers condolences
No Mamma No Pappa No Uncle Sam
And genocide never forgotten Damn.

North tested on South then perfected on Indian
Home Depot dream for employees therein
No Mamma No Pappa No Uncle Sam
Pay them less because you can Damn.

Two hour max in Garden during Summer heat wave ardor
Bard must go away after this stay because of poor Arthur
No Mamma No Pappa No Uncle Sam
Keep in Garden or he goes home Damn.

Shift ended when store closed but stayed late
HC needed help said to wait
No Mamma No Pappa No Uncle Sam
Wait and late don't give a Damn.

Olive on last shift as HC exhausted in woe
Boyfriend tried to bring coffee stores all closed
No Mamma No Pappa No Uncle Sam
Starbucks and Dunkin closed at 7PM Friday Damn.

Leaders serve managers serve employees serve customers
At Depot reverse train so lame such hustlers
No Mamma No Pappa No Uncle Sam
No Kaizen who gives a Damn.

Atlanta leaders know they great why Depot rates
Haughty spirit assures destruction wait and see mate
No Mamma No Pappa No Uncle Sam
They don't give a Damn.

Janet wanted to remain in Garden
Bard gave pardon marched to PRO like a Spartan
No Mamma No Pappa No Uncle Sam
PRO or Garden who gives a Damn.

Frederick Henry mourned bride in book appertaining
Dan buried and like Henry it was raining
No Mamma No Pappa No Uncle Sam
Dan did rain on their parade after all Damn.

Vendors arranged Garden for Memorial Day like Pixy's pasture
Customers and employees make more like a force majeure
No Mamma No Pappa No Uncle Sam
Pretty as a picture Damn.

Jesse had a register problem item would not ring
Asked Bard if he could make it sing
No Mamma No Pappa No Uncle Sam
Bard helped because Jesse gives a Damn.

Andrea in PRO reached time to leave
Took returns her drink retrieved
No Mamma No Pappa No Uncle Sam
Andrea never talks Damn.

Customer left buggy and flatcar in middle of causeway
Came in but Customer Service sent him away
No Mamma No Pappa No Uncle Sam
Abandon cart and buggy in middle of causeway Damn.

Post pictures of cashiers of the month in this domain
Four quit three transferred few remain
No Mamma No Pappa No Uncle Sam
Cashier of the month no real thing Damn.

Little old lady mutilated by truck one Sunday morn
Did not survive Depot released black balloons mourn
No Mamma No Pappa No Uncle Sam
Black balloons released next to wildlife refuge Damn.

Covid fraud revealed in price of sanitizer
Dropped from nine to two dollars no appetizer
No Mamma No Pappa No Uncle Sam
And a worthless sham kills no virus Damn.

Little Christy suffering in misery
Bard took SCO so sits at register briefly
No Mamma No Pappa No Uncle Sam
Little Christy in misery Damn.

Mary autistic made cashier of month
For once realistic up front
No Mamma No Pappa No Uncle Sam
Well deserved Damn.

Janet commented Bo Peep and Amber hardly working
Then complained about timing of breaks shirking
No Mamma No Pappa No Uncle Sam
Janet sees they don't give a Damn.

Unseasonably cool in Garden this Memorial Saturday
Yo Yo left alone there to work and make hay
No Mamma No Pappa No Uncle Sam
Yo Yo really cold Damn.

Rocky complimented for improvements in Plumbing
Inventory left on floor by receiving causing much grieving
No Mamma No Pappa No Uncle Sam
Rocky determined to fix Plumbing Damn.

Receiving covers Bar Codes some kind of game
Makes cashier run out of options and exclaim
No Mamma No Pappa No Uncle Sam
Receiving does not give a Damn.

Donna left phone in buggy unanswered
Reminded phone not substandard
No Mamma No Pappa No Uncle Sam
Why phone in buggy Damn.

Cop came in covered with mask
Needed to drink from big flask
No Mamma No Pappa No Uncle Sam
Are you serious Damn.

Wind from door blew gift cards all over
Bard moved them to more peaceful clover
No Mamma No Pappa No Uncle Sam
Gift cards blown away don't give a Damn.

Bo Peep with men of her age likes passive aggression
When finished normally an unwanted possession
No Mamma No Pappa No Uncle Sam
Poor Nick never stood a chance against this Damn.

Dumb like a brick an old adage braying
At Home Depot passes for management saying
No Mamma No Pappa No Uncle Sam
Bricks don't give a Damn.

HC first time on audit did not count heads
Seems Amber simply too full of dread
No Mamma No Pappa No Uncle Sam
Bard helped her to count to three Damn.

No coverage in annex for customer with two loads
Bard had him make two trips and not explode
No Mamma No Pappa No Uncle Sam
Opened gate and filled his order Damn.

Mary ebony queen moved buggies from corral
Said too tough for her morale
No Mamma No Pappa No Uncle Sam
Mary learned buggies are heavy Damn.

Memorial Day weekend at Store 0884 all new
Much more like a mausoleum than normal holiday zoo
No Mamma No Pappa No Uncle Sam
And no one in the store Damn.

Millie in paint full of restraint moving back to cashier
Wants to flee Christy cookie monster so dear
No Mamma No Pappa No Uncle Sam
First Hunter then Sumner now Millie Damn.

Customer mad over chain did exclaim
Amber declined to extinguish flame
No Mamma No Pappa No Uncle Sam
PR and Amber not one and the same Damn.

Explained to Amber why Garden open to Sunday close
Light remains customers come to load by the gross
No Mamma No Pappa No Uncle Sam
Keep Garden open in light Amber Damn.

I am an outlaw and on highway I make my run
At Home Depot they do this just for fun
No Mamma No Pappa No Uncle Sam
These Eagles don't give a Damn.

Management may act like apes dragging knuckles on ground
When they do employees know not to be found
No Mamma No Pappa No Uncle Sam
Oh just give them a banana Damn.

Amber flustered and confused on audit night news
Unable to focus for fear of bad reviews
No Mamma No Pappa No Uncle Sam
Amber afraid and who gives a Damn.

Nick the silent spoke about no one in Garden stay
Amanda ignored customer and walked away
No Mamma No Pappa No Uncle Sam
When Nick speaks you better listen Amanda Damn.

Amanda believes in great escape
Avoids work hides well in this landscape
No Mamma No Pappa No Uncle Sam
What Amanda work Damn.

Employees take care of each other in these wilds
Management paddles own canoes like Rothschilds
No Mamma No Pappa No Uncle Sam
Red Shields don't give a Damn.

Charlie and Nick not a sight to see
Act like fell off Zeider zee
No Mamma No Pappa No Uncle Sam
Burned out and don't give a Damn.

Fatal error register locking customer and cashier
Had to reboot and re-key act like a seer
No Mamma No Pappa No Uncle Sam
Customer understood did not work Damn.

Three customers said hi to Bard in store as arrived
Made him feel great to be alive
No Mamma No Pappa No Uncle Sam
Customers say hi with no apron on Damn.

Jesse left $750 in Garden register till
Said would give it to robber for thrill
No Mamma No Pappa No Uncle Sam
Jesse risking life are you serious Damn.

Donna sent all tubes to Garden with no pardon
Amber stressed feared for job over this jargon
No Mamma No Pappa No Uncle Sam
They can't manage tubes Damn.

Unidentified newbie in Paint alone tonight
No training nor help from Christy not a delight
No Mamma No Pappa No Uncle Sam
Replace Millie with this Christy Damn.

Depot told Bard stay home on holiday Monday
Gave double pay to newbies as if a buffet
No Mamma No Pappa No Uncle Sam
This buffet does not give a Damn.

Algorithms on Holidays go to employees with least pay
Company saves difference OK
No Mamma No Pappa No Uncle Sam
Worry about three buck difference Damn.

Monkey see monkey hear monkey do no evil
Management acts much more like Evel Knievel
No Mamma No Pappa No Uncle Sam
These monkeys don't give a Damn.

Put on apron glaze eyes stop ears
You will never be brought to tears
No Mamma No Pappa No Uncle Sam
These don't give a Damn.

Employees know when management nice watch out
Very similar to smile on hungry shark cookout
No Mamma No Pappa No Uncle Sam
Hungry sharks don't give a Damn.

Amber needed help organizing audit with SCO machines
Told to let them cool then might come clean
No Mamma No Pappa No Uncle Sam
No one told Amber how to do this Damn.

You got to walk that lonesome valley
Amber discovered better rally
No Mamma No Pappa No Uncle Sam
Poor Amber alone on audit night Damn.

Lot attendant called out in AM
Said too drunk from PM
No Mamma No Pappa No Uncle Sam
Drink after shift not before Damn.

Stoics do not always have much to say
At Home Depot told to go away
No Mamma No Pappa No Uncle Sam
Stoics do not give a Damn.

Some employees retain masks wear them fast
Probably because afraid to be unmasked
No Mamma No Pappa No Uncle Sam
Masks don't work and hurt Damn.

Forgot to make 30-minute closing announcement
Amber could offer twenty-six-minute endowment
No Mamma No Pappa No Uncle Sam
Amber's train has left rails Damn.

Plants discounted old fashioned way
Customers and cashiers confused how much to pay
No Mamma No Pappa No Uncle Sam
And system does not change price Damn.

Allocate hours but never manage
Par for course using this adage
No Mamma No Pappa No Uncle Sam
This adage does not give a Damn.

Melisha wanted to stay and make more pay
Amber asked Bard to go away
No Mamma No Pappa No Uncle Sam
Bard glad to oblige Damn.

What can shall go wrong in Murphy's Law
Permanent resident in this store's rickshaw
No Mamma No Pappa No Uncle Sam
Murphy had this store in mind Damn.

Consanguineous in this store often found
Make sure know who from whom bound
No Mamma No Pappa No Uncle Sam
They all have family connections Damn

Bard had Amber count to four he might leave
Exited store greased sieve to three
No Mamma No Pappa No Uncle Sam
Getting off Titanic not dumb Damn.

Bo Peep called for buggy jamboree
No one free to answer plea
No Mamma No Pappa No Uncle Sam
Boy Scouts today don't give a Damn.

Customers in Garden ask to pass with merchandise
Remind them customers not thieves edgewise
No Mamma No Pappa No Uncle Sam
Customers reminded appreciate Damn.

Front end HC Phone 190 refused sign-ins
Busy tone means one calling take on shin
No Mamma No Pappa No Uncle Sam
Phone 190 not working again Damn.

Edmund Fitzgerald sank in winter storm one year
Home Depot losing this cargo not pay dear
No Mamma No Pappa No Uncle Sam
Some cargo lost who gives a Damn.

Home Depot no future only a past
Present consumes future and fast
No Mamma No Pappa No Uncle Sam
Consume present and future Damn.

Connor new one in Hardware scene quiet always pristine
Manages customers very quietly never enters quarantine
No Mamma No Pappa No Uncle Sam
Connor gets it done well Damn.

Saw Lon Chaney not walking with queen
Quite the sight in evening to be seen
No Mamma No Pappa No Uncle Sam
Werewolves not real right Damn.

SKU on one gallon paint rang up picture of five
Customer had to rant before agreeing with this jive
No Mamma No Pappa No Uncle Sam
SKU screwy they don't give a Damn.

Required accuracy check test watched rest
Used separate cart easy no mess
No Mamma No Pappa No Uncle Sam
Work test never let it work you Damn.

Oscar and customer loading cement bags
Twisted and turned producing really bad drag
No Mamma No Pappa No Uncle Sam
Oscar will be very sore from this Damn.

Explained to cashier about health and strips
Customer and thief might get in shooting tiff
No Mamma No Pappa No Uncle Sam
John Wayne is dead Damn.

April all a-titter with way Front end now glitters
Reminded Bard now had much less to consider
No Mamma No Pappa No Uncle Sam
It means little now Damn.

James in Lot called out for not having help
Terrible spot like being stuck in kelt
No Mamma No Pappa No Uncle Sam
Come to work James Damn.

Customer in PRO on third trip of day
Paid 12 8 and 6 hundred in separate forays
No Mamma No Pappa No Uncle Sam
She used Depot card Damn.

Nebuchadnezzar arrived at 10 and entered in 4
Practice applied to equipment on floor
No Mamma No Pappa No Uncle Sam
Ten-four and out who gives a Damn.

Valdez oil tanker captain drunk failed to steer ran aground
Home Depot that boat steered seems similarly bound
No Mamma No Pappa No Uncle Sam
At least he was drunk Damn.

Rain may be falling on their heads
Never envisioned sprinklers watering Bread
No Mamma No Pappa No Uncle Sam
Bread does not give a Damn.

Hunter left store from flooring April wanted someway
Burned by Christy refused to stay another day
No Mamma No Pappa No Uncle Sam
Hunter's license revoked Damn.

Chemistry brings action reaction and byproduct
Management yields consequences got it
No Mamma No Pappa No Uncle Sam
Consequences don't give a Damn.

Ace in Flooring chair when Christy absent
Checks process remains passionate
No Mamma No Pappa No Uncle Sam
Ace reviewing for whom Damn.

This store but a nursery in school says Josh
Are customers then Oshkosh B'Gosh
No Mamma No Pappa No Uncle Sam
Oshkosh B'Gosh does not give a Damn.

Blame game by management supervision water running down hill
No one owns anything very lame big chill
No Mamma No Pappa No Uncle Sam
Blame grunts and don't give a Damn.

The SEC says just means so much more
At this Depot store silly numbers galore
No Mamma No Pappa No Uncle Sam
SEC does not give a Damn.

How to measure customer satisfaction
Management not interested in determining reaction
No Mamma No Pappa No Uncle Sam
Numbers matter customers don't Damn.

Henpecked by April and Emily over delivery
Surrendered and complied an act of sheer chivalry
No Mamma No Pappa No Uncle Sam
Chivalry is not dead Damn.

Depot like gaming casino
One has odds other profits on shingles
No Mamma No Pappa No Uncle Sam
Odds better at casino Damn.

Oscar de la Renta not found in Lumber
No perfume just dust and must asunder
No Mamma No Pappa No Uncle Sam
John made him stay till 9 Damn.

JC result on his lung deemed stage zero
No problem free to go to Point Barrow
No Mamma No Pappa No Uncle Sam
JC OK Damn.

Aerospace retiree ex-Marine talked inventory control
Joyce appeared inventory her black hole
No Mamma No Pappa No Uncle Sam
Solve inventory at Depot ha ha Damn.

Amanda passed by looked far less than neat
No longer able to skip hard work beat
No Mamma No Pappa No Uncle Sam
Amanda learning to work Damn.

Hire them male female and whatever
Too many become useless clutter
No Mamma No Pappa No Uncle Sam
You think this gives a Damn.

Sylvia angry at JC for not coming off break for customer help
Called ASM hatched plan to make him whelp
No Mamma No Pappa No Uncle Sam
JC not getting his break Damn.

Bryan and Sylvia left PRO for break leaving Bard at stake
Managed customers without fault did not have to make
No Mamma No Pappa No Uncle Sam
Sylvia and Bryan happy Damn.

Lumber aisles smell of fresh wood
Reminded the way it should
No Mamma No Pappa No Uncle Sam
Fresh wood for sale gives a Damn.

Spoke with Hollywood about sister
Offered money and help in secret he differed
No Mamma No Pappa No Uncle Sam
Declined sugar for this lemon Damn.

Row row row your boat gently down stream
At Home Depot lost paddles and scream
No Mamma No Pappa No Uncle Sam
Home Depot sells neither boats nor oars Damn.

Charlie pitched fit over returns at Customer Service
April wanted housekeeping in his Garden circus
No Mamma No Pappa No Uncle Sam
Just doing what instructed Damn.

Safety at Depot like barrel to Niagara
Men swallow Viagra ladies wear mascara
No Mamma No Pappa No Uncle Sam
Niagara Falls does not give a Damn.

Another newbie for Christy and Flooring
Turnover there just like when in front end soaring
No Mamma No Pappa No Uncle Sam
Turnover like Front End Damn.

Sales in Flooring hit skids looking bad at this jot
Compare when Christy there with when she not
No Mamma No Pappa No Uncle Sam
High turnover less sales and who gives a Damn.

Customer talked of stimulus checks and people work
Ones that do taxed all the more to be jerks
No Mamma No Pappa No Uncle Sam
This customer is mad Damn.

Hoarding lumber to maximize price
Depot put customers in vice
No Mamma No Pappa No Uncle Sam
Hoarders don't give a Damn.

Home field advantage in sports all the way
Then why send so many customers away
No Mamma No Pappa No Uncle Sam
They just walk out the door Damn.

PRO collecting extra flat carts choking front
Flooring no sales no need for them to be blunt
No Mamma No Pappa No Uncle Sam
Carts and sales both flat in Flooring Damn.

Good day when customers act and enjoy
Makes it fun to be employed
No Mamma No Pappa No Uncle Sam
Nice Customers fun Damn.

Sling and cane approached register with much to explain
Tore rotator broke arm ruptured knee no small thing
No Mamma No Pappa No Uncle Sam
Looked like chicken bones snapped in pieces Damn.

One came to register because of smile
Drew them there walk a mile
'No Mamma No Pappa No Uncle Sam
Walked a mile in their shoes Damn.

Where have customers gone
Store empty bang the gong
No Mamma No Pappa No Uncle Sam
Gong show does not give a Damn.

Customer referenced Christy for review
Told now in Flooring adjust skew
No Mamma No Pappa No Uncle Sam
Did not know Christy moved Damn.

Don't know where you been or are going
Anyplace will do don't try knowing
No Mamma No Pappa No Uncle Sam
Any place will do and don't give a Damn.

Wearers beware masks have graphene
Sucked into lungs may cause gangrene
No Mamma No Pappa No Uncle Sam
And you wear this Damn.

Store more empty than church at midnight
Customers have all taken flight
No Mamma No Pappa No Uncle Sam
An empty church does not give a Damn.

Bo Peep keeps mask very tight her way
Makes her look mysterious at work today
No Mamma No Pappa No Uncle Sam
Quit being scared Damn.

Christy in twenty years Amber in ten insane
Bo Peep look in mirror or become same
No Mamma No Pappa No Uncle Sam
Watch out Bo Peep Damn.

Donna brought three newbies to PRO described
Bard told not in PRO and Lot do or die
No Mamma No Pappa No Uncle Sam
Lot moves them up or out Damn.

Puppy dog eyes Lauren missing in Paint
Sent home for Red Virus now she ain't
No Mamma No Pappa No Uncle Sam
Really miss those sad eyes Damn.

April Wiseman not of the three front end ornamented
Never distended employees usually contented
No Mamma No Pappa No Uncle Sam
And eat your heart out Christy Damn.

A joke on Bo Peep by Bard made wonder
Ditched wig after chemo down under
No Mamma No Pappa No Uncle Sam
Gotcha Bo Peep Damn.

Met Kimmie with small gift for Omega
Read Malachi 3 and deliver expressa
No Mamma No Pappa No Uncle Sam
Play it forward Omega Damn.

Dakota involved Bard plot asked Bo Peep knowing
Worked through chemo looked great new hair showing
No Mamma No Pappa No Uncle Sam
Bo Peep will believe Dakota Damn.

Told Bo Peep chemo made Bard weak
Reduced to four days a week for more sleep
No Mamma No Pappa No Uncle Sam
Bo Peep almost believes Damn.

Having ball at work these days
Management wants to have replay
No Mamma No Pappa No Uncle Sam
And their monkeys belong to them Damn.

Jasmine the jewel in paint never cruel
Smart as a tack always cool
No Mamma No Pappa No Uncle Sam
This Jasmine a diamond Damn.

Kevin and customer had discussion over load
Measuring tape made it impossible Lo
No Mamma No Pappa No Uncle Sam
Kevin says wishful thinking must go Damn.

Where have all young men gone
Not to glory can't be found
No Mamma No Pappa No Uncle Sam
Seeger does not give a Damn.

Shared time with Jesse in PRO
Been there for seven she ready to go
No Mamma No Pappa No Uncle Sam
Jesse red streaked weak Damn.

Bit by mosquito and highly allergic
Spent lunch taking Benadryl now liturgic
No Mamma No Pappa No Uncle Sam
Benadryl does not give a Damn.

Customer stopped to discuss gangrene
Saw Joey's arm Jesse grew faint screamed
No Mamma No Pappa No Uncle Sam
Joey's arm getting well but smell Damn.

Men want to be this Jesse's boy
Line up to compete with ploys
No Mamma No Pappa No Uncle Sam
Jesse an attractor Damn.

Amber wanted break in two on a five-hour shift
Did not want to mess up dinner gift
No Mamma No Pappa No Uncle Sam
Dinner matters Damn.

Explained no meniscus bone on bone over concrete
Unable to work 3 more after early break complete
No Mamma No Pappa No Uncle Sam
Suck it up they don't give a Damn.

Needed cash for register Amber at dinner
Christy from Flooring brought winner
No Mamma No Pappa No Uncle Sam
Christy helped Bard Damn.

Bard last male part-time cashier
One full-time one HC all that's left to revere
No Mamma No Pappa No Uncle Sam
Do tokens really give a Damn.

Another empty Saturday with hardly a roar
Customers have left for vacations and more
No Mamma No Pappa No Uncle Sam
Sales plan doomed Damn.

Asked Millie why left paint for register play
Cashier full-time enabled transfer that way
No Mamma No Pappa No Uncle Sam
Concrete monster has Millie now Damn.

Kevin in lumber filling orders holding court
Great to see having fun again in this port
No Mamma No Pappa No Pappa No Uncle Sam
Kevin happy a good thing Damn.

Little old lady on phone walked toward Ballymore silent
Bard stopped her before run over violent
No Mamma No Pappa No Uncle Sam
Ballymore rental had no alarm Damn.

Failed to reboot registers each day
Fatal flaw hit all Saturday very obscene way
No Mamma No Pappa No Uncle Sam
Why won't they listen and do Damn.

Company sends out cyber 24-hour mandate
If not installed registers abate
No Mamma No Pappa No Uncle Sam
Cyberattacks all over wake up Damn.

Behr brought storage bin into PRO
No one told Bard explained when go
No Mamma No Pappa No Uncle Sam
Behr not told no surprise Damn.

Fatal error a cyber deal from Home Office
Must reboot each day or be locked in paralysis
No Mamma No Pappa No Uncle Sam
Let the customer stand and wait Damn.

Rebooting register after Fatal Donna arrived to use phone smugly
Asked Bard broke again replied her device still in buggy
No Mamma No Pappa No Uncle Sam
She can't keep phone with her Damn.

Kilmer and over the hill gang one last limp down field
Whiskey and Bard never do quite yield
No Mamma No Pappa No Uncle Sam
Woke killed the Redskins Damn.

April said no one to help as she did Christy
You do not have you voodoo offered strong whiskey
No Mamma No Pappa No Uncle Sam
Whiskey does not give a Damn.

Wasco drenched outside for an hour insane
Customer buying lawnmower in driving rain
No Mamma No Pappa No Uncle Sam
Find an umbrella Damn.

Wasco in locker room completely drained
Very tired of rain and this inane game
No Mamma No Pappa No Uncle Sam
Wasco drained of his give Damn.

Jesse ending shift from PRO stopped in middle
Laughed that Bard able to heat her griddle
No Mamma No Pappa No Uncle Sam
Jesse has Punch and Judy Damn.

Tina out with Lyft in parking spot
Closed overhead with her in rain thanks a lot
No Mamma No Pappa No Uncle Sam
Sorry Tina very bad Damn.

Asked Bo Peep why still with mask
Replied fear and preparing for inoculation task
No Mamma No Pappa No Uncle Sam
Fear and inoculation do not give a Damn.

Amanda came to and fro like woman worn
Work making her wish never born
No Mamma No Pappa No Uncle Sam
Worn woman does not give a Damn.

Josh told to wave flags in front of Ballymore
Waved them suffering with bursitis forevermore
No Mamma No Pappa No Uncle Sam
Limp flag spotting does not give a Damn.

Melisha came to Middle with Bard
Discussed declining role with USPS canard
No Mamma No Pappa No Uncle Sam
This Postmaster a Trump appointee an idiot Damn.

Explained my plight with knee and meniscus
Bone on bone swells early breaks make vicious
No Mamma No Pappa No Uncle Sam
Meniscus does not give a Damn.

Amber gave Bard choice early break or five straight
Dinner for her or Bard to ache what a shake
No Mamma No Pappa No Uncle Sam
Amber does not give a Damn.

Employees and customers greet Bard when arrives
Calls them by name they exclaim with high-fives
No Mamma No Pappa No Uncle Sam
Shame no one else calls them by name Damn.

Mop and bucket fraud sale on Internet big sweat
Customers mad Depot not honor this threat
No Mamma No Pappa No Uncle Sam
Kick the bucket Damn.

Explained that after five yesterday with no break just grieve
Knee swollen given four no break then allowed to leave
No Mamma No Pappa No Uncle Sam
Use you up no breaks and don't give a Damn.

Customers at register with Bard simply offer more
Return again to bring more cash to store
No Mamma No Pappa No Uncle Sam
Customers Bard and cash Damn.

April took charge over a five-dollar item four-minute delay
Apologized boss had way before could go away
No Mamma No Pappa No Uncle Sam
Just ring it up and take money Damn.

Melisha stopped customer over ten-cent pencil
Stood on table to hail stencil
No Mamma No Pappa No Uncle Sam
A ten-cent pencil are you serious Damn.

Leaving store Charlie asked why exiting
Replied AWOL new form of text messaging
No Mamma No Pappa No Uncle Sam
AWOL does not give a Damn.

Depot offers vacation paid time off even a dose of bonus
Scales don't balance but this helps even onus
No Mamma No Pappa No Uncle Sam
Wages still too low Damn.

Bo Peep this sheep leaving flock
Counted to four said thanks a lot
No Mamma No Pappa No Uncle Sam
Bo Peep needs only two not four sheep Damn.

Melisha very precise and neat in packing bags
Bard doubled she wanted to nag
No Mamma No Pappa No Uncle Sam
Melisha tight with bags Damn.

Legion of the Damned rock band repute and fame
At Depot employees stay evermore in shame
No Mamma No Pappa No Uncle Sam
Legion of the Damneded don't give a Damn.

Do Not Call DNC very much in play for Bard
Management decision and result too hard
No Mamma No Pappa No Uncle Sam
They don't miss Bard Damn.

Meeting with Ace with plan to consider
Keep Bard in pocket to make Flooring sales bigger
No Mamma No Pappa No Uncle Sam
Bard can sell and Christy needs that Damn.

Two wolves and lamb decide what to eat
At Home Depot employees know they meat
No Mamma No Pappa No Uncle Sam
Ben Franklin does not give a Damn.

Melanie said no cashier should be full-time
Made many to make that lie almost a crime
No Mamma No Pappa No Uncle Sam
Not exactly does not give a Damn.

Awash with cashiers hours hard to gleam
Day will come when again be a need indeed
No Mamma No Pappa No Uncle Sam
When have need still won't give a Damn.

Corporate never lies declared like bagpipers
Except when tongues move behind face diapers
No Mamma No Pappa No Uncle Sam
Face diapers and liars don't give a Damn.

Receiving covers SKU on packages and boxes
Must think it funny to do this to cashiers and bosses
No Mamma No Pappa No Uncle Sam
Receiving has their joke Damn.

For but a few Depot treadway train to nowhere
Years pass names do not last then the end beware
No Mamma No Pappa No Uncle Sam
This Chicago overcoat does not give a Damn.

Customers parked under PRO awning in rain
Another came for pick up and gridlocked same
No Mamma No Pappa No Uncle Sam
Pickups in the rain insane Damn.

Making popcorn in Employee Lounge
Many used as excuse to scrounge
No Mamma No Pappa No Uncle Sam
Popcorn smells good Damn.

Amanda and young Josh from PRO play in rain
Came back like drowned rats quite insane
No Mamma No Pappa No Uncle Sam
Parkas do have hoods children Damn.

Sent to Garden Janet asked to beg her pardon
Bard returned inside HC put him out to harden
No Mamma No Pappa No Uncle Sam
Aim to please Damn.

Woman with child asked for board to be cut awhile
Told her saw closed at six to test guile
No Mamma No Pappa No Uncle Sam
Yes we did cut her board Damn.

Foot traffic absent lumber stacked to roof
This store's goof in for serious reproof
No Mamma No Pappa No Uncle Sam
About time to discount lumber Damn.

Depot presents booklet of tests to complete
Cashiers worried Bard said ignore change beat
No Mamma No Pappa No Uncle Sam
Right or wrong answers don't give a Damn.

Charm offensive for Bard from HC FES and ASM
This alphabet soup quite insane no hope for gain
No Mamma No Pappa No Uncle Sam
Alphabet soup scrambled does not give a Damn.

Coop and Bergman in For Whom the Bell Tolls
For FES imitate her cut hair a style to behold
No Mamma No Pappa No Uncle Sam
For Whom the Bell tolls it is for thee Damn.

Isaac the rooster came to PRO engaged in talk
Pretty good sign EEOC no conspiracy on clock
No Mamma No Pappa No Uncle Sam
Since when did roosters give a Damn.

One register open at PRO Emily had three to go
Bard took two to middle to ease flow
No Mamma No Pappa No Uncle Sam
Explained and they appreciated Damn.

Left note for Sylvia about sweeping floor
Unable to do with no broom for use indoor
No Mamma No Pappa No Uncle Sam
Sylvia will laugh at the message Damn.

Paul did not bring in carts tonight
Bard afraid might have caught blight
No Mamma No Pappa No Uncle Sam
Paul not bringing in carts Damn.

Stood by PRO door to close and lock
Had to restrain Paul must watch clock
No Mamma No Pappa No Uncle Sam
This racehorse wants to run Damn.

Drongo birds use ants for bath
Depot still trying to learn math
No Mamma No Pappa No Uncle Sam
Math and bath don't give a Damn.

Carlos took peyote rode coyote to Ixtlan
Lophophora williamsii cacti not sold under brand
No Mamma No Pappa No Uncle Sam
Carlos Castaneda does not give a Damn.

Bo Peep called Garden with need for pabulum
Must send another craving to Garden
No Mamma No Pappa No Uncle Sam
Craving does not give a Damn.

Schedule splintered into pieces from 18 to 12
Expect Saturday and Sunday no other days oh well
No Mamma No Pappa No Uncle Sam
And they give hours to others Damn.

Sullins brought story and key to open Garden gate
Said turkeys gather in rain like customers of late
No Mamma No Pappa No Uncle Sam
Turkeys are turkeys Damn.

Hanlon's razor very dull shave insipidly
Never attribute Depot malice for acts of stupidity
No Mamma No Pappa No Uncle Sam
Hanlon does not give a Damn.

Sumner before Autumn or rain left paint in pain
Steve made whole while Christy sought bane
No Mamma No Pappa No Uncle Sam
Another one gone in Flooring Damn.

Depot treats part-time employees very shrill
If reversed would not enjoy this drill
No Mamma No Pappa No Uncle Sam
Shrill teaches part-times to never give a Damn.

Rain and water splatter garden merchandise
Some customers consider this paradise
No Mamma No Pappa No Uncle Sam
Rainy day in Garden paradise Damn.

Bought four pieces of wood for $162
Determined not afford nails nor screws
No Mamma No Pappa No Uncle Sam
This is not good Damn.

EEOC has Depot on clock tick tock
30 days to respond or may lose chalk
No Mamma No Pappa No Uncle Sam
Tempus Fugit Damn.

EEOC offers Mediation alternative with Depot
Not binding no blame no way for this credo
No Mamma No Pappa No Uncle Sam
Mediation will not work Damn.

Walmart effect rules customers at Depot
Take off masks believe it or not
No Mamma No Pappa No Uncle Sam
Walmart does not wear masks Damn.

Make Bard weekend warrior with glee
Never discussed or explained you see
No Mamma No Pappa No Uncle Sam
Retaliation for EEOC huh Damn.

No masks required for over a month
No cases reported Red Virus lost punch
No Mamma No Pappa No Uncle Sam
Wearing a mask a fraud Damn.

Complete indifference by employees aggrieved
Wonder why customers not better received
No Mamma No Pappa No Uncle Sam
Aggrieved employees do not give a Damn.

Lumber arrived unneeded piled high to rafters
Beginning of housing boom coming in tatters
No Mamma No Pappa No Uncle Sam
Where to stock and don't give a Damn.

Connor in hardware ready to serve best way
Controlled and cool always manages to convey
No Mamma No Pappa No Uncle Sam
Connor keeps hardware secure Damn.

Dre new in Lot works as if running Grand Prix
Caught in rain barely knew where to leave
No Mamma No Pappa No Uncle Sam
This Dre gives a Damn.

Helping customer at close with a huge load
Bard stayed at PRO refused to lock door or go
No Mamma No Pappa No Uncle Sam
Not locking him out Damn.

Bo Peep rather under weather
Unable to make feel any better
No Mamma No Pappa No Uncle Sam
Bo Peep sick Damn.

New schedule reduced days from four to three
They must think Bard will climb up tree
No Mamma No Pappa No Uncle Sam
This tree does not give a Damn.

Removed beef jerky and split candy in PRO
Customer can reach and buy except jerky a big blow
No Mamma No Pappa No Uncle Sam
At least candy accessible Damn.

Kitchen drawers now on display behind PRO register
Looks neat and clean not a non-sequitur
No Mamma No Pappa No Uncle Sam
These drawers nice Damn.

Mary cashier of month spent time with Bard
Heard about Red China how Red Guards hard
No Mamma No Pappa No Uncle Sam
Make Red China pay Mary Damn.

Phyllis updated on Omega and battle with cancer
Glad Bard already helped find answer
No Mamma No Pappa No Uncle Sam
Cancer does not give a Damn.

Jerky of beef for sale again back on shelf
Customer could not wait to help themself
No Mamma No Pappa No Uncle Sam
Jerky and Depot do match right Damn.

Amber fussing and fuming about meeting brewing
Find out why Bard losing time and days accruing
No Mamma No Pappa No Uncle Sam
Fuming and gives a Damn.

Suckers moved from display with insecticide
Parents now find less difficult to buy
No Mamma No Pappa No Uncle Sam
Suckers displayed with insecticide Damn.

Christy passed by had a bit to say
Customer not treated her well that day
No Mamma No Pappa No Uncle Sam
Need conscience of a burglar Christy Damn.

IED took off leg now holds merchandise
Emptied and rang up not easy nor nice
No Mamma No Pappa No Uncle Sam
Winless war and this poor man do not give a Damn.

Customer with four full carts during close
Had to work fast to help move load
No Mamma No Pappa No Uncle Sam
Lights out and four carts to scan Damn.

Dre helping load outside after store closed
Kept door unlocked and remained on spot reposed
No Mamma No Pappa No Uncle Sam
Dre working Damn.

Bo Peep inquired if Bard asleep with store deplete
Wait on Dre then make returns complete
No Mamma No Pappa No Uncle Sam
Bo Peep appreciated Bard gives a Damn.

Cut Little Christy schedule to minimal hours and days
Interviewing with Old Charlie's hopes they will pay
No Mamma No Pappa No Uncle Sam
Christy has learned not to give a Damn.

Mexican family wanted $4000 lawnmower outside unlocked
Called manager for key failed to appear and balked
No Mamma No Pappa No Uncle Sam
They only wanted to buy it Damn.

Jagr and Brianna having fun packing doors
Had to remind them lines straight as oars
No Mamma No Pappa No Uncle Sam
Fun to watch kids doing chores Damn.

Aisle to lumber blocked carts freight stalking
Forklift abandoned carts clogged blocking
No Mamma No Pappa No Uncle Sam
Housekeeping where are you Damn.

Jagr tried to help customer with wide load
Succeeded in making door and baskets explode
No Mamma No Pappa No Uncle Sam
Kids don't drive worth a Damn.

Amber said Bo Peep sought to go astray
Hoped Bard would not join her that way
No Mamma No Pappa No Uncle Sam
Have a nice night Bo Peep Damn.

Some shifts wonder why bother to stay
No customers no management little pay ole
No Mamma No Pappa No Uncle Sam
And apathy does not give a Damn.

Choking on lumber with no end to number
Future contracts dropping faster than prenumber
No Mamma No Pappa No Uncle Sam
Greed and avarice no reward Damn.

Major update on registers or they shall fail
Managed to reboot three but rest remain veiled
No Mamma No Pappa No Uncle Sam
Guess which registers not to use tomorrow Damn.

Lumber futures and brokers hemorrhaging in red
Soon to drag earnings out of their bed
No Mamma No Pappa No Uncle Sam
Made your bed now lie down in it Damn.

Ruritania knows no Depots
No intrigue romance adventure shows
No Mamma No Pappa No Uncle Sam
Alexander Pope does not give a Damn.

Why make Bard a weekend warrior
Probably better to make him courier
No Mamma No Pappa No Uncle Sam
Weekend and warrior do not give a Damn.

Management to help raise funds for stricken Omega
Did not want to make this run Ichyostega
No Mamma No Pappa No Uncle Sam
Shamed them to act like they give a Damn.

Falsehoods empty words useless gossip vomit
What management considers useful comment
No Mamma No Pappa No Uncle Sam
This useful comment does not give a Damn.

Whispering rumors about Bard and EEOC
Depot employees will one day come to see
No Mamma No Pappa No Uncle Sam
These rumors impaled on cross of truth Damn.

Those that consumed Bard's gifts and cookies
Now lift their mouths like a gang of bullies
No Mamma No Pappa No Uncle Sam
Betrayed by all Damn.

Cut hours by eight because they choose
Why ask why when dealing with fools
No Mamma No Pappa No Uncle Sam
Increased call-out and who gives a Damn.

Vengeance is mine I shall repay said He
At Depot this will be a very long line oh gee
No Mamma No Pappa No Uncle Sam
Vengeance does not give a Damn.

Battle ax buried between shoulders aware
Taunted and bullied by Depot compared
No Mamma No Pappa No Uncle Sam
Taunts and reproach don't give a Damn.

He the author of refuge and strength
Will cast down this awful stink
No Mamma No Pappa No Uncle Sam
Refuge and strength do give a Damn.

Endless list of shifts to fill each week
Why not schedule and reduce this peak
No Mamma No Pappa No Uncle Sam
Scheduling does not give a Damn.

Cut reliables from four to three days for newbies
Wonder why have more shifts to fill like rubies
No Mamma No Pappa No Uncle Sam
Reliables and newbies do not give a Damn.

Make part-time reliables work every Saturday
Rest scheduled other days to play
No Mamma No Pappa No Uncle Sam
Then call this fair right Damn.

This store rewards cashiers who don't come to work
Burden those that do more with shirk
No Mamma No Pappa No Uncle Sam
Cashiers that won't do not give a Damn.

Shifts available list remains much adrift
Just like last year and the year before no facelift
No Mamma No Pappa No Uncle Sam
Same result year to year Damn.

Shift available list just like last year
Nothing changed from Christy to April clear
No Mamma No Pappa No Uncle Sam
Shifts available don't give a Damn.

Christy figured it out walked away
April tried but result same anyway
No Mamma No Pappa No Uncle Sam
Christy right all along Damn.

Told by HR in 2020 no full-time cashiers to add
Placed four in month another lie how sad
No Mamma No Pappa No Uncle Sam
Truth ruined by lies again Damn.

Hindus bow down for sacred cows
Monday to Friday full-time cashiers take vows
No Mamma No Pappa No Uncle Sam
Retail seven not five days a week Damn.

Home Depot a hopeless conundrum
Half-trillion company that schedules dumdum
No Mamma No Pappa No Uncle Sam
Dumdum not very smart Damn.

Customer needed lumber and molding cut no employee available
Christy arrives ran saw cut clean malleable
No Mamma No Pappa No Uncle Sam
Is there any machine she cannot run Damn.

Paul in Hardware came by Bard at break
Talked of his lover and her heartbreak
No Mamma No Pappa No Uncle Sam
Shut up and listen Damn.

Winds snapped power poles like toothpicks
Hail pounded roof like falling bricks
No Mamma No Pappa No Uncle Sam
One mile of poles snapped like toothpicks Damn.

Phyllis explained why Bard a good catch
Money job possessions what in it for him natch
No Mamma No Pappa No Uncle Sam
What in it for him does not give a Damn.

Customer arrived from restaurant at close
Had to find generator because of storm woes
No Mamma No Pappa No Uncle Sam
And all their meat will be ruined Damn.

Green Mountain band forced English from their land
No furniture made here just a new employee in Lot stand
No Mamma No Pappa No Uncle Sam
Ethan Allen does not give a Damn.

Generac generators king of the storm
Customers wished had one now mourn
No Mamma No Pappa No Uncle Sam
And Mother Nature takes no prisoners Damn.

Nick brought ladder step to main aisle for flag
Left it blocking customers quite a drag
No Mamma No Pappa No Uncle Sam
How are customers and buggies to move Damn.

Phyllis asked Bard for twenty to buy stuff
When to repay when ready not tough
No Mamma No Pappa No Uncle Sam
Phyllis got stuff Damn.

Lauren in paint kicked away cans
Husband promoted retreated to vault land
No Mamma No Pappa No Uncle Sam
Lauren not in paint Damn.

Think like an owner a real boner
Bolsheviks make sure soon goner
No Mamma No Pappa No Uncle Sam
Bolsheviks don't give a Damn.

Depot merchandise a front for CCP PLA
Foremost line for profit never buy orange blarney
No Mamma No Pappa No Uncle Sam
Funding Red Chinese People's Liberation Army Damn.

Depot their very own cargo ship
That way think sales will not slip
No Mamma No Pappa No Uncle Sam
Loaded in Red China right Damn.

Ships have planks to walk for those that balk
Management will learn when their fault
No Mamma No Pappa No Uncle Sam
Planks walked on a ship don't give a Damn.

Depot declines to learn lesson of Red China
Find suppliers or suffer from endless angina
No Mamma No Pappa No Uncle Sam
Treason by trade and don't give a Damn.

Nothing but a winner in store built to lose
Makes stomach wretch sing blues
No Mamma No Pappa No Uncle Sam
Al Jolson does not give a Damn.

0884 never wins makes no sense to begin again
Management spin looks down never up how grim
No Mamma No Pappa No Uncle Sam
Looking down does not give a Damn.

Ashley bailed on night work
Now runs day shift enjoys perk
No Mamma No Pappa No Uncle Sam
What Ashley wants Damn.

Employee finds fix to a problem
Management requires their pardon
No Mamma No Pappa No Uncle Sam
Problems solved do not give a Damn.

Why ask why when fair rules feelings and fear
Quite intolerant and not of good cheer
No Mamma No Pappa No Uncle Sam
Fair verses why who gives a Damn.

Flooring appeared at PRO 28 cases each fifty
Really helped make day and plan quite nifty
No Mamma No Pappa No Uncle Sam
Sales like this help plan Damn.

They could schedule three weeks out and avoid rout
Prefer to leave open till that week then have out
No Mamma No Pappa No Uncle Sam
Schedule chaos and don't give a Damn.

Interstates to beach and mountain gridlocked
Leaves fewer customers for store unlocked
No Mamma No Pappa No Uncle Sam
Vacation after two years Damn.

Management plays Chinese checkers marbles missing
Men that are old use Calculus leaves them hissing
No Mamma No Pappa No Uncle Sam
Calculus does not give a Damn.

Warehouse mentality not best way to succeed
Often becomes little more than endless greed
No Mamma No Pappa No Uncle Sam
Warehouse does not give a Damn.

Management like the walking dead
Employees follow as zombies that dread
No Mamma No Pappa No Uncle Sam
You think zombies or walking dead give a Damn.

Christy removed mask and worked all day
Smiled at Bard warming cold heart hooray
No Mamma No Pappa No Uncle Sam
Bard with heart who knew Damn.

Old men or men that are old
Snow on roof but furnace not cold
No Mamma No Pappa No Uncle Sam
Men that are old know how to give a Damn.

Store 0884 corporate creature time forgot
Layout not at all what they want in their plot
No Mamma No Pappa No Uncle Sam
This creature does not give a Damn.

Passion and ownership skills for best
Depot would prefer employees do less
No Mamma No Pappa No Uncle Sam
Own job but don't give a Damn.

Practiced longer than others even born
Disdained dismissed ignored left in scorn
No Mamma No Pappa No Uncle Sam
What could this practitioner possibly know Damn.

Bean Counter lost in figures and beans
Cannot understand what Store 0884 means
No Mamma No Pappa No Uncle Sam
End of the line Damn.

Meme and profit on docket
At Depot always seek to pocket
No Mamma No Pappa No Uncle Sam
Meme does not give a Damn

Received email from Depot on paid time off
Paying me for not watering trough
No Mamma No Pappa No Uncle Sam
Pay me extra for just coming in Damn.

America traded prosperity for posterity
Depot pockets former in barbarity
No Mamma No Pappa No Uncle Sam
Since when did barbarians give a Damn.

When sales up Management all around
When down or depressed rarely found
No Mamma No Pappa No Uncle Sam
Ain't management great Damn.

Depot manages with only half a deck
And you wonder why such a wreck
No Mamma No Pappa No Uncle Sam
Never play with half a deck Damn.

3 Days off with 4 in a row up next
Are they kidding this senseless jest
No Mamma No Pappa No Uncle Sam
3 straight off and 4 straight on who gives a Damn.

Fundraiser coming Smash Mouth burger for raise
Help associate in need reduce haze
No Mamma No Pappa No Uncle Sam
Smash Mouth burgers might give a Damn.

Home Depot ship like Noah's Ark
Neither had rudder nor captain's bark
No Mamma No Pappa No Uncle Sam
No rudder no captain who gives a Damn.

Prometheus a great craftsman gave Zeus quite a thrill
Sent Pandora to open box that made Depot ill
No Mamma No Pappa No Uncle Sam
Pandora does not give a Damn.

Foot traffic and sales hit skids
Management no clue how to lift lids
No Mamma No Pappa No Uncle Sam
An empty store is an empty store Damn.

Wind and hail caused damage to roof
Will management look or simply goof
No Mamma No Pappa No Uncle Sam
Wind and hail do not give a Damn.

When success achieved Home Depot believes
Failure arrives blame employees lie like thieves
No Mamma No Pappa No Uncle Sam
Guess that means no success sharing Damn.

Depot has stores that win and those that don't
A few reserved for status as ones that won't
No Mamma No Pappa No Uncle Sam
Won't never wins nor gives a Damn.

Constancy of purpose for improvement product and service
This would make management extremely nervous
No Mamma No Pappa No Uncle Sam
Nervous does not give a Damn.

Bought a golfer's hat with cooling bend
Let Depot have some money to send
No Mamma No Pappa No Uncle Sam
This hat does not give a Damn.

Adopt new philosophy at afternoon tea
Leadership fails to achieve or even believe
No Mamma No Pappa No Uncle Sam
Left an orphan and they don't give a Damn.

Stop awarding business on basis of price alone
Depot thinks not nice will proceed to stone
No Mamma No Pappa No Uncle Sam
Cheap uber alles and don't give a Damn.

Constant process improvement for product and service always
Process means cheap Depot wins you lose survey
No Mamma No Pappa No Uncle Sam
Process improvement at Depot are you serious Damn.

Training and education inculcated schooled
Not indoctrination how to and why through
No Mamma No Pappa No Uncle Sam
Depot training does not give a Damn.

They come in at end of day
Bard helps them quickly hurry away
No Mamma No Pappa No Uncle Sam
Day is ending Damn.

Adopt and institute leadership with vision
Makes for far more intelligent decisions
No Mamma No Pappa No Uncle Sam
And more than bean counting Damn.

Olive making requests to answer phone
Called to tell her nobody home
No Mamma No Pappa No Uncle Sam
When Olive uses her voice just say yes Damn.

Drive out fear crystal clear
Depot must abandon sneer
No Mamma No Pappa No Uncle Sam
Fear does not give a Damn.

Mandy and Joey held court between Lumber and Hardware
Both left before store closed their departments nadir
No Mamma No Pappa No Uncle Sam
As usual no one left in Hardware or Lumber Damn.

Break down barriers and smash silos
Depot must think pure loco
No Mamma No Pappa No Uncle Sam
Silos are silos and don't give a Damn.

Cease dependence on inspection as quality
Depot never inspects causes groans audibly
No Mamma No Pappa No Uncle Sam
Inspection does not give a Damn.

No slogans targets nor exhortations to auger
Work smarter not harder stop cannon fodder
No Mamma No Pappa No Uncle Sam
Cannon fodder does not give a Damn.

Isaac gave Bard a choice of three
PRO Middle or Garden really up a tree
No Mamma No Pappa No Uncle Sam
Isaac in need of help Damn.

Mentioned to Isaac about schedule thinned
Made no sense to come in and grin
No Mamma No Pappa No Uncle Sam
Isaac understands Damn.

Exterminate bean counting and sales quotas
Manage process reduce variation improve outcomes focus
No Mamma No Pappa No Uncle Sam
Quotas don't give a Damn.

Remove barriers to ownership or ship will sink
Home Depot prefers not to blink
No Mamma No Pappa No Uncle Sam
Own not but do your job Damn.

Catherine from Customer Service great
Really knows how to make customers relate
No Mamma No Pappa No Uncle Sam
Catherine gives a Damn.

Self improvement not part of Home Depot
Believes people sheeple
No Mamma No Pappa No Uncle Sam
Provide self-improvement and give a Damn.

Amanda cut hair added red donned spectacles
Looked like a new receptacle
No Mamma No Pappa No Uncle Sam
First blonde now red streaked Damn.

Jagr too on Mohican look
Keeps cool for Summer chinook
No Mamma No Pappa No Uncle Sam
This last of the Mohicans gives a Damn.

Take action to accomplish transformation
Not an issue nor debate much less causation
No Mamma No Pappa No Uncle Sam
This transformation will give a Damn.

Ethan brought out electric blower
No one recharged no airflow there
No Mamma No Pappa No Uncle Sam
Ethan used a broom Damn.

Be proactive and act on things you can
Not especially present in Depot's den
No Mamma No Pappa No Uncle Sam
Proactive may give a Damn.

Joey full of jelly in belly from being sick
Laughed called himself Old Saint Nick
No Mamma No Pappa No Uncle Sam
Jelly Belly does not give a Damn.

Begin with end in mind
At Depot playing from way behind
No Mamma No Pappa No Uncle Sam
Depot has no end nor mind Damn.

Garden no answer and not in place
Provided customers succor at Customer Service place
No Mamma No Pappa No Uncle Sam
No One in Garden and no phone answered Damn.

Put first things first to move ahead
Management prefers worst instead
No Mamma No Pappa No Uncle Sam
Worst does not give a Damn.

Andrea arrived clad with face diaper
Young healthy innocent ditch mask cypher
No Mamma No Pappa No Uncle Sam
Putting good health at risk thanks Depot Damn.

Think win win boy really gets under skin
Win lose how begin and practice sin
No Mamma No Pappa No Uncle Sam
Win win at Depot are you serious Damn.

Behr outraged car window shot by BB
Controlled anger worked like a Seabee
No Mamma No Pappa No Uncle Sam
This Seabee works hard Damn.

Think first to understand then understood
Sacrilege in this neighborhood
No Mamma No Pappa No Uncle Sam
But first you have to give a Damn.

SCO with cash said no dice nor give up wad
Sullins wanted two cashiers in middle squad
No Mamma No Pappa No Uncle Sam
We only had two cashiers ASM Damn.

Synergize preferred way to make this run
At Depot they think this battery undone
No Mamma No Pappa No Uncle Sam
Synergize does not give a Damn.

Management and supervision in season brawl
Taking bets on which will soon fall
No Mamma No Pappa No Uncle Sam
No one in charge can you say Vietnam Damn.

Sharpen the saw at Depot means one in hall
For employees get ready to bawl
No Mamma No Pappa No Uncle Sam
This saw does not give a Damn.

Sent to Garden in heat register chose not to compete
Asked Amber despaired pretty much beat
No Mamma No Pappa No Uncle Sam
Amber full of what might have been Damn.

Discussed Christy what she knew behaved and betrayed
Believe April will know same within year and go away
No Mamma No Pappa No Uncle Sam
April learning does not matter if you do give a Damn.

Amber said offered full-time play wanted shifts
Reminded no one in building coveted this job's gifts
No Mamma No Pappa No Uncle Sam
No One wants to be a HC Damn.

HR on vacation encountered additional family misery
Increased store despair little more than history
No Mamma No Pappa No Uncle Sam
Can't manage a vacation Damn.

Management has not been on roof
Damage may need visual proof
No Mamma No Pappa No Uncle Sam
Roof leaks grab a bucket Damn.

Polio on crutches came to Garden for a cart
Explained inside store walk more hit heart
No Mamma No Pappa No Uncle Sam
This customer has spirit Damn.

Depot lies in every way even in schedule display
Never deliver on what they say more like foreplay
No Mamma No Pappa No Uncle Sam
Speak with forked tongue Damn.

HR said no new full-time employees in Front end
Turned around added six not lying a sin
No Mamma No Pappa No Uncle Sam
Truth what they say right Damn.

Returns piled up for days floors not swept
Flowers dry as a desert entire place unkept
No Mamma No Pappa No Uncle Sam
Not one cashier cleans up Damn.

Lisa not Mona hired as cashier
Drove truck until no longer see clear
No Mamma No Pappa No Uncle Sam
Yet another unneeded cashier Damn.

Four days past due still no schedule published
Bean Counter considered nothing but rubbish
No Mamma No Pappa No Uncle Sam
Another example of they don't give a Damn.

Bri on sprees all over Garden needs help
Met calls all did not break no problem nor yelp
No Mamma No Pappa No Uncle Sam
Filled all needs in Garden wow Damn.

After three hours Amber called asked to close indisposed
Walked inside found moribund about to decompose
No Mamma No Pappa No Uncle Sam
Amber done in Damn.

Schedule comes from Atlanta to 0884 for review
HR squared on vacation no one bothers not shrewd
No Mamma No Pappa No Uncle Sam
Schedules don't matter Damn.

Asked Yo Yo if wanted to stay in Garden
No no ran inside with heavy Spanish jargon
No Mamma No Pappa No Uncle Sam
Yo Yo wants air conditioning Damn.

America once melting pot providing unity
Depot more chamber than melt not a community
No Mamma No Pappa No Uncle Sam
And you think a chamber pot gives a Damn.

Mary in PRO had stroke of bad luck
Seems her appendix ran amok
No Mamma No Pappa No Uncle Sam
That appendix does not give a Damn.

Little Christy came to give Bard a break
Sat with him shared scheduling heartache
No Mamma No Pappa No Uncle Sam
Christy abused by management Damn.

Worked inside for hour after three outside
Arthur arrived crawled over most of Bard's hide
No Mamma No Pappa No Uncle Sam
Amber let Bard go as quickly as could Damn.

EEOC asking for mediation with Depot
Bard binding arbitration quid pro quo
No Mamma No Pappa No Uncle Sam
Make it binding Damn.

Emailed April to see what up with scheduling in store
Asked Missy and Bean Counter who for
No Mamma No Pappa No Uncle Sam
Bard made them respond Damn.

Diversity at this Pot nothing more than non-white
Different thought opinion or view not right
No Mamma No Pappa No Uncle Sam
Diversity does not give a Damn.

Broke pledge moved buggies outside anyway
Just had to help Lot for all they did today
No Mamma No Pappa No Uncle Sam
Bard just has to give a Damn.

Donna saw Bard at register in PRO
Did not come close remained on the go
No Mamma No Pappa No Uncle Sam
Afraid of Bard Damn.

Bo Peep did not want to be HC tonight
Would have loved to run register as rite
No Mamma No Pappa No Uncle Sam
Bo Peep and Amber sick of closing Damn.

Kim Jung and Craig have one thing in common
Rely on Red China for power and wealth strawmen
No Mamma No Pappa No Uncle Sam
Craig's list calligraphy Damn.

Dept offered Bard Father's Day gift knife or cookout set
Made by Red Chinese slaves headed for organ harvesting bet
No Mamma No Pappa No Uncle Sam
Father of Red China I think not Damn.

Melisha reading book on North Korea exiles
Reminds what employees in Depot face all while
No Mamma No Pappa No Uncle Sam
Melisha has it figured Damn.

Agreed she passive aggressive
Believes Bard increase aggression made restive
No Mamma No Pappa No Uncle Sam
Melisha more than OK Damn.

Asked Bo Peep to leave flock
Reminded Bard needed on clock
No Mamma No Pappa No Uncle Sam
Race you out the door Bo Peep Damn.

Replacing part-times with full toothpaste tube squeeze
How to cut full-time later causes management heaves
No Mamma No Pappa No Uncle Sam
Cannot reduce full-time hours Damn.

Rains came and stayed in Garden wind blew onto machines
Bard covered with plastic managed to maintain scene
No Mamma No Pappa No Uncle Sam
Keep Garden open and wet merchandise outside Damn.

Garden closed as rains ended made sure nothing hidden
Brought inside where had four doing bidding
No Mamma No Pappa No Uncle Sam
An Orange gaggle gathering Damn.

Management must approve leave regardless of numbers
Millie offered to call Roland unencumber
No Mamma No Pappa No Uncle Sam
Bard just stayed wasted coverage Damn.

Six in circle at SCO thirty minutes to go
Kumbaya blocking poor customers slow
No Mamma No Pappa No Uncle Sam
Orange aprons combined don't give a Damn.

Sav off clock due to growing tumors
Surgery and treatment constant rumors
No Mamma No Pappa No Uncle Sam
These tumors don't give a Damn.

Ethan War of Northern Genocide caused by slavery
Responded all about tariffs from ports livery
No Mamma No Pappa No Uncle Sam
Victors own history Damn.

Logan explained manager at Tractor Supply sane
Assistant manager Amanda an angry Panda their bane
No Mamma No Pappa No Uncle Sam
Depot getting great hires Damn.

Logan worked in rain helped customers all the same
Thanked for help agreeing to remain
No Mamma No Pappa No Uncle Sam
Three numbers and only Logan answered Damn.

Ethan studying at JSU to have sports view
Playoffs and Notre Dame need complete review
No Mamma No Pappa No Uncle Sam
Knows his stuff Damn.

Customer checked out with family in rain
Locked key in car had to remain
No Mamma No Pappa No Uncle Sam
Leaving key in car with family in rain Damn.

Bought his kids some candy while waited
Daughter remembered Bard from checkouts abated
No Mamma No Pappa No Uncle Sam
These customers will be back for sure Damn.

Koyaanisqatsi world unbalanced say Hopi
At Depot way business played dopey
No Mamma No Pappa No Uncle Sam
Depot prefect in Koyaanisqatsi Damn.

Melisha discussed Culver's hamburgers and custard
Wisconsin-based cheese always passes muster
No Mamma No Pappa No Uncle Sam
Custard like this worth a Damn.

Why cut us from four to three and make us weak
Do they not understand makes everything bleak
No Mamma No Pappa No Uncle Sam
Weak and bleak don't give a Damn.

Reduce hours to twelve from twenty-two
Must mean really like turning screws
No Mamma No Pappa No Uncle Sam
These screws turned don't give a Damn.

Why schedule Bard for every Saturday
Only way to make payday
No Mamma No Pappa No Uncle Sam
Saturday scheduled does not give a Damn.

Never discussed being weekend force
Guess want to ruin this horse
No Mamma No Pappa No Uncle Sam
This horse does not give a Damn.

Store closes at 9 so why work to 10:30 then
HR said OK new policy no longer bends
No Mamma No Pappa No Uncle Sam
Cashier with no customers Damn.

Leave shifts unfilled expect reliables fill in
Think own our private lives hit on chin
No Mamma No Pappa No Uncle Sam
Schedule unfilled does not give a Damn.

Keep devices in pocket new socket
No clocks on floor adjust to docket
No Mamma No Pappa No Uncle Sam
This docket does not give a Damn.

Hindu cows at register during week
Make weekends more difficult peak
No Mamma No Pappa No Uncle Sam
These Brahmans do not give a Damn.

Cashiers scheduled for self-checkout
Must deal with middle register workout
No Mamma No Pappa No Uncle Sam
Cashiers not allowed at SCO Damn.

HCs never touch a register on floor calm down
Head is adjective to cashier noun don't frown
No Mamma No Pappa No Uncle Sam
Adjectives and nouns don't give a Damn.

Missed two shifts in almost three years
Not one person in management ever did cheer
No Mamma No Pappa No Uncle Sam
No cheer in three years Damn.

Replace part with full-time costs extra 300 thousand
Three thousand hours lost for no reason Herr Hausen
No Mamma No Pappa No Uncle Sam
300 hundred thousand reasons very dumb Damn.

Full-times cannot work additional hours
Must shave schedule or be in briars
No Mamma No Pappa No Uncle Sam
Briars don't give a Damn.

When schedule cracks splinters patch
Full-times extend beyond waste hours natch
No Mamma No Pappa No Uncle Sam
This patch waste Damn.

Reducing and eliminating part-times whatever
Never told nature of this endeavor
No Mamma No Pappa No Uncle Sam
Disclosure and truth don't laugh Damn.

John asked Blanca to flee Appliances
Ace trying to help make receiving allowances
No Mamma No Pappa No Uncle Sam
They do figure her out Damn.

Can't cut full-time hours in January swoon
Must continue to feed with spoon
No Mamma No Pappa No Uncle Sam
Wasting shareholder dividends Damn.

Amber and Bo Peep stop losing sleep
Nobody wants their job much less keep
No Mamma No Pappa No Uncle Sam
Sleep and keep do not give a Damn.

Additional duties abound by fiat in this endless gambit
Do more for less under duress management greedy bandits
No Mamma No Pappa No Uncle Sam
These bandits don't give a Damn.

Promises and policies often provided
Integrity and word but puffing decided
No Mamma No Pappa No Uncle Sam
Their word is just a word Damn.

Customers amazed Garden open in wind and rain
Explained why continue to come in
No Mamma No Pappa No Uncle Sam
Wind and rain customers reign Damn.

Woman approached Bard in middle buggy full of paint
Relative at another Depot charged more made her faint
No Mamma No Pappa No Uncle Sam
Does this Depot give a Damn.

They want to be fair to us each day
You know determine their way
No Mamma No Pappa No Uncle Sam
Fair to them right Damn.

Management simple in theory at Depot
It is OK until not their guiding credo
No Mamma No Pappa No Uncle Sam
Credo does not give a Damn.

Bard had patience tested in science
Result negative explains defiance
No Mamma No Pappa No Uncle Sam
Science does not give a Damn.

Management new scheduling rules
Takes three days to get eight hours who knew
No Mamma No Pappa No Uncle Sam
And it does not matter Damn.

When asked by management what doing
Explain doing nothing no blushing
No Mamma No Pappa No Uncle Sam
It is work to do nothing Damn.

When customer approaches register stare straight ahead
Ask if brought money makes them dread
No Mamma No Pappa No Uncle Sam
Gets their attention Damn.

Run like winded work bended
Management will never call splendid
No Mamma No Pappa No Uncle Sam
You think winded gives a Damn.

Management asks what am I doing
Respond by asking what did hear brewing
No Mamma No Pappa No Uncle Sam
Doing does not give a Damn.

When stretching to flex on floor
Sounds like goat chewing aluminum cans with celery more
No Mamma No Pappa No Uncle Sam
And no need to dial 911 Damn.

Never interrupt someone else proper advice
Getting excited over remembering more than nice
No Mamma No Pappa No Uncle Sam
Interrupt so they can share excitement Damn.

Bard has saying for employees when in store
Abandon all hope when enters the door
No Mamma No Pappa No Uncle Sam
And those poor employees Damn.

Sixty not really the new forty
Any more than nine new twelve sporty
No Mamma No Pappa No Uncle Sam
And old is old Damn.

Something unexpected arrives makes heart race
Rest assured not found in Depot place
No Mamma No Pappa No Uncle Sam
This race does not give a Damn.

As age accrues time passes faster
Helps get through Depot disaster
No Mamma No Pappa No Uncle Sam
And a faster clock is nice at Depot Damn.

Oldsters think in decades
Youngsters live in current haze
No Mamma No Pappa No Uncle Sam
Decades do not give a Damn.

Walk a mile in my shoes probably rude
Spend minute in Bard's mind a real treat dude
No Mamma No Pappa No Uncle Sam
Shoes do not give a Damn.

Andrea fresh out of high school
Bard fifty years removed how cruel
No Mamma No Pappa No Uncle Sam
A half-century Damn.

Age apparent when realize doing forever
Before those around born endeavor
No Mamma No Pappa No Uncle Sam
Forever beyond giving a Damn.

The blind dumb and lame stood in line
Depot taking money will be fine
No Mamma No Pappa No Uncle Sam
For this line you think they give a Damn.

EEOC asked Bard about mediation
Stated all needed is letter of remediation
No Mamma No Pappa No Uncle Sam
EEOC thinks they can settle Damn.

Olive returned as HC 8 days in a row
Did not ask before delivering this blow
No Mamma No Pappa No Uncle Sam
Business as usual Damn.

Asked by EEOC what needed to settle
Bard said sign letter of apology mettle
No Mamma No Pappa No Uncle Sam
Bard will write the letter Damn.

Edgar a force of obsidian at night
Moved carts helped customers using might
No Mamma No Pappa No Uncle Sam
Answers phone and comes running Damn.

Kevin askant over Bard's scheduling demise
Indicated hardly worth working no surprise
No Mamma No Pappa No Uncle Sam
This cheese is binding Damn.

Andrea removed mask breathed again
Found task much easier to spin
No Mamma No Pappa No Uncle Sam
She took Bard's advice Damn

Shields from registers removed
Fauci's affecting lies disproved
No Mamma No Pappa No Uncle Sam
Bard moved them out of the way for months Damn.

Pallet of remnant insulation sold in middle of aisle
Donna took Bard aside listened to jive
No Mamma No Pappa No Uncle Sam
Bard helped wrap and mark for Donna Damn.

Bard gave EEOC letter for Depot supervision and management
Included admission of wrongdoing leading to lament
No Mamma No Pappa No Uncle Sam
Lament who cares Damn.

Scheduling simple to begin and end
Fail to schedule induce call-ins list shifts to blend
No Mamma No Pappa No Uncle Sam
You think beck and call give a Damn.

Garden closed by weather six cashiers plus HC on duty
Who can possibly explain employee booty
No Mamma No Pappa No Uncle Sam
Line them up needlessly Damn.

That will be the day John Wayne did say
For Depot usually means get paid
No Mamma No Pappa No Uncle Sam
That day does not give a Damn.

Alex helping Edgar paused to say hi
Enjoys new role much more than cashier sigh
No Mamma No Pappa No Uncle Sam
Alex likes to keep on the move Damn.

How to make brown eyes blue
Simply come in and watch this zoo
No Mamma No Pappa No Uncle Sam
Brown or blue they don't give a Damn.

Edgar brought energy to front end
Teamed with Alex delivered service therein
No Mamma No Pappa No Uncle Sam
Yet another good Lot man Damn.

Olive explained had but ten hours in shifts
Begged for more to cover car note swift
No Mamma No Pappa No Uncle Sam
Car notes do not give a Damn.

Wasco arrived in Garden with purpose
Declined to help customer lawnmower circus
No Mamma No Pappa No Uncle Sam
Supervisors won't help customers Damn.

Charlie limped on peg leg and snarled
No room for customers appareled
No Mamma No Pappa No Uncle Sam
Snarl does not give a Damn.

Ex ASM in Garden with Walmart lapel
Interviewing Amanda for job bombshell
No Mamma No Pappa No Uncle Sam
Walmart a siren to Amanda Damn.

Bo Peep serious about dinner bell
If late she will loudly yell
No Mamma No Pappa No Uncle Sam
Make sure Bo Peep fed on time Damn.

Amber told Bard could not contact
Pitched fit with management she cracked
No Mamma No Pappa No Uncle Sam
Hearsay and rumors directed at Bard Damn.

EEOC agreed to phone and offer Bard's letter
Agreed to move forward if management not better
No Mamma No Pappa No Uncle Sam
Home Depot admit wrong ha ha Damn.

Require apology for interviewing falsely
Management will scream and deny hoarsely
No Mamma No Pappa No Uncle Sam
And good luck with that EEOC Damn.

Several part-time cashiers reduce hours lost bucks
Management simply cares not how much sucks
No Mamma No Pappa No Uncle Sam
As usual they don't give a Damn.

Old people in Garden strangled in face diapers
Can't see think or breathe makes them hyper
No Mamma No Pappa No Uncle Sam
Take off diapers and breathe Damn.

Red Virus D making rounds for abound
Attacks those where inoculation found
No Mamma No Pappa No Uncle Sam
Breeders for a new round Damn.

Admit falsehood on another interviewing better
Admit to truth makes them less debtor
No Mamma No Pappa No Uncle Sam
No confidentiality either Damn.

Discriminated based on age they must say
Peace can then come that way
No Mamma No Pappa No Uncle Sam
Truth very painful for them Damn.

Yo Yo in PRO fit to be tied
Bard listened to her endless diatribe
No Mamma No Pappa No Uncle Sam
Yo Yo never gets mad Damn.

They not appreciate Bard nor take time to thank
Ignored and abhorred while on floor in this tank
No Mamma No Pappa No Uncle Sam
Appreciation rarer than manhole covers Damn.

Ignored as a human received less value
Refuse to say sorry choose gallows
No Mamma No Pappa No Uncle Sam
These gallows will never give a Damn.

Yo Yo and JC asked Bard when more cookies arrive
Oatmeal for Yo Yo all kinds for JC provide
No Mamma No Pappa No Uncle Sam
And Christmas must be in July Damn.

Bard no longer moves buggies to row in Garden
Customers remove returns for buggy offers no pardon
No Mamma No Pappa No Uncle Sam
Bard was right on these buggies Damn.

Arrived in store near front door asked why no buggies
Walked fifty feet or more very ugly
No Mamma No Pappa No Uncle Sam
Why no buggies around entrance Damn.

Acknowledge and apologize very wise
Easier to capsize ship they surmise
No Mamma No Pappa No Uncle Sam
Don't acknowledge much less apologize Damn.

Amber asked Bard to go to Garden
Discussed options to reduce bother no pardon
No Mamma No Pappa No Uncle Sam
Bard took Garden for three Damn.

Ramshack did not want to leave sought reprieve
Threatened with water spray she did then flee
No Mamma No Pappa No Uncle Sam
How to negotiate with Ramshack Damn.

Christy gladdened day with face and heart
Made time for Bard not the least tart
No Mamma No Pappa No Uncle Sam
These crumbs are really fine Damn.

Phyllis in good mood today talking to mates
Gave all she had to associates
No Mamma No Pappa No Uncle Sam
Phyllis high on life Damn.

Omega arrived for brief time in
Skinny as rail from cancer where begin
No Mamma No Pappa No Uncle Sam
Omega true grit Damn.

Thanked Joy for all help
No phone working she alone did not yelp
No Mamma No Pappa No Uncle Sam
Joy alone on phone not good Damn.

Store must close if Kimme and Olive not there
No one can match their wares
No Mamma No Pappa No Uncle Sam
You better hope store closed if not there Damn.

Beware if too well thought of by men
Depot will quickly call this sin
No Mamma No Pappa No Uncle Sam
Well thought of by men Damn.

Heisman said better never born than fumble
At Depot never fail or you will stumble
No Mamma No Pappa No Uncle Sam
Don't fumble nor fail Damn.

Turn fans on in Garden bring air
Hard to talk to customers there
No Mamma No Pappa No Uncle Sam
Like talking in front of a prop Damn.

Trying to help Yoslyn expenses avoid bends
Car seats clothes playpens it never ends
No Mamma No Pappa No Uncle Sam
Passes through not from me Damn.

Experts admit ignorance not ever happening
Depot admit wrong never championing
No Mamma No Pappa No Uncle Sam
Admit wrong are you serious Damn.

Joy in Garden decided to give stuff away
Clean out shelves in every bay
No Mamma No Pappa No Uncle Sam
Improved housekeeping Damn.

First in war peace and hearts of countrymen
Hard to find in Depot's pen
No Mamma No Pappa No Uncle Sam
No profit in these right Damn.

Post office has those that go postal
Front makes one Dan's hopeful
No Mamma No Pappa No Uncle Sam
Dan's hopeful does not give a Damn.

Front end suffering from HC blues
Do not have enough to see shifts through
No Mamma No Pappa No Uncle Sam
Bard tried to help right Damn.

EEOC on phone to negotiate letter
Depot working up large lather
No Mamma No Pappa No Uncle Sam
Foaming at mouth rabies Damn.

Kingdom dweller visited Bard at garden register
Came to bring joy and comfort as His messenger
No Mamma No Pappa No Uncle Sam
Wow what a blessing Damn.

Cutting up with prescribed customers quite a thrill
Other cashiers enthralled with scene of this drill
No Mamma No Pappa No Uncle Sam
Remind customers they are customers Damn.

Depot teaches Associates blind and deaf
Probably why act like UNICEF
No Mamma No Pappa No Uncle Sam
Trained not to see nor hear Damn.

Customer dug through garbage for broken vase
Agreed to have her take without pause
No Mamma No Pappa No Uncle Sam
You can give away garbage Damn.

When Bard moves toward Bo Peep retreats
One way to make conversation complete
No Mamma No Pappa No Uncle Sam
Bo Peep still great Damn.

Associates made dissociative Depot motive
Determine orthodoxy double-speak locomotive
No Mamma No Pappa No Uncle Sam
Dissociative does not give a Damn.

Deadened detached from life memories and self
Depot can easily keep on shelf
No Mamma No Pappa No Uncle Sam
You think this can give a Damn.

Town criers sang out news of the day
More rubbish for Depot to clear away
No Mamma No Pappa No Uncle Sam
Town criers don't give a Damn.

Truth intimidates in this store
No one wants to hear much less keep score
No Mamma No Pappa No Uncle Sam
Truth has resonance Damn.

People confuse Bard with Him inside
Perhaps another form of Who died
No Mamma No Pappa No Uncle Sam
He gives a Damn.

Management earned contempt enjoyed
Content with this standard employed
No Mamma No Pappa No Uncle Sam
Earned contempt and have it Damn.

Feed babies food with spoon
Associates at Depot receive broom
No Mamma No Pappa No Uncle Sam
Broom for more than sweeping Damn.

What Depot says all that matters
Think otherwise be prepared to scatter
No Mamma No Pappa No Uncle Sam
This matter does not give a Damn.

Phyllis told Bard a heart somewhere inside
Responded sold for gold that now resides
No Mamma No Pappa No Uncle Sam
Heart for gold made fool Damn.

Right speech from Orwellian Delphi
Make sure to turn up check WiFi
No Mamma No Pappa No Uncle Sam
Right speech does not give a Damn.

Segregate isolate quarantine dissenters
Put in ghettos prevent other cominglers
No Mamma No Pappa No Uncle Sam
Ghettoes do not give a Damn.

Disparage ostracize ridicule and disdain
Helps turn them into little more than stain
No Mamma No Pappa No Uncle Sam
The disdained don't give a Damn.

Use Open Door as lock and key
Make sure communication never free
No Mamma No Pappa No Uncle Sam
Lock and key don't give a Damn.

Threaten jobs and employment opportunities
Subordinated regurgitated extremities
No Mamma No Pappa No Uncle Sam
Threats don't give a Damn.

French Foreign Legion motto March or Die
At Depot make them buy or cry
No Mamma No Pappa No Uncle Sam
The Legion was France Damn.

Zager and Evans sang what you think in pill today
Home Depot believes all in what they say
No Mamma No Pappa No Uncle Sam
Zager and Evans don't give a Damn.

Recant under force publicly for all to hear
Confession maintains orthodoxy on funeral bier
No Mamma No Pappa No Uncle Sam
Funeral biers do not give a Damn.

Roof leaks require buckets all over floor
Why not fix or this too much of a chore
No Mamma No Pappa No Uncle Sam
Cobbler to shoes and Depot to roof Damn.

Air in building full of humidity and mold
Air conditioning left off by home office told
No Mamma No Pappa No Uncle Sam
Humidity and mold don't give a Damn.

Two days off in a row quite a blow
They think pest will really go
No Mamma No Pappa No Uncle Sam
Pest rested still does not give a Damn.

Never wonder what management may think
Most likely found in canned drink
No Mamma No Pappa No Uncle Sam
They have to think to give a Damn.

Letter promised meeting with April and Donna
More likely Bard will meet Bwana
No Mamma No Pappa No Uncle Sam
Promises never give a Damn.

Lies and statistics both make Depot ballistic
Watch out or they may call mystic
No Mamma No Pappa No Uncle Sam
Mystic does not give a Damn.

Never deviate from proper Orange speech
Most likely to then cause real grief
No Mamma No Pappa No Uncle Sam
Orange speech does not give a Damn.

Red Guards dragged bourgeoise through streets
Depot would love to duplicate this feat
No Mamma No Pappa No Uncle Sam
Red Guards don't give a Damn.

What we say Orange orthodoxy
Truth relative sold like epoxy
No Mamma No Pappa No Uncle Sam
Epoxy does not give a Damn.

Two plus two equals five drilled into mind
Use to grind Associates into mental bind
No Mamma No Pappa No Uncle Sam
This mind does not give a Damn.

War a continuation of policies by alternative means
Business conducted by Depot through many schemes
No Mamma No Pappa No Uncle Sam
Clausewitz does not give a Damn.

Left God's money with Bo Peep for friend Yoslyn
Came through but not from Bard Goose Gosselin
No Mamma No Pappa No Uncle Sam
Yoslyn and child matter Damn.

If floor doesn't get you the steel box will if not customers will
If not Depot will if not life will your chosen drill
No Mamma No Pappa No Uncle Sam
This drill does not give a Damn.

Tower of Siloam collapsed and fell
Opportunity for Depot to send Beth El
No Mamma No Pappa No Uncle Sam
Siloam does not give a Damn.

EEOC says Depot will post letter with approved changes
All managers and supervisors sign across ranges
No Mamma No Pappa No Uncle Sam
And Devil in detail Damn.

Returned Bard to four from three per week
Guess they figured three might make them weak
No Mamma No Pappa No Uncle Sam
Three or four or more who gives a Damn.

Little Christy trying Door Dash seeking cash
Few hours scheduled causes backlash
No Mamma No Pappa No Uncle Sam
Chase out door and don't give a Damn.

Sell right and wrong for sales and profit
What could ever go wrong filling their pocket
No Mamma No Pappa No Uncle Sam
Fill your pockets and don't give a Damn.

Condo in Florida collapsed from within
Depot happy to sell materials there again
No Mamma No Pappa No Uncle Sam
Fallen condo profit and don't give a Damn.

Compose with those that oppose
Depot makes them seek repose
No Mamma No Pappa No Uncle Sam
They don't give a Damn.

Take it home tonight real delight
Makes Bean Counter exclaim right
No Mamma No Pappa No Uncle Sam
This delight just not quite right Damn.

Customer arrived at 8:45 for delivery
Explained loading not act of chivalry
No Mamma No Pappa No Uncle Sam
Employees not chivalrous Damn.

Promote with arrogance demote Depot can
Why Associates feel in frying pan
No Mamma No Pappa No Uncle Sam
Frying pans don't give a Damn.

Receive adversity with no complaint
Depot's rants without restraint
No Mamma No Pappa No Uncle Sam
Rants don't give a Damn.

Promises of deliverance unto justice
Hardly ever found in Depot's lustrous
No Mamma No Pappa No Uncle Sam
This light does not give a Damn.

Orders on carts blocked register surroundings
Moved to cover overhead foundings
No Mamma No Pappa No Uncle Sam
Do some organizing gang Damn.

Meek in spirit never weak
Depot simply cannot compete
No Mamma No Pappa No Uncle Sam
Weak does not give a Damn.

Meek may receive salvation in fullness of time
At Home Depot they cannot spend a dime
No Mamma No Pappa No Uncle Sam
Can't buy and sell time Damn.

Bo Peep in need of sleep
Worked five in a row now in a heap
No Mamma No Pappa No Uncle Sam
Too tired for shepherd's hook Damn.

Kyobi put tools on sale but register did not obey
Donna fixed over played Bard corrected right way
No Mamma No Pappa No Uncle Sam
Kyobi Japanese in English land Damn.

Lisa had quandary with customer on screen
Called Bard to fix before they screamed
No Mamma No Pappa No Uncle Sam
Bard made it right Damn.

Bo Peep made Bard blush when said nice
Melted much of heart's very cold ice
No Mamma No Pappa No Uncle Sam
Ice does not give a Damn.

G-man made an appearance in Aisle 14
Now full-time but rarely seen
No Mamma No Pappa No Uncle Sam
And moved into a better apartment Damn.

A new kid in Lot brain not quite clear or sane
Damaged but works hard all same
No Mamma No Pappa No Uncle Sam
He makes you feel blessed a lot Damn.

Invited Millie to tell all in Christy's house
Many tales to tell without being a louse
No Mamma No Pappa No Uncle Sam
This would be of interest Damn.

Old grey mule not what she used to be
Hear grey cart screech like banshee
No Mamma No Pappa No Uncle Sam
This auditory toothache does not give a Damn.

Mentioned to customer store closed in ten
Hurried to checkout brought cart back in
No Mamma No Pappa No Uncle Sam
A great customer Damn.

Bo Peep will cry when paycheck received
Unable to make all hours scheduled left peeved
No Mamma No Pappa No Uncle Sam
Full-time is real work Damn.

Champlain a Great Lake off New York
Now a collapsed condo in Florida Court
No Mamma No Pappa No Uncle Sam
Collapsed from building materials Damn.

Air conditioner left off by Atlanta for savings
Leaves employees with hopeless cravings
No Mamma No Pappa No Uncle Sam
No air conditioning they don't give a Damn.

Jesus used whip on bean counting scribes
Depot will one day be so ascribed
No Mamma No Pappa No Uncle Sam
Whip is judgment Damn.

Self-sacrificeat Depot's bane
Causes many employees to act insane
No Mamma No Pappa No Uncle Sam
Self-sacrificeuseless at Depot Damn.

Predicted coastal plain eustasy three years
Home Depot then flooded with tears
No Mamma No Pappa No Uncle Sam
Eustasy not nice Damn.

Hardly any employees on Sunday
Customers like birds of prey
No Mamma No Pappa No Uncle Sam
The picked-over don't give a Damn.

Jesse said bye as Bard arrived
Said no way to stay in her jive
No Mamma No Pappa No Uncle Sam
Jesse did not want to be Bard's partner Damn.

Store empty of customers on Saturday eve
Mortuary has more this you can believe
No Mamma No Pappa No Uncle Sam
And Depot a mausoleum Damn.

Emperor burned books to consolidate power
At Depot done to make employees cower
No Mamma No Pappa No Uncle Sam
Emperor undone by illiterates Damn.

Why to Depot like truth to hate speech
Presence of either increases heat
No Mamma No Pappa No Uncle Sam
This fact does not give a Damn.

Pittsburgh Depot had exorcism for lumber
Customers think evil spirits outnumber
No Mamma No Pappa No Uncle Sam
Exorcism for lumber Damn.

At Depot have it their way
Your way matters not they say
No Mamma No Pappa No Uncle Sam
Never can have it your way Damn.

Little Christy misty at Pro tonight
Wondered if victim of sinister plot
No Mamma No Pappa No Uncle Sam
And Play Misty for Me Damn.

Amber Sunday audit hold phone
Bite dust better stoned
No Mamma No Pappa No Uncle Sam
Another audit night for Amber Damn.

Atta person board empty not updated
Management blind or constipated
No Mamma No Pappa No Uncle Sam
Atta persons don't give a Damn.

Kill chicken scare monkeys
Depot management's way when hungry
No Mamma No Pappa No Uncle Sam
This chicken does not give a Damn.

Stuck in line for twenty over two pieces of wood
Seems no one could ring them up or should
No Mamma No Pappa No Uncle Sam
Not coming back again Damn.

When lights dim at store close OK to grin
Good to go be gone like the wind
No Mamma No Pappa No Uncle Sam
Gone with the wind Damn.

Followed up with April over proposed meeting
Still waiting on greeting not grieving
No Mamma No Pappa No Uncle Sam
Promised this meeting Damn.

Viet vet in store for online buy
Told no over twenty in a pig's eye
No Mamma No Pappa No Uncle Sam
This real Viet vet denied over twenty Damn.

Ethan collapsed on Paint desk stand
Unable meet customer's demands
No Mamma No Pappa No Uncle Sam
Ethan collapsed does not give a Damn.

Lot partied all Friday night called out Saturday morn
Left store in great big mourn
No Mamma No Pappa No Uncle Sam
Lot in heat no place for hungover Damn.

New employee in paint mother of Ethan quaint
Instructing what not to do hardly a saint
No Mamma No Pappa No Uncle Sam
Mom instructing child how not to work Damn.

Fatigue makes cowards of us all
At Depot means never having a ball
No Mamma No Pappa No Uncle Sam
Exhausted and victorious but don't give a Damn.

Depot marketing loved by Henry Ford
Have anything desired if black adored
No Mamma No Pappa No Uncle Sam
Henry Ford does not give a Damn.

Depot capped at one half trillion
Why no new store vermillion
No Mamma No Pappa No Uncle Sam
Accept red and don't give a Damn.

Church bells ring their solemn knell
Depot simply more things to sell
No Mamma No Pappa No Uncle Sam
No church bells for sale Damn.

Camus wrote nothing matters in life
At Depot just get over strife
No Mamma No Pappa No Uncle Sam
Albert never gave a Damn.

Store future to sell a few items more
Does anyone care about what's in store
No Mamma No Pappa No Uncle Sam
Sell more and future don't give a Damn.

Two rules guide store and activity
Never wrong never apologize captivity
No Mamma No Pappa No Uncle Sam
Never wrong and don't give a Damn.

Who cares about Home Depot pay
Never enough anyway
No Mamma No Pappa No Uncle Sam
Pay less get more understand Damn.

Floor in Paint covered by fallen white
Pound tops on cans tight avoid blight
No Mamma No Pappa No Uncle Sam
Can't anything remove this paint Damn.

We did not start fire simply guns for hire
Depot wants things sold so aspire higher
No Mamma No Pappa No Uncle Sam
Hired guns do not give a Damn.

Donner's train consumed wrong kind of meat
Depot never operates under this beat
No Mamma No Pappa No Uncle Sam
Donner's train does not give a Damn.

Cycle of life for Depot career
Demoralize destabilize crisis normalize unclear
No Mamma No Pappa No Uncle Sam
Neither Marx nor Lenin gives a Damn.

Eperchomai a gift for those alive
At Depot they rather cast die
No Mamma No Pappa No Uncle Sam
A die cast gives not a Damn.

Ephrathah fruitfulness in that day
Not inventory for Depot's buffet
No Mamma No Pappa No Uncle Sam
Ephrathah does not give a Damn.

Management does what it does and says
Shame two never interphase
No Mamma No Pappa No Uncle Sam
Say and do don't give a Damn.

Mediation failed impaled by no fault
Depot now in real tough spot
No Mamma No Pappa No Uncle Sam
They won't admit wrongdoing Damn.

Wasco came to Garden register
Customer attempting theft pester
No Mamma No Pappa No Uncle Sam
Theft does not give a Damn.

Customer at register heard Wasco's statements
Bard explained only stuff not entertainments
No Mamma No Pappa No Uncle Sam
These entertainments don't give a Damn.

Enforcement on front burner
EEOC may tear Depot asunder
No Mamma No Pappa No Uncle Sam
Enforcement may make Depot give a Damn.

Depot's crafty mischievous treachery deceit
Hard to stand before much less defeat
No Mamma No Pappa No Uncle Sam
These tongues do not give a Damn.

Offered to look in eye on telescreen
Sometimes Depot antics really scream
No Mamma No Pappa No Uncle Sam
Look me in eye on television Damn.

Shadows in pantomime futile and empty
At Depot selected for this community
No Mamma No Pappa No Uncle Sam
Futile and empty do not give a Damn.

Cheerless churlish dark in despair
Depot way beyond repair
No Mamma No Pappa No Uncle Sam
Despair does not give a Damn.

JC taking leg in for repair on Thursday
Just falling apart from age poor baby
No Mamma No Pappa No Uncle Sam
Another procedure again Damn.

Arrogance in play showed again today
EEOC told Depot apologize on TV hooray
No Mamma No Pappa No Uncle Sam
Nuts you say and don't give a Damn.

Einstein had theory of relativity
Depot usually lacks civility
No Mamma No Pappa No Uncle Sam
Relativity does not give a Damn.

Woman with limited English no splat
Treated like outcast from Poker Flat
No Mamma No Pappa No Uncle Sam
Bret Harte does not give a Damn.

Goggusmos practiced normalcy at Depot
Management's preferred credo
No Mamma No Pappa No Uncle Sam
Management Greek to employees Damn.

Depot thinks only returns and cash
Bard wants neither holocaust
No Mamma No Pappa No Uncle Sam
Holocaust does not give a Damn.

Delight in Depot's will and wealth
Quickly reduced to stench and stealth
No Mamma No Pappa No Uncle Sam
Stand upwind Damn.

Rocks for sale sealed in plastic
Better there than in head fantastic
No Mamma No Pappa No Uncle Sam
Rocks in head don't give a Damn.

Miry clay froth and slime
Sold at Depot for more than a dime
No Mamma No Pappa No Uncle Sam
Miry clay for sale does not give a Damn.

Depot trades in beads and trinkets
Employees never rethink it
No Mamma No Pappa No Uncle Sam
And this not Manhattan Damn.

Customer brought row of flowers chagrined
Barcode not on file bargain yet again
No Mamma No Pappa No Uncle Sam
Just another barcode not on file Damn.

Yoslyn concerned over gift received
From God for her accede
No Mamma No Pappa No Uncle Sam
This money His money Damn.

Make Christy store manager nothing to lose
What could be worse than current ruse
No Mamma No Pappa No Uncle Sam
Christy for store manager hooray Damn.

Charley moving lawn mowers to front from drive-thru
Sweating more than slaves seeking gold of Karfu
No Mamma No Pappa No Uncle Sam
Too many cervezas Damn.

Canoodling never confused as canoeing
At Depot more like spaghetti no fooling
No Mamma No Pappa No Uncle Sam
Canoodling does not give a Damn.

Management believes store serendipity
Employees know house of stupidity
No Mamma No Pappa No Uncle Sam
Stupidity does not give a Damn.

Lumber not moving out door
No pine straw coins on floor
No Mamma No Pappa No Uncle Sam
What can be said Damn.

Alex only help in Garden tonight
Why have other numbers contrite
No Mamma No Pappa No Uncle Sam
Alex The Great Damn.

Alex wore new climber boots
Their comfort returned to her roots
No Mamma No Pappa No Uncle Sam
Alex has incredible boots Damn.

Erica organizing and arranging Flooring
Keeping area spotless simply adoring
No Mamma No Pappa No Uncle Sam
Erica gives a Damn.

Four-hour inspection conducted by big brass
No one will ask why so long too crass
No Mamma No Pappa No Uncle Sam
EEOC and four-hour store inspections Damn.

Rumor abounds about things at the top
Nobody able to ever make this stop
No Mamma No Pappa No Uncle Sam
Rumors do not give a Damn.

Equal opportunity for all privilege to none
Experience teaches rarely in Depot done
No Mamma No Pappa No Uncle Sam
Privilege does not give a Damn.

EEOC and Bard want rumors to stop
Want truth to finally come out on top
No Mamma No Pappa No Uncle Sam
Truth does gives a Damn.

Castles in sky not for you nor me
Home Depot reserves for stock see
No Mamma No Pappa No Uncle Sam
Castles and sky don't give a Damn.

Hive mind not hard to find in this store
Synapses burned lesson learned never bored
No Mamma No Pappa No Uncle Sam
Depot a hive never mind Damn.

Depot grows like a tree in native soil
Soon an end to mindless toil
No Mamma No Pappa No Uncle Sam
Trees do die in soil Damn.

Management wolves employees sheep
Wolves decide which sheep shall eat
No Mamma No Pappa No Uncle Sam
Wolves and sheep don't give a Damn.

Coin shortage returned avenging
Money not flowing through Depot's engine
No Mamma No Pappa No Uncle Sam
Coins not circulating don't give a Damn.

Bard at three for sixteen instead of four
Management scheduling a real big chore
No Mamma No Pappa No Uncle Sam
Three sixteen and they don't give a Damn.

When terminated most receive pink
At Depot use orange makes you blink
No Mamma No Pappa No Uncle Sam
Orange slip does not give a Damn.

Call of the Wild by London did write
For Depot little more than child with spite
No Mamma No Pappa No Uncle Sam
Jack London does not give a Damn.

Depot labor woes quitting in droves
Going to Mary Jane up in smoke treasure troves
No Mamma No Pappa No Uncle Sam
Mary Jane does not give a Damn.

Never wonder why in this din
It will only make head spin
No Mamma No Pappa No Uncle Sam
Head spinning and don't give a Damn.

If Depot a bank won't keep money there
One in whatever don't dare beware
No Mamma No Pappa No Uncle Sam
And can't count change either Damn.

Ten percent kept on every transaction
Now hold change all arranged keep infraction
No Mamma No Pappa No Uncle Sam
Infraction does not give a Damn.

Bard in mirror looked like a frog
Decided to diet whole hog
No Mamma No Pappa No Uncle Sam
Slaughter this hog Damn.

Little Christy cooled her teapot
Decided to leave let Depot rot
No Mamma No Pappa No Uncle Sam
The teapot unplugged Damn.

Red pill for debit to credit
Depot wormhole just like Reddit
No Mamma No Pappa No Uncle Sam
Worm hole without end Damn

Hitler bunker and God thunder
When management fired no wonder
No Mamma No Papa No Uncle Sam
Thunder and bunker don't give a Damn.

Christy losing weight of late
Looking to make things great
No Mamma No Pappa No Uncle Sam
Never too late Damn.

Credibility sacrificed promises unkept
Ignore everything do your thing inept
No Mamma No Pappa No Uncle Sam
No credibility and who gives a Damn.

Lumber prices collapse supply expands
Depot caught too many loose ends
No Mamma No Pappa No Uncle Sam
And still there is no demand Damn.

April turning around in silo
Realizing really no place to go
No Mamma No Pappa No Uncle Sam
Can't turn around a silo Damn.

Iatrogenic in medical world a plague
Depot customer service equally vague
No Mamma No Pappa No Uncle Sam
Plagues don't give a Damn.

Being on time written key to success
Regrettably Depot always settles for far less
No Mamma No Pappa No Uncle Sam
Be on time your option Damn.

Coaching sessions and notes in file new norm
Vile and bile taking store by storm
No Mamma No Pappa No Uncle Sam
If called out how to coach Damn.

Threaten notes and counseling for those that don't perform
Promises unkept and policies not followed established norm
No Mamma No Pappa No Uncle Sam
Promises unkept don't give a Damn.

Don't be early or late recent writing
HCs and cashiers ignore when inviting
No Mamma No Pappa No Uncle Sam
Early late or not at all who gives a Damn.

Breaks for fifteen and not more
No clocks found in store
No Mamma No Pappa No Uncle Sam
Count to fifteen whatever Damn.

Cell phones out not allowed
Company treats as personal foul
No Mamma No Pappa No Uncle Sam
Cell phones do not give a Damn.

Greet entreat for surveys offer credit mammon
Customers will soon suffer from famine
No Mamma No Pappa No Uncle Sam
Bleed like leeches and don't give a Damn.

Common sense and reason calling on phone
Management and process completely unknown
No Mamma No Pappa No Uncle Sam
Answer the phone Damn.

Life in Depot very simple and hollow
Customers in goods out sales follow
No Mamma No Pappa No Uncle Sam
Simple and hollow don't give a Damn.

Emma Peel enigma paired dilemma
Depot never found on agenda
No Mamma No Pappa No Uncle Sam
Diana Rigg never gave a Damn.

Employees walk out the door
Soon forgotten by all evermore
No Mamma No Pappa No Uncle Sam
Remembered never Damn.

Coin shortage an interesting game
Money supply not moving insane
No Mamma No Pappa No Uncle Sam
No velocity less sales Damn.

Ask leader for picture of company in five years
Only have numbers for answers cheers
No Mamma No Pappa No Uncle Sam
And coins piled no picture Damn.

Customers shrewd seldom rude
Store and employees bad mood
No Mamma No Pappa No Uncle Sam
These customers figured Damn.

Treated as number or item of inventory
Hard for employees to enjoy customer story
No Mamma No Pappa No Uncle Sam
Treat as a number what to expect Damn.

Hard to win in store built for loss
Does not matter who is boss
No Mamma No Pappa No Uncle Sam
They don't want to win Damn.

Little Christy added water to pot
Decided to remain in Home Depot spot
No Mamma No Pappa No Uncle Sam
Little Christy staying at Depot Damn.

Store a building design no longer used
Any store behind really abused
No Mamma No Pappa No Uncle Sam
They have another purpose for this store Damn.

Depot wants open borders all around
Helps drive wages down so sound
No Mamma No Pappa No Uncle Sam
Sell America sovereignty for profit Damn.

Nike traitors by and for Red Chinese
Depot eunuch for those Commies
No Mamma No Pappa No Uncle Sam
Eunuch for profit Damn.

CCP celebrating century of genocide
Depot wants products for sale inside
No Mamma No Pappa No Uncle Sam
Cheap is cheap regardless of cost Damn.

English literacy not practiced in store
Better at speaking Spanish on floor
No Mamma No Pappa No Uncle Sam
And Cinco de Mayo not Fourth of July Damn.

All run together past present and whatever
Like mixing colors in a large can together
No Mamma No Pappa No Uncle Sam
And it is an open turnstile Damn.

Management in store never move up only out
Company makes sure never catch gout
No Mamma No Pappa No Uncle Sam
This store of the Damned Damn.

Don't be judgmental or harsh about Depot
Meet shareholder demands avoid veto
No Mamma No Pappa No Uncle Sam
Got to keep those bonuses Damn.

Wasco red as a beet in very little heat
Afraid may become a beet complete
No Mamma No Pappa No Uncle Sam
Red Wasco does not give a Damn.

Told customers could not check out goods
Then showed them that I would
No Mamma No Pappa No Uncle Sam
Customers believed Damn.

Had no coverage July three
Asked all to stay except thee
No Mamma No Pappa No Uncle Sam
Can you say discrimination again Damn.

Published to work only shifts and time
Why then make Bard stay way past time
No Mamma No Pappa No Uncle Sam
Four straight in Garden enough Damn.

Jesse unable to stay needed to go to barbecue
Declined to manage terrible schedule skew
No Mamma No Pappa No Uncle Sam
Barbecue does not give a Damn.

Letter on podium says work only time selected
No one came to Garden to relieve Bard so elected
No Mamma No Pappa No Uncle Sam
Ignore own rules and don't give a Damn.

Lisa in Customer Service cancer in Lymph
Starting treatment next week wondrous nymph
No Mamma No Pappa No Uncle Sam
An epidemic in store Damn.

Customer wanted a full pallet of sod
No one in Garden nor store available to prod
No Mamma No Pappa No Uncle Sam
And sent to Customer Service Damn.

Customer spilled bird seed all over Garden
Sam came running accepted pardon
No Mamma No Pappa No Uncle Sam
This one works and well Damn.

Dre and Bear arrived in Garden to empty trash
Drained water therein with a gash
No Mamma No Pappa No Uncle Sam
They give a Damn.

Sam alias Samantha in Garden noticed by guys
Short black hair with wondrous brown eyes
No Mamma No Pappa No Uncle Sam
Short but she gives a Damn.

Jesse ran through four freezes and roaring fan
Thought she might flee to Kazakhstan
No Mamma No Pappa No Uncle Sam
Four freezes in an hour Damn.

Letter by April posted on register
Many errors better strip cash or face divestiture
No Mamma No Pappa No Uncle Sam
Strip cash Damn.

Logan making hard run through Garden
Date said leave undone not fun
No Mamma No Pappa No Uncle Sam
Put a stop to Logan's Run Damn.

Jesse gobbles freezes as she pleases
Bard receives cold shoulder must have diseases
No Mamma No Pappa No Uncle Sam
Frozen out on hot summer day Damn.

Register in Garden almost died
Jesse asked Bard to help keep alive
No Mamma No Pappa No Uncle Sam
And they refuse to reboot Damn.

Thief beat Bard today stole tool
Used flower to make him a fool
No Mamma No Pappa No Uncle Sam
A thief a thief Damn.

Part-time employees numbers on spreadsheet
Depot too cheap for paper complete
No Mamma No Pappa No Uncle Sam
Wonder why they don't give a Damn.

Management provides meal on holidays
Treat employees to cheap from Walmart their way
No Mamma No Pappa No Uncle Sam
Go cheap why employees don't give a Damn.

April missing from weekend warrior parade
More stuff belonging to charade
No Mamma No Pappa No Uncle Sam
Charades don't give a Damn.

Asked father if could treat daughter to candy
She said no sugar no cookie but did take chips handy
No Mamma No Pappa No Uncle Sam
This child a real keeper Damn.

Phyllis said two grumpy old men on way
Discovered regulars who stay
No Mamma No Pappa No Uncle Sam
These grumpy old men great Damn.

Customer crossed through heat to return cart
Gave him free water thanked for upstart
No Mamma No Pappa No Uncle Sam
What a customer Damn.

OK for them to say their people to us
Not allowed our people their way fuss
No Mamma No Pappa No Uncle Sam
Rules of speech vary Damn.

Emptied trash cans for Dre thankful
Instructed to remind cashiers there handle
No Mamma No Pappa No Uncle Sam
Make cashiers do their jobs Damn.

Phyllis fled register roamed through store
For door lock that worked and more
No Mamma No Pappa No Uncle Sam
Why complain they don't give a Damn.

Phone unsheathed at register
Turned into extended court jester
No Mamma No Pappa No Uncle Sam
Phone jester too busy for customers Damn.

Table with flowers said $7.98
Register rang up $10.98 not great
No Mamma No Pappa No Uncle Sam
Once again prices don't track Damn.

Bo Peep asked if conflict with Phyllis abhorred
Asked if happened Peep squeaked nevermore
No Mamma No Pappa No Uncle Sam
Never never means Bo Peep Damn.

Bloodworth on computer broken
Expect more than friendly token
No Mamma No Pappa No Uncle Sam
More like a blood curdling Damn.

Purgatory an imagined Catholic Hell
Four and more with Phyllis as well
No Mamma No Pappa No Uncle Sam
Thanks Bo Peep Damn.

Kids think in days middle-aged a blink
Old in decades never quite in sync
No Mamma No Pappa No Uncle Sam
Where is wisdom Damn.

Complained about price not nice
Asked if wanted merchandise or no dice
No Mamma No Pappa No Uncle Sam
Tough love Damn.

Phyllis said Amish kids abused in life
Come to work no devices never cause strife
No Mamma No Pappa No Uncle Sam
These kids know life Damn.

Fired four from cashiers for not coming in
Work not an option where do they begin
No Mamma No Pappa No Uncle Sam
And they claimed entitled victimhood Damn.

Connor decided hardware rescind
Chose to leave that the end
No Mamma No Pappa No Uncle Sam
Another good one out the door Damn.

Register went where no one dared
Took a long time to make repair
No Mamma No Pappa No Uncle Sam
Even registers go rogue Damn.

Lumber and employee nearly exclusive
Department now little more than reclusive
No Mamma No Pappa No Uncle Sam
Nothing but lumber Damn.

Customer at PRO with Garden in basket
Believe when told this tragic
No Mamma No Pappa No Uncle Sam
Believe most anything right Damn.

Question of the day for FES
Does she ever work weekend fest
No Mamma No Pappa No Uncle Sam
Have not seen her on weekends Damn.

Part-timers sick of Saturday blues
Suggested all call-out give them news
No Mamma No Pappa No Uncle Sam
Bet that makes them give a Damn.

Call-outs and absences fixed in a jiffy
If management mans posts pretty nifty
No Mamma No Pappa No Uncle Sam
That would fix call-outs in a hurry Damn.

Part-timers abused on weekends unite
Call out together in spite
No Mamma No Pappa No Uncle Sam
Spite makes might Damn.

When Motley schedules expect foolish schedule
No one ever heard of using a level
No Mamma No Pappa No Uncle Sam
Foolishness does not give a Damn.

HR squared out for reasons unknown
Missy scheduling prepares groan
No Mamma No Pappa No Uncle Sam
No backup for HR squared Damn.

Bloodworth schedules like a Kenilworth
At least on time easy to read Butterworth
No Mamma No Pappa No Uncle Sam
Butterworth poured over flapjacks Damn.

Frenzy on floor now no more
Moved to turn over all over store
No Mamma No Pappa No Uncle Sam
Turnover frenzy unchecked don't give a Damn.

Inventory raced employee to door
Employee winning in great roar
No Mamma No Pappa No Uncle Sam
Employee leaves faster than inventory Damn.

Explained to Paul in hardware run astray
Tools on sale customers need him to stay
No Mamma No Pappa No Uncle Sam
Paul alone in tools and no one gives a Damn.

Employees a vapor then quickly gone
Never makes Depot least bit strong
No Mamma No Pappa No Uncle Sam
Anyone remember last month's flower Damn.

Donna came by asked if Bard great
So happy wanted to work late
No Mamma No Pappa No Uncle Sam
Should see shock on her face Damn.

Jesse in Garden next day
Asked if wanted inside said no way
No Mamma No Pappa No Uncle Sam
Consume those freezes in empty Garden Damn.

Let them eat cake royals once said
Depot store managers same thread
No Mamma No Pappa No Uncle Sam
Royals don't give a Damn.

Management kind on July fourth
Walmart corn sugar cookies set forth
No Mamma No Pappa No Uncle Sam
Corn sugar for obese Damn.

Turnover adored by management in frenzy
Makes them channel McKenzie
No Mamma No Pappa No Uncle Sam
McKenzie Break does not give a Damn.

Brought a meal in on July 5th to browse
Fleece weekend warriors reward Hindu cows
No Mamma No Pappa No Uncle Sam
Weekend warriors only a cookie Damn.

Success share has become big scare
Seems this store south of nowhere
No Mamma No Pappa No Uncle Sam
No success and less share Damn.

Big benefit provided to employees a game
Can use 1% of salary for stock purchase gain
No Mamma No Pappa No Uncle Sam
And Bard can buy two-thirds of one share Damn.

Management serves employees on plate
Employees to customers replicate
No Mamma No Pappa No Uncle Sam
These plates do not give a Damn.

Store needs sign hung from rafters
Proclaim House of Stupidity a disaster
No Mamma No Pappa No Uncle Sam
Rafters don't give a Damn.

Millie agreed to meet for lunch over Christy
Want to share what Bard been shown we'll see
No Mamma No Pappa No Uncle Sam
Millie cares about Christy Damn.

Later decided could not be bothered
Wanted to keep Christy dishonored
No Mamma No Pappa No Uncle Sam
Millie does not give a Damn.

Fourth of July in store little more than wake
Employees had trouble finding cupcake
No Mamma No Pappa No Uncle Sam
Wakes do not give a Damn.

Myths and legends often unfold
At Depot tied to promises all told
No Mamma No Pappa No Uncle Sam
Promises made don't give a Damn.

Gonna raise a fuss wanna make a holler
At Depot old news just grab dollar
No Mamma No Pappa No Uncle Sam
Fuss and holler at Depot Damn.

No hope for folks nowhere to go
Come and see this Depot show
No Mamma No Pappa No Uncle Sam
Nowhere in mind and who gives a Damn.

This store world grey and cold
Strawmen neither warm nor bold
No Mamma No Pappa No Uncle Sam
Strawmen don't give a Damn.

Jimmy came by to say goodbye
His shift over had to fly
No Mamma No Pappa No Uncle Sam
Jimmy leaving still gives a Damn.

Phyllis doubled over in pain
Appears to have stone moving exclaim
No Mamma No Pappa No Uncle Sam
This real pain Damn.

Doing six when seventy not very heavenly
Concrete floor lean on legs and back heavily
No Mamma No Pappa No Uncle Sam
Heavily not heavenly Damn.

Make happy customers black white brown whoever
Other employees admire think very clever
No Mamma No Pappa No Uncle Sam
They here to give Depot money Damn.

Paul and lumber expert got in tiff
Bard able to cast them adrift
No Mamma No Pappa No Uncle Sam
It's just wood Damn.

Proclaim our store what a bore
We know means simply in for more
No Mamma No Pappa No Uncle Sam
Store does not give a Damn.

Wonder what she's doing tonight
Just move freight join in spite
No Mamma No Pappa No Uncle Sam
Tommy James does not give a Damn.

April came for electric cart in PRO
Declined to stay or speak to Bard though
No Mamma No Pappa No Uncle Sam
April went away Damn.

Melanie HR squared still missing in action
Missie scheduling to satisfaction
No Mamma No Pappa No Uncle Sam
Schedules done on time Damn.

Darth Vader arrived threatened Dark Star
Bard responded now no longer spar
No Mamma No Pappa No Uncle Sam
The Force be with us Damn.

Most employees have good reason
Management considers high treason
No Mamma No Pappa No Uncle Sam
High treason does not give a Damn.

Newbies arrive working for gain
Very soon discover truth lame
No Mamma No Pappa No Uncle Sam
Lame does not give a Damn.

Negotiate with customer keep them blessed
Money then flows into Depot's chest
No Mamma No Pappa No Uncle Sam
Make them human collect cash Damn.

Thanked Missy for stepping up with functions
Looked as if Bard suggested unction
No Mamma No Pappa No Uncle Sam
Break out the oil Damn.

Gave water to customer in need
Treated like Moses at well indeed
No Mamma No Pappa No Uncle Sam
The little things matter Damn.

Sullins watched Darth Vader ingrate
Bard positioned him to appreciate
No Mamma No Pappa No Uncle Sam
Just send Bard the tough ones Damn.

Kimme hysterical by what she saw
Told Bard she in awe
No Mamma No Pappa No Uncle Sam
Doing this for fifty years Damn.

Sam I Am working for green eggs and ham
Found it better to reach for canned spam
No Mamma No Pappa No Uncle Sam
Spam does not give a Damn.

Stupidocracy practiced by management cruel
Employees refuse to play by these rules
No Mamma No Pappa No Uncle Sam
Stupidocracy does not give a Damn.

Lisa starting chemo today at three
Kimme agreed to send help for free
No Mamma No Pappa No Uncle Sam
Hate cancer and the author Damn.

Now only Friday Saturday Sunday scheduled
Trying to test Bard's steely mettle
No Mamma No Pappa No Uncle Sam
Stay cool and win Damn.

This store won't or don't because it can't
Rather lose than win don't bother to rant
No Mamma No Pappa No Uncle Sam
Won't don't and can't don't give a Damn.

Bard told Sullins cut to three why no see
Appreciated yeah like skunk up tree
No Mamma No Pappa No Uncle Sam
Who needs this appreciation Damn.

Bard schedule a weekend retreat repeat
No good enough to work during week
No Mamma No Pappa No Uncle Sam
Not good enough for Monday through Thursday Damn.

April works week and over
Bard remains only in weekend hover
No Mamma No Pappa No Uncle Sam
Weekend warriors do not give a Damn.

Over river and through woods
Home Depot only sells goods
No Mamma No Pappa No Uncle Sam
Management a fairytale rhyme Damn.

Sometimes shut mouth walk away no more to say
Stupidity not worth more time nor stay
No Mamma No Pappa No Uncle Sam
Just clam up and leave Damn.

Rory new in Hardware making noise
Customers enjoy being around his poise
No Mamma No Pappa No Uncle Sam
Rory loud and gives a Damn.

Many young'uns enjoy work complete
Always in motion rarely off feet
No Mamma No Pappa No Uncle Sam
If they put down devices Damn.

Employees have feelings and bleed
Chain to weekend bring to knees
No Mamma No Pappa No Uncle Sam
Busted knees don't give a Damn.

Rock casbah crazy boogie sound blares
Depot's new way to sell more wares
No Mamma No Pappa No Uncle Sam
Rock Casbah does not give a Damn.

Part-time untouchable class disease
Do with them as you please
No Mamma No Pappa No Uncle Sam
Caste system does not give a Damn.

Never discussed nor agreed to weekend warrior
Management believes this quarrier
No Mamma No Pappa No Uncle Sam
Break rocks and don't give a Damn.

Three days a week never agreed nor discussed
Four by management left in dust
No Mamma No Pappa No Uncle Sam
Do whatever because they can Damn.

Three sons of Japheth had dream
Unfortunately turned into Depot scream
No Mamma No Pappa No Uncle Sam
This dream does not give a Damn.

Sixteen hours minimum for partial plate
Hours at fifteen exculpates promulgate
No Mamma No Pappa No Uncle Sam
Promulgate and exculpate don't give a Damn.

Management scheduling tool weekly
Adjust schedules as needed meekly
No Mamma No Pappa No Uncle Sam
Won't use this tool Damn.

Gave management up to twenty-four
Responded by saying go out door
No Mamma No Pappa No Uncle Sam
Does not need covered hours Damn.

Defendants make pleas in court
Depot prefers to easily abort
No Mamma No Pappa No Uncle Sam
Defendants don't give a Damn.

Private life and call-outs owned by employee
Not an asset for management deployed
No Mamma No Pappa No Uncle Sam
Discretion by management does not give a Damn.

Come to work own job incentivize customers
Management reduces hours forms pustulars
No Mamma No Pappa No Pappa No Uncle Sam
Carbuncles do not give a Damn.

Absence of malice silver chalice
No looking glass here don't tell Alice
No Mamma No Pappa No Uncle Sam
Alice does not give a Damn.

Store on treadmill stuck in rut
Spend their time looking for smut
No Mamma No Pappa No Uncle Sam
This rut does not give a Damn.

Here from government want to help
Depot home office a blight to yelp
No Mamma No Pappa No Uncle Sam
Here to help and don't give a Damn.

Arrived at Depot hat caved in doo da
Left store with bucket full of tin ha
No Mamma No Pappa No Uncle Sam
You think Stephen Foster gives a Damn.

Hard to make customer laugh when needs not met
Makes it tough for Depot to cover bet
No Mamma No Pappa No Uncle Sam
Supply dislocation does not give a Damn.

Lumber price dropped 40% last month
No change none sold anymore blunt
No Mamma No Pappa No Uncle Sam
Take losses on those contracts Damn.

Depot reed blowing in wind
Not for customers to come in
No Mamma No Pappa No Uncle Sam
Blowing in wind does not give a Damn.

Hours time days reduced after meeting of May third
Expected outcome from nerds have you heard
No Mamma No Pappa No Uncle Sam
Nerds don't give a Damn.

Garden not hit by hot summer sun
New cashiers still think it fun
No Mamma No Pappa No Uncle Sam
They will learn soon Damn.

Hindu cows off this week on sacred pilgrimage
Left Depot with cow feathers plumaged
No Mamma No Pappa No Uncle Sam
Don't touch those cows Damn.

Quacks looks and sounds like a duck
Management has run out of luck
No Mamma No Pappa No Uncle Sam
These ducks do not give a Damn.

Management would like Bard to leave never return
Can then spend more time churning churn
No Mamma no Pappa No Uncle Sam
Churns don't give a Damn.

Quixote jousted windmills for beloved Dulcinea
Employees treated more like tortillas
No Mamma No Pappa No Uncle Sam
Miguel Cervantes does not give a Damn.

Workplace hostility harassment discrimination no civility
Expected outcome received in this facility
No Mamma No Pappa No Uncle Sam
This facility does not give a Damn.

Bard's heart deadened by life made cold
Employees come running to help warm cockles behold
No Mamma No Pappa No Uncle Sam
Cockles of heart warmed may give a Damn.

Amicably come to terms through mutual agreement
For this store an impossible achievement
No Mamma No Pappa No Uncle Sam
Just another nail in coffin Damn.

Stuck in middle again oh fiddle
No way to explain this crazy riddle
No Mamma No Pappa No Uncle Sam
Second fiddle who gives a Damn.

Numbers replace knowledge their view
Soon numbers will be few
No Mamma No Pappa No Uncle Sam
Knowledge not numbers gives a Damn.

When scans and barcode numbers fail
Find another way to help customer sail
No Mamma No Pappa No Uncle Sam
Enjoy your inventory right Damn.

Store has what numbers conclude
Inventory in much more somber mood
No Mamma No Pappa No Uncle Sam
And reality an awful thing Damn.

Pin tail on donkey child's game played
Used as technique to make employees go away
No Mamma No Pappa No Uncle Sam
Child's game played does not give a Damn.

Two things constant in this store's mess
Never say thanks use names less
No Mamma No Pappa No Uncle Sam
Numbers on spreadsheets have names Damn.

Scheduling Bard like this hostile in discrimination
May lead to much later Depot recrimination
No Mamma No Pappa No Uncle Sam
Recrimination will give a Damn.

Looked as if management once been nice
Discovered later scratching for lice
No Mamma No Pappa No Uncle Sam
Lice don't give a Damn.

Three kings of Orient gifts galore
Stuff for Depot's boat to engorge
No Mamma No Pappa No Uncle Sam
These kings don't give a Damn.

Depot decided Bard fit only for weekends
No good enough to pick other pecans
No Mamma No Pappa No Uncle Sam
Pecans and nuts do not give a Damn.

Where might they be in five years or ten
A few still working in this den
No Mamma No Pappa No Uncle Sam
Not good Damn.

Offered Christy four-year degree
Ran screaming like Simon Legree
No Mamma No Pappa No Uncle Sam
Harriet Beecher Stowe does not give a Damn.

Management work with employee
Right after Rapture we'll see
No Mamma No Pappa No Uncle Sam
After Rapture who gives a Damn.

Lisa from chemo returned to work very next day
Living a difficult life in an extraordinary way
No Mamma No Pappa No Uncle Sam
One tough cookie Damn.

Went to store to deliver funds for Lisa
Six employees greeted spoke loosely
No Mamma No Pappa No Uncle Sam
Bard so blessed Damn.

Schedule those that may not come in not those that do
Why employees feel like bolts and screws
No Mamma No Pappa No Uncle Sam
Management scrambled does not give a Damn.

Visited store brought in electric cart
James saw and appreciated jump start
No Mamma No Pappa No Uncle Sam
Off the clock got your back Damn.

Olive and Kimme kept record intact
Store not open unless there to act
No Mamma No Pappa No Uncle Sam
Gluttons for punishment Damn.

Ashley smiling broadly with morning routine
Showed Bard's schedule disliked his cuisine
No Mamma No Pappa No Uncle Sam
Good to see Ashley Damn.

Ramshack and Phyllis holding court in resort
Baited by Bard ready repartee for retorts
No Mamma No Pappa No Uncle Sam
And customers will enjoy this repartee Damn.

Friday morning in store as civilian
Very few customers available for kindling
No Mamma No Pappa No Uncle Sam
And they don't even have a quorum Damn.

April out until Sunday opening
Bard will appear to do some exposing
No Mamma No Pappa No Uncle Sam
Fix the schedule Damn.

The girl with no curl Christy
When nice spice naughty Palma Christi
No Mamma No Pappa No Uncle Sam
Twirls hair and does not give a Damn.

Depot not an orange delight
Many think terrible blight
No Mamma No Pappa No Uncle Sam
Delight blighted does not give a Damn.

Not good enough for Monday through Thursday
How any better for Friday through Sunday
No Mamma No Pappa No Uncle Sam
Customers sure don't understand Damn.

Madi in Customer Service no reservist
Small in stature measures up with service
No Mamma No Pappa No Uncle Sam
This reservist provides service Damn.

Gave funds for Lisa to Kimme anonymous
Asked if this meant posthumous
No Mamma No Pappa No Uncle Sam
Dead don't give Damn.

Inventory audit about to commence
Tends to make management sphinx
No Mamma No Pappa No Uncle Sam
Count all nails Damn.

Rain and humidity made evening empty
No one wants to shop under this assembly
No Mamma No Pappa No Uncle Sam
Rain and humidity don't give a Damn.

Dreadfully slow on Friday eve rightly so
Millwork at ease complete no show
No Mamma No Pappa No Uncle Sam
Do not even answer phone Damn.

Christy working banker's hours in flooring
Weekend schedule simply has no mooring
No Mamma No Pappa No Uncle Sam
Eight to five and don't give a Damn.

Weekend time for gathering of part-times
Nobody else works or shares in these crimes
No Mamma No Pappa No Uncle Sam
Part-timers only on weekends Damn.

Leaving work Sullins slapped forehead
Bard exclaimed he should have a V8
No Mamma No Pappa No Uncle Sam
V8 great Damn.

Depot like New Orleans cemetery
Concrete not living contrary
No Mamma No Pappa No Uncle Sam
Cemeteries don't give a Damn.

Bo Peep on Friday mission to leave
Had registers closed without one reprieve
No Mamma No Pappa No Uncle Sam
Bo Peep on mission to leave Damn.

Took road angels feared to tread
Chose to come into Depot instead
No Mamma No Pappa No Uncle Sam
Robert Mitchum does not give a Damn.

SCO screams customer needs assistance in stereo
Bo Peep and Yoslyn decided to let it go
No Mamma No Pappa No Uncle Sam
SCO unleashed and they don't give a Damn.

Teapot cameo in PRO for tubes
Complained schedule remains crude
No Mamma No Pappa No Uncle Sam
Joins Bard as weekend warrior Damn.

Keeping spider wraps under lock and key
Simply makes no sense think and see
No Mamma Pappa No Uncle Sam
Spiders locked up Damn.

Vultures to carrion part-times to weekends
Customers hardly ever know how to begin
No Mamma No Pappa No Uncle Sam
Vultures don't give a Damn.

Cobblers' children never have shoes
Depot employees sing blues
No Mamma No Pappa No Uncle Sam
Blues and shoes who gives a Damn.

No backup power though it sells
Been this way forever no end swell
No Mamma No Pappa No Uncle Sam
Lights go out who gives a Damn.

Public enjoys Depot image and hokum
Wait till they read this show them
No Mamma No Pappa No Uncle Sam
Hokum sham and does not give a Damn

Forensic audit performed on inventory how grand
What to send received on hand unplanned
No Mamma No Pappa No Uncle Sam
No one knows Damn.

Endless search for yellow tag pick-ups
Not pulled nor lost creates large hiccup
No Mamma No Pappa No Uncle Sam
Must be here somewhere Damn.

Rainy Sunday afternoon without end or clowning
Customers stuffed under PRO awning avoid drowning
No Mamma No Pappa No Uncle Sam
Raining really hard Damn.

Saturday biggest day of sales during week
Stock with part-times to make store weak
No Mamma no Pappa No Uncle Sam
Management throws up their hands Damn.

No coverage in Lot through morning
Made Behr work hard to catch up restoring
No Mamma No Pappa No Uncle Sam
Behr in rain does give a Damn.

April explained warrior weekend strain
Full-times in part-times out new game
No Mamma No Pappa No Uncle Sam
Are they really this crazy Damn.

Part-times cost ten an hour for each flock
Full-times nearly triples cost real crock
No Mamma No Pappa No Uncle Sam
Triple cost and don't give a Damn.

Order fulfillment failed feared practice
Better to land in tub of cactus
No Mamma No Pappa No Uncle Sam
Order fulfillment cluster Damn.

Depot like large peanut M&M candy
Core greed chocolate management shell employee dandy
No Mamma No Pappa No Uncle Sam
Melts in your hand Damn.

When will-call employed to fulfill needs
You can expect store to quickly bleed
No Mamma No Pappa No Uncle Sam
Will-calls won't give a Damn.

Generac keeps homes from dark hulks
Depot too cheap to install these bulks
No Mamma No Pappa No Uncle Sam
Who needs power at store right Damn.

When lights go out in Georgia
Depot will seek new Borgia
No Mamma No Pappa No Uncle Sam
Borgia stick does not give a Damn.

Good customer arrived wanted to rent generator
Told him to buy return when done fabricator
No Mamma No Pappa No Uncle Sam
Buy and return who gives a Damn.

Concord makes for great grape jelly
At Depot little more than woe Nelly
No Mamma No Pappa No Uncle Sam
Keith Jackson does not give a Damn.

Like pigs at first frost management commits troth
Depot shall somehow consume this broth
No Mamma No Pappa No Uncle Sam
Pigs and frost don't give a Damn.

Depot expects employees to always claque
Disappointed when crack and quack
No Mamma No Pappa No Uncle Sam
Claques don't give a Damn.

Orange at zenith and apex close to Sun
Daedalus would tell them soon no fun
No Mamma No Pappa No Uncle Sam
Pay attention Orange Damn.

April let slip management embarks on new trip
Full-time only part-times gone what a rip
No Mamma No Pappa No Uncle Sam
Orange slips for part-time Damn.

Nothing more savage than grizzly dripping rain
For this Behr more than little pain
No Mamma No Pappa No Uncle Sam
Grizzlies in rain don't give a Damn.

Chris arrived at 2 to serve as Indian to chiefs in Lumber
Very tired of working with Bard each weekend penumbra
No Mamma No Pappa No Uncle Sam
Chris tired of weekends only Damn.

Paint covered with Jasmine
Promised to avoid all razzing
No Mamma No Pappa No Uncle Sam
This Jasmine not usual shrub Damn.

Charles like softened peanut butter
Spreads employee and customer
No Mamma No Pappa No Uncle Sam
Smooth not chunky Damn.

Two in PRO barely needed one
Maybe home office will end run
No Mamma No Pappa No Uncle Sam
Nothing to do Damn.

Two HCs and April plus six cashiers
Management watching hours ha ha sneer
No Mamma No Pappa No Uncle Sam
Ludicrous and they don't give a Damn.

ASM in rear with ORG
Employees fear form new Borg
No Mamma No Pappa No Uncle Sam
Borgs don't give a Damn.

Bridge over Kwai railroad and wood
Depot madness never understood
No Mamma No Pappa No Uncle Sam
Pierre Boulle does not give a Damn.

Hammer in morning hammer in evening
No wonder customers and employees leaving
No Mamma No Pappa No Uncle Sam
Trini Lopez does not give a Damn.

Christy arrived in store with friends of Ham
Picked up order never before like lamb
No Mamma No Pappa No Uncle Sam
Christy in a dress Damn.

Things unlikely include meteor hitting store
More probable than new building here Endor
No Mamma No Pappa No Uncle Sam
Bulldozers will never demolish Damn.

Locker room visit by Roland bringing freezes
Jesse could eat them all as pleases
No Mamma No Pappa No Uncle Sam
Just give her three hours Damn.

April as HC flayed away on deserving extra dollar
Deaf to Bard about 16 hours wants to holler
No Mamma No Pappa No Uncle Sam
Holler and dollar don't give a Damn.

Schedule now miser Bard two shifts
Last cut worst burst no gifts
No Mamma No Pappa No Uncle Sam
This miser does not give a Damn.

Afghanistan air base property left behind
Depot charges off next in line
No Mamma No Pappa No Uncle Sam
Next in line does not give a Damn.

Insults reproaches shame make broken hearts
At Depot often done insane lame not smart
No Mamma No Pappa No Uncle Sam
Numbers on sheet don't give a Damn.

Donna jumped out of skin when said hello
Inventory audit made her unmellow
No Mamma No Pappa No Uncle Sam
And this is a crack of doom Damn.

Customer stole tool very great vice
Company only allows good day be nice
No Mamma No Pappa No Uncle Sam
Just like San Francisco Damn.

Let numbers on printouts become snare
Wolves then shall enter lair
No Mamma No Pappa No Uncle Sam
These wolves don't give a Damn.

Yo Yo arrived at PRO told Bard to go
Signed him out laughed face aglow
No Mamma No Pappa No Uncle Sam
Yo Yo got one on Bard Damn.

English and Yo Yo often not mesh
Moves hands dances with feet creche
No Mamma No Pappa No Uncle Sam
Yo Yo can communicate Damn.

Jesse in PRO during Sunday rain
So very tired real shame
No Mamma No Pappa No Uncle Sam
Worked into ground they don't give a Damn.

Bo Peep arrived at 12 to work till eight
One look at face you knew this not great
No Mamma No Pappa No Uncle Sam
Was he worth it last night Bo Peep Damn.

Kids adults young and dumb
Depot does not understand need for fun
No Mamma No Pappa No Uncle Sam
Pretty soon kids don't give a Damn.

Sir Arthur paid visit today during shift
Made Bard stiff very much adrift
No Mamma No Pappa No Uncle Sam
Breaks inaugurate Arthur Damn.

Jesse going to school she no fool
Looking to make engineering golden rule
No Mamma No Pappa No Uncle Sam
An Electrical Engineer Damn.

Mary autistic left alone in storm flood
Water drenched unkempt just shrug
No Mamma No Pappa No Uncle Sam
Well at least she did not drown Damn.

Arrow up deliverance in sky hope
When down as is above so below you dope
No Mamma No Pappa No Uncle Sam
Up or down does not give a Damn.

Depot less station more pot
Hard to catch train at this spot
No Mamma No Pappa No Uncle Sam
All aboard and don't give a Damn.

Melisha at PRO in soggy mood
Cut like knife to make all blue
No Mamma No Pappa No Uncle Sam
Soggy blue mood does not give a Damn.

Asthma at work in April wheezing
Inhalers work to reduce sneezing
No Mamma No Pappa No Uncle Sam
Asthma does not give a Damn.

Sell rocks in bag for customer use
Not a shelter to comfort in Zeus
No Mamma No Pappa No Uncle Sam
No rocks in this head Damn.

Wrath and indignation poured on management
Make this source of eternal banishment
No Mamma No Pappa No Uncle Sam
Banishment does not give a Damn.

When strength spent power fails
Don't expect Depot to ever prevail
No Mamma No Pappa No Uncle Sam
No strength left and who gives a Damn.

Rumors swirl attack Bard all over
Not about to leave in high clover
No Mamma No Pappa No Uncle Sam
Rumors don't give a Damn.

Blame and shame content of Depot game
Reproach scorn adversarial dishonor blame
No Mamma No Pappa No Uncle Sam
And this system is more than lame Damn.

Pursue persecute employees smitten
How process manual written
No Mamma No Pappa No Uncle Sam
Employees smitten don't give a Damn.

Enjoy watching management sweat
Inventory audit makes regret
No Mamma No Pappa No Uncle Sam
Reality is awful right Damn.

Great troubles and sore quickened in store
Still Depot moves to create even more
No Mamma No Pappa No Uncle Sam
Great troubles don't give a Damn.

God is gold and altar rising stock
When falls covetousness becomes shock
No Mamma No Pappa No Uncle Sam
This shock and awe won't give a Damn.

Turn backward those that seek revenge on job
Desire delight in hurt *thingamabob*
No Mamma No Pappa No Uncle Sam
Thingamabob does not give a Damn.

Part-time employees to be phased out
Leaves store little more than flinging grout
No Mamma No Pappa No Uncle Sam
Who thought this one up Damn.

Treat Lot attendant like board of director
Watch sales rise in this sector
No Mamma No Pappa No Uncle Sam
Are you serious not happening Damn.

Fall leaves and Depot have much in common
Neither will ever meet or greet Hamann
No Mamma No Pappa No Uncle Sam
Uncle Mordechai does not give a Damn.

Woman with beauty and brain a dangerous thing
Depot makes sure such must act insane
No Mamma No Pappa No Uncle Sam
Beauty and brains at Depot don't give a Damn.

Paint spills now happening each week
Really makes floor look like a freak
No Mamma No Pappa No Uncle Sam
Pound the lids Damn.

Corporatism new religion practiced with zeal
Make sure employees know real
No Mamma No Pappa No Uncle Sam
Baal worship does not give a Damn.

Leadership similar to Nero playing fiddle
Conflagration ignored focus on little
No Mamma No Pappa No Uncle Sam
Nero does not give a Damn.

Hypocrisy practiced each and every day
Corporatism truth applied that way
No Mamma No Pappa No Uncle Sam
Conscience need not apply Damn.

Many heroes in store today
Saw them work fully assayed
No Mamma No Pappa No Uncle Sam
Depot Hell for these heroes Damn.

Vision occasionally glimpses as flash
Souls revealed then sealed not balderdash
No Mamma No Pappa No Uncle Sam
These glimpses do give a Damn.

Associates poor sorrowful and pained
Corporate source for additional gain
No Mamma No Pappa No Uncle Sam
These associates don't give a Damn.

Numbers should support theory in query
Depot forces numbers to theory be leery
No Mamma No Pappa No Uncle Sam
Numbers what they say Damn.

Sometimes breath refuses to work
Depot believes this shirk
No Mamma No Pappa No Uncle Sam
Shirk does not give a Damn.

Part-time employees cost ten an hour
Full-time three times more go shower
No Mamma No Pappa No Uncle Sam
Increase labor cost and don't give a Damn.

Sav eaten with tumor pestilence inside
No one offered help she may die
No Mamma No Pappa No Uncle Sam
Get it done Bard Damn.

Depot promises employee benefactor
Ends up Associate malefactor
No Mamma No Pappa No Uncle Sam
Malefactors don't give a Damn.

Management bones lie at gate of Sheol
Snared in nets like fish and eel
No Mamma No Pappa No Uncle Sam
A fine kettle of fish Damn.

Good years Depot promises much delivers little
Bad years tells us play fiddle
No Mamma No Pappa No Uncle Sam
Fiddles don't give a Damn.

Hear teach deliver and save
Not Depot's preferred way
No Mamma No Pappa No Uncle Sam
Their ways don't give a Damn.

When Depot says here to help
Employees know encased in kelp
No Mamma No Pappa No Uncle Sam
Kelp does not give a Damn.

Depot calls them Associates not employees
Assoc. abbrieve independent contractor believe
No Mamma No Pappa No Uncle Sam
Obscure and don't give a Damn.

Scorn and scoffing fill life of proud
At ease in this store wearing shroud
No Mamma No Pappa No Uncle Sam
Proud don't give a Damn.

A train wrecked cannot back up
At Depot simply make stuff up
No Mamma No Pappa No Uncle Sam
A real trainwreck Damn.

Hey brother can you spare dime refrain
At Depot keep change blame
No Mamma No Pappa No Uncle Sam
Can't spare a dime Damn.

Depot sells tin and straw for men
Bring Dorothy and lion in then
No Mamma No Pappa No Uncle Sam
Not in Kansas anymore Damn.

Wax and wane yin and yang anything claimed
Depot no clue how to play game for shame
No Mamma No Pappa No Uncle Sam
And Tao does not give a Damn.

Bird escaped from snare of fowlers
Management taught to practice howler
No Mamma No Pappa No Uncle Sam
Snared don't give a Damn.

Sharpened tongues serpent adders poison under lips
Management no end to these useless trips
No Mamma No Pappa No Uncle Sam
Adders don't give a Damn.

Depot dinner table covered in linen
Few seats most disheveled call Lenin
No Mamma No Pappa No Uncle Sam
And bread lines in St. Petersburg don't give a Damn.

Depot announces end of sign-in questionnaire
Trying to become more debonaire
No Mamma No Pappa No Uncle Sam
Work if you're sick they don't give a Damn.

Bread of anxious toil brought by late sleep
Depot will never give rest nor let keep
No Mamma No Pappa No Uncle Sam
Anxious does not give a Damn.

Asia three monkeys that do not see hear nor speak
At Home Depot featured each week
No Mamma No Pappa No Uncle Sam
Three monkeys don't give a Damn.

Management grass growing on house top
Scorched and withered before grows up
No Mamma No Pappa No Uncle Sam
Name manager five years ago Damn.

Store like huge crossword puzzle
No one connects pieces use shovel
No Mamma No Pappa No Uncle Sam
This puzzle does not give a Damn.

New form of employee appearing
One and done no show veneering
No Mamma No Pappa No Uncle Sam
No shows don't give a Damn.

Depot exalts name over all things
One day called upon to explain
No Mamma No Pappa No Uncle Sam
Watch what you exalt Damn.

Three off in row makes life go slow
Four in row tends to ruin show
No Mamma No Pappa No Uncle Sam
You call this scheduling Damn.

Always take time for little humor
Helps lift store's endless stupor
No Mamma No Pappa No Uncle Sam
Stupor does not give a Damn.

Free speech and new ideas hand in hand
Politburo always ready to ban and brand
No Mamma No Pappa No Uncle Sam
Politburo does not give a Damn.

Depot daughter of Babylon
Neither provide employees bon bons
No Mamma No Pappa No Uncle Sam
And Semiramis had no daughters Damn.

Fireworks fail to launch very near
Like new hires that never appear
No Mamma No Pappa No Uncle Sam
Failed fireworks don't give a Damn.

Justice for oppressed food for hungry
Depot considers advanced misandry
No Mamma No Pappa No Uncle Sam
Misandry does not give a Damn.

Bureaucrats rule home office
Unable to smooth any pumice
No Mamma No Pappa No Uncle Sam
Pumice rock in their heads Damn.

April said schedule not nice take advice
Will straighten out be nice
No Mamma No Pappa No Uncle Sam
Advice and nice do not give a Damn.

Schedules treated as well as inventory
No wonder both appear very hoary
No Mamma No Pappa No Uncle Sam
Schedules and inventory who cares Damn.

Watch out if thought well of by them
Almost never treated for long as gem
No Mamma No Pappa No Uncle Sam
You are just a number Damn.

Dentists may make crown
Christy and Depot get out of town
No Mamma No Pappa No Uncle Sam
Get out of town Damn.

There is a wisdom that descends to woe
And woe to madness for Depot to hoe
No Mamma No Pappa No Uncle Sam
This wisdom not so wise Damn.

Pappa Joe says Xinjiang supply chain sin
For you Craig where have you been
No Mamma No Pappa No Uncle Sam
Cancel that ship lease Craig Damn.

Phillip inquired of Sparta if friend or foe said neither
Depot management prefers employees believer
No Mamma No Pappa No Uncle Sam
Leave it to Alexander Damn.

Before King poor showed sack asked for flour
Employees lack sack no flour work by hour
No Mamma No Pappa No Uncle Sam
Empty sacks who gives a Damn.

Quota pars operis tanti nobis committitur
Management practices nothing but fear
No Mamma No Pappa No Uncle Sam
Velikovsky does not give a Damn.

Money to burn everywhere except when earned
Management learned how to bury in urns
No Mamma No Pappa No Uncle Sam
Urns don't give a Damn.

New schedule online not so fine
Hours now eight must be a fine
No Mamma No Pappa No Uncle Sam
Cut to eight why bother Damn.

April said patience wait on schedule fix
Hardly seems fair for them to play these tricks
No Mamma No Pappa No Uncle Sam
Starve them of hours and don't give a Damn.

Scheduling asphyxiation tearing apart store nation
Driving part-timers out with no justification
No Mamma No Pappa No Uncle Sam
Depot does not give a Damn.

If scheduled for only eight why participate
What's in it for me just tell them straight
No Mamma No Pappa No Uncle Sam
Worth more to stay home now Damn.

Ask HR squared if outplacement offered
Employment hour starvation made awkward
No Mamma No Pappa No Uncle Sam
Find your own job Damn.

Schedules inventory and hours allowed run same
No schedules inventory unknown hours exclaimed
No Mamma No Pappa No Uncle Sam
Truly all this practiced insane Damn.

When doing physical inventory audit
No one knows anything about it
No Mamma No Pappa No Uncle Sam
Don't even know what is in store Damn.

Starve employee with schedules of eight
How are they to customer going to appreciate
No Mamma No Pappa No Uncle Sam
Treated this way what can I say Damn.

Management says don't do to customers what done to you
Provide them very best we give you less don't ridicule
No Mamma No Pappa No Uncle Sam
The ridiculed don't give a Damn.

Inventory audit determines what should already know
Means before merely putting on show
No Mamma No Pappa No Uncle Sam
Run store with inventory unknown Damn.

Walking tightrope across Niagara Falls
easier than surviving this bunch of pitfalls
No Mamma No Pappa No Uncle Sam
Niagara Falls does not give a Damn.

Part-timers wonder what management might say
If their hours and pay reduced this way
No Mamma No Pappa No Uncle Sam
They squeal like pigs Damn.

Do unto others what you might want from them
At Depot almost always take crumbs
No Mamma No Pappa No Uncle Sam
Crumbs don't give a Damn.

Unions and Depot deserve each other
Made very similar in druthers brother
No Mamma No Pappa No Uncle Sam
Unions don't give a Damn.

Reduced pay by 60% on part-times that way
What might they do if it was their pay
No Mamma No Pappa No Uncle Sam
Better you than me and don't give a Damn.

Promote good attitudes by cutting pay
Attitude toward customers likely sway
No Mamma No Pappa No Uncle Sam
This sway won't give a Damn.

Customer in Garden seizure collapsed to floor
Bard offered help provided more
No Mamma No Pappa No Uncle Sam
Fell to the ground Damn.

Fire and rescue arrived at scene
Made sure man did not go obscene
No Mamma No Pappa No Uncle Sam
Man OK and sent to hospital hooray Damn.

Store number four in region of seven
Other stores definitely lost leaven
No Mamma No Pappa No Uncle Sam
Good boys not stores go to Heaven Damn.

Store 0884 creature layout time forgot
Make others worry with fraught
No Mamma No Pappa No Uncle Sam
Those other stores really bad Damn.

Antiquated layout number four in sales
Refuse to make new with hammer and nails
No Mamma No Pappa No Uncle Sam
Replace this runt and give a Damn.

Depot and enormous deemed essential
Too big to fail receive bailout potential
No Mamma No Pappa No Uncle Sam
And Leviathan consumes Damn.

Leeches and Depot shared goal
One takes blood other life from foal
No Mamma No Pappa No Uncle Sam
These leeches do not give a Damn.

April relayed what Bean Counter said
Numbers this year to last compared not red
No Mamma No Pappa No Uncle Sam
Ahead of last year numbers are you serious Damn.

Millie with wool jacket draped
Wearing in 90 degree heat wait
No Mamma No Pappa No Uncle Sam
Really cold-blooded Damn.

Christopher with apron off playing cop
Chased thief like Rimsky Korsakov
No Mamma No Pappa No Uncle Sam
Thief walked out anyway Damn.

Behr called in to finish Lot at close
Made sure did not look bulldozed
No Mamma No Pappa No Uncle Sam
Behr in his den for sure Damn.

Nick upset over something overheard took aim
Apologized covered back explained all the same
No Mamma No Pappa No Uncle Sam
Keep him happy Damn.

April not allowed to call anyone for call-outs
Tell management to man registers come about
No Mamma No Pappa No Uncle Sam
That will promote change Damn.

Depot has wheel called values and justice
Another way to turn screws and fuss at us
No Mamma No Pappa No Uncle Sam
This wheel more rack and Inquisition Damn.

Doing right thing one sector on wheel
Associates know this but empty spiel
No Mamma No Pappa No Uncle Sam
Spiels do not give a Damn.

Building strong relationships not exactly
Depot wins Associates lose factly
No Mamma No Pappa No Uncle Sam
Not exactly a relationship Damn.

Giving back principal espoused in house
Your back your giving Mickey Mouse
No Mamma No Pappa No Uncle Sam
Backaches and empty pockets don't give a Damn.

Respect for all people tune used
Some more respected than others ruse
No Mamma No Pappa No Uncle Sam
People more equal don't give a Damn.

Taking care of our people bellow and boast
Cut pay 60% make others toast
No Mamma No Pappa No Uncle Sam
Ex-employees don't give a Damn.

House built on sand hard to stand
Part and parcel to Home Depot brand
No Mamma No Pappa No Uncle Sam
You think this brand gives a Damn.

Excellent customer service proclaimed in signs
Cut staff in two save real design
No Mamma No Pappa No Uncle Sam
Corporate hypocrisy does not give a Damn.

Managers grieved over what Bard had seen
Wanted to make sure did not vent spleen
No Mamma No Pappa No Uncle Sam
Man recovered give thanks Damn.

Supervisors and employees jointly adoring
Never to company or management warring
No Mamma No Pappa No Uncle Sam
Just get along somehow Damn.

This Wheel not of fortune more of rack
Turns employees into sad sack quacks
No Mamma No Pappa No Uncle Sam
And Pat Sajak does not give a Damn.

Employees improved bad actors mostly removed
Methods employed more than crude
No Mamma No Pappa No Uncle Sam
Achieved their ends Damn.

It is said have a cross to bear
Depot management will stop and stare
No Mamma No Pappa No Uncle Sam
Stare does not give a Damn.

Sales announced as good as yesteryear
Then why abuse employees with so much fear
No Mamma No Pappa No Uncle Sam
Enough never enough right Damn.

Profit and greed source of creed
Management never leaves this awful deed
No Mamma No Pappa No Uncle Sam
This creed does not give a Damn.

April brought customer for credit app for usury
Only had passport made offer illusory
No Mamma No Pappa No Uncle Sam
Almost ensnared in usury Damn.

Angels at work in Garden last night
Caught customer collapsing helped lay right
No Mamma No Pappa No Uncle Sam
Straight down on concrete not hurt Damn.

Creating shareholder value through numbers and smoke
Eventually exposed will go broke
No Mamma No Pappa No Uncle Sam
Pay those big bonuses Damn.

Bo Peep said Bard so old school on computer link
Replied old schools taught think in their rink
No Mamma No Pappa No Uncle Sam
Old schools know how to think Damn.

Entrepreneurial spirit wears frown
Must always come from corporate down
No Mamma No Pappa No Uncle Sam
Heaven help new idea Damn.

Nectar to bees so very sweet
Young men to Bo Peep how neat
No Mamma No Pappa No Uncle Sam
Bo Peep the honey pot Damn

You know they took pay dollars
Now expect not to bother or holler
No Mamma No Pappa No Uncle Sam
Just tell customers Damn.

Roland asked about Sav thought ointment
Explained tumors power of appointment
No Mamma No Pappa No Uncle Sam
Sav forgotten and needing help Damn.

Market cap halfway to trillion and glory
Bags managed like schedule and inventory
No Mamma No Pappa No Uncle Sam
Can't even order bags Damn.

SCO said no coins all night their might
Send all cash payers to middle great fright
No Mamma No Pappa No Uncle Sam
And tomorrow is Saturday oh no Damn.

Bo Peep has suitor asking her out
Making him ask often to earn bout
No Mamma No Pappa No Uncle Sam
Don't wait too long for yes Bo Peep Damn.

Talmadge not Benjamin came by ending jam
Wires bands up on weekends ma'am
No Mamma No Pappa No Uncle Sam
Worth a Continental Damn.

Yo Yo in PRO asked Bard to take returns
Promised to be happy not do a burn
No Mamma No Pappa No Uncle Sam
Take the returns Damn.

Darth Vader in store asked for Bard with Kimme
Sullins decided Bard amazing at kibbutzie
No Mamma No Pappa No Uncle Sam
Add sugar to lemons Damn.

Autism pre-birth damage rewires brain
Helps overcome make quite sane
No Mamma No Pappa No Uncle Sam
Amazing how body overcomes Damn.

Noah in Lot suffers from touch
Customer came up said more than clutch
No Mamma No Pappa No Uncle Sam
Overcomes and humbles Damn.

Dogs good cats a treat
This store sells cookers that heat
No Mamma No Pappa No Uncle Sam
These cookers do meat Damn.

Customer arrived two dogs in tow
Ran to Bard to sniff before go
No Mamma No Pappa No Uncle Sam
More sniffing dogs Damn.

Not everyone pet lover or afficionado
Those don't won't count in this bravado
No Mamma No Pappa No Uncle Sam
And this kennel is loud Damn.

Las Navas de Tolosa where much settled
Home Depot would prefer to sell kettles
No Mamma No Pappa No Uncle Sam
Just sell history Damn.

Amber in charge of Saturday enclave
Wanted very much to be elsewhere and play
No Mamma No Pappa No Uncle Sam
Amber laughing does her job Damn.

Melisha came in heat to PRO with beef
Bard explained tired of grief
No Mamma No Pappa No Uncle Sam
Little Christy saw and heard Damn.

Phyllis gave away Amish peanuts
Thought might make zealot
No Mamma No Pappa No Uncle Sam
Amish don't grow peanuts Damn.

Lisa accepted peanuts said thanks
Anything to help out of tank
No Mamma No Pappa No Uncle Sam
Help her anyway we can Damn.

Home office compliance about hours and pay
Very certain will make it go away
No Mamma No Pappa No Uncle Sam
Backfill and go away as usual Damn.

Lisa struggling with chemo tough
Worked an hour left for home rough
No Mamma No Pappa No Uncle Sam
Really drained Damn.

PRO just a mess at 10 AM clear aisle fill water
Bring in carts take chest out real barter
No Mamma No Pappa No Uncle Sam
And ASMs don't walk store or give a Damn.

Andrea not schooled on PRO tools
Stands by register as if barstool
No Mamma No Pappa No Uncle Sam
Barstools don't give a Damn.

Contractor asked for pallet of cement
Noon on Saturday forklift at lunch lament
No Mamma No Pappa No Uncle Sam
No one responded as usual Damn.

Customers no bags staff reduction and pay cuts
Very sympathetic and wish lots of luck
No Mamma No Pappa No Uncle Sam
Explains the limited service Damn.

If you don't like deal leave
Sums up Depot's spiel and creed
No Mamma No Pappa No Uncle Sam
Loyalty for profit who gives a Damn.

Ramshack and Phyllis covering middle great sport
Gave Bard no opportunity for lengthy retort
No Mamma No Pappa No Uncle Sam
Ramshack just messin' Damn.

Store needs class try piano and tuxedo
Customers arriving may say Holy Toledo
No Mamma No Pappa No Uncle Sam
Class in Depot will never give a Damn.

Melisha bucking for full-time spare climb
Schedules cut hours deleted much impeded sublime
No Mamma No Pappa No Uncle Sam
Another full-time cashier not happening Damn.

Little Christy reviewing Doordash foray
Believes some good money made
No Mamma No Pappa No Uncle Sam
Doordash better than Depot Damn.

Behr foraging throughout store
Ethan joined made neat once more
No Mamma No Pappa No Uncle Sam
Wow these two really give a Damn.

April and Little Christy doing Doordash
Full- or part-time not enough in Depot hash
No Mamma No Pappa No Uncle Sam
April cannot make ends meet Damn.

Christy mixing paint and pounding cans Saturday
Hair no longer golden now rust red display
No Mamma No Pappa No Uncle Sam
Munchausen does not give a Damn.

ASM picks music to hear over PA
Not exactly uplifting better say neigh
No Mamma No Pappa No Uncle Sam
This music does not give a Damn.

Dog beaten night and day by owner
Why bites others real no boner
No Mamma No Pappa No Uncle Sam
And employees the dog Damn.

Expect more schedule less decline to confess
Why this soon becomes perfect mess
No Mamma No Pappa No Uncle Sam
Confession does not give a Damn.

Anger to thought then action must avoid
Not smart in Depot to employ
No Mamma No Pappa No Uncle Sam
Don't take it serious or personal Damn.

Explain pay and staff cuts to customers Depot hustler
Helps them understand why service little to muster
No Mamma No Pappa No Uncle Sam
A hustler does not give a Damn.

Asked 12 questions about schedule and pay
Requested answers for wheel's decay
No Mamma No Pappa No Uncle Sam
No answers coming Damn.

Locker room displayed Olive and Chance
Going to Nashville for romance
No Mamma No Pappa No Uncle Sam
Young and in love Damn.

JC exit in ten months from full-time
Hope decides to continue part-time
No Mamma No Pappa No Uncle Sam
Plumbing without JC worse than Dan Damn.

Joey why apron underneath shirt
Only way can relieve from spurt
No Mamma No Pappa No Uncle Sam
No friends in bathroom Damn.

Bo Peep arrived to replace Amber wearing diaper
Promised Bard could leave on time sweet cider
No Mamma No Pappa No Uncle Sam
Bo Peep at helm again Damn.

Four days off coming around yet again
Time to make Christmas cookies in July attain
No Mamma No Pappa No Uncle Sam
Enjoy the cookies Damn.

Will-calls and pickups had difficulty
Sprouted wings flew critically
No Mamma No Pappa No Uncle Sam
Worse than paperchase Damn.

When customers arrive say welcome to Pot
Hope when through will say thanks a lot
No Mamma No Pappa No Uncle Sam
This pot stirred does not give a Damn.

Remind customers on their own self-serve
Depot cut most employees forlorn beware
No Mamma No Pappa No Uncle Sam
Beware and don't give a Damn.

Employees compacted service redacted
How customers expected to not be impacted
No Mamma No Pappa No Uncle Sam
Impacted customers won't give a Damn.

When service demanded and none there
Recommend Big Blue not very fair
No Mamma No Pappa No Uncle Sam
If we only had employees Damn.

What to do when employees few
Hope customers don't learn to feud
No Mamma No Pappa No Uncle Sam
The few don't give a Damn.

Spare us Orange Life value vignettes
Better to swim in mud of Metz
No Mamma No Pappa No Uncle Sam
A pot is nothing but a croc Damn.

Call to arms solution display badge of truth
Depot took 65% of pay forsooth
No Mamma No Pappa No Uncle Sam
Let world know about this Damn.

Neither customer nor Associate control store
Reason just too few left anymore
No Mamma No Pappa No Uncle Sam
Silent and empty Damn.

Stonewall a rock at Manassas Junction
Depot sells rocks part of their function
No Mamma No Pappa No Uncle Sam
Stonewall Jackson does not give a Damn.

Associate may encounter bad health and stroke
Depot prefers to roll dice make them broke
No Mamma No Pappa No Uncle Sam
Stroke and broke don't give a Damn.

If don't like deal then leave Depot retort
Gave their word means nothing purport
No Mamma No Pappa No Uncle Sam
Retort does not give a Damn.

Depot practices few ethics or morals
Never receive from employees laurels
No Mamma No Pappa No Uncle Sam
No morals nor ethics don't give a Damn.

Depot free to act and run business as deemed
Just stop with other neither smoke nor steam
No Mamma No Pappa No Uncle Sam
Smoke and steam don't give a Damn.

U2 sang of sad Sunday long ago
Employees know this weekly blow
No Mamma No Pappa No Uncle Sam
U2 band does not give a Damn.

These conditions expect at least
Lot mess work less no codes Judas priest
No Mamma No Pappa No Uncle Sam
Judas priest won't give a Damn.

Paul in Hardware rode bike to work
Showed where to park enjoy perk
No Mamma No Pappa No Uncle Sam
Seventy years old riding a bike Damn.

Employees great management nothing but ingrate
Appreciate customers remains on slate
No Mamma No Pappa No Uncle Sam
Those ingrates really don't give a Damn.

Depot has goal in deceptive obsession
Treat world like employees desired intercession
No Mamma No Pappa No Uncle Sam
Obsessors don't give a Damn.

Christy and Schlage fought bout over keys locks
Frustrated her made it a rout
No Mamma No Pappa No Uncle Sam
Schlage won the bout Damn.

Bard arrived at front customer said hi
Glad to see soon on register to stem tide
No Mamma No Pappa No Uncle Sam
Customers greet Bard Damn.

Dre in Lot tonight not much to do
Filled drink machines buggies returned on cue
No Mamma No Pappa No Uncle Sam
Nothing happening this eve Damn.

Donna appeared on floor after store closed
Customers gone moving pallets unopposed
No Mamma No Pappa No Uncle Sam
Pallets don't buy Damn.

Customer from afar arrived to pick up tile
Weight too much no trailer went wild
No Mamma No Pappa No Uncle Sam
Pallets of tile weigh a ton Damn.

Jesse in middle blue hair like ice
Better hair than skin still not nice
No Mamma No Pappa No Uncle Sam
Hair ice blue sickles Damn.

Amanda tried to solve trailer issue
Unable to rent used tissue
No Mamma No Pappa No Uncle Sam
Amanda did care Damn.

Christy occupying paint brought customer
Said best employee in building for sure
No Mamma No Pappa No Uncle Sam
Flummoxed Christy again Damn.

Chris arrived welcomed fellow weekend warrior
Both hoped might soon see destroyer
No Mamma No Pappa No Uncle Sam
Every Sunday in lumber Damn.

Stopped a would-be thief by giving grief
Rejected check made him wreck no relief
No Mamma No Pappa No Uncle Sam
Asked to pay and fled Damn.

Microburst swallowed parking in moment
Depot sales started moaning atonement
No Mamma No Pappa No Uncle Sam
Anybody knows what to do Damn.

Mille arrived for break talking food
Really helped improve Bard's mood
No Mamma No Pappa No Uncle Sam
Millie and food give a Damn.

Single female arrived asked to check her out
Realized this might not mean intended about
No Mamma No Pappa No Uncle Sam
Watch those double meanings ouch Damn.

Gave us cards for customer gift
Had so few remained short shrift
No Mamma No Pappa No Uncle Sam
No customers no gift needed Damn.

Emily almost always fun to work under
Makes sure store mush never causes blunder
No Mamma No Pappa No Uncle Sam
Emily makes very few blunders Damn.

ASM went on run for bags
Other stores never come to rag
No Mamma No Pappa No Uncle Sam
Just order them Damn.

Noise you hate to hear at close
Saw going full blast cutting rows
No Mamma No Pappa No Uncle Sam
The saw does not give a Damn.

Alone with nothing to do when customer arrives
Scan manually to increase items gain high-fives
No Mamma No Pappa No Uncle Sam
Boredom awful Damn.

Half a league onward rode six hundred
Depot considered major blunder
No Mamma No Pappa No Uncle Sam
Alfred Tennyson does not give a Damn.

Five minutes to close looking for hot wire
Told to ground purchase desire
No Mamma No Pappa No Uncle Sam
No staff no answer closing time Damn.

Marketing to Depot very simple in mind
Sell cheap never come from behind
No Mamma No Pappa No Uncle Sam
Cheap does not give a Damn.

Oh say can you see by eve's first blight
Neither customers nor employees at twilight
No Mamma No Pappa No Uncle Sam
Home alone in PRO Damn.

Long list of customers known by name
Appreciate what say do take aim
No Mamma No Pappa No Uncle Sam
Customers know Bard by name

Depot many cashiers few count change
Hard to believe must see on screen
No Mamma No Pappa No Uncle Sam
Lost if customer rounds up Damn.

Spanish only brochure thrown away
English once spoken in USA
No Mamma No Pappa No Uncle Sam
No Habla English and who gives a Damn.

Stuck in middle with you song words
HC and cashier on busy day bluebirds
No Mamma No Pappa No Uncle Sam
Bluebirds don't give a Damn.

Depot offered 401k offered to match in preferred beat
Using Black Rock climate destroyers how sweet
No Mamma No Pappa No Uncle Sam
Once again vultures flock together Damn.

Black rock in Mecca's holy camp
Aladdin's lamp their stamp
No Mamma No Pappa No Uncle Sam
Rub the lamp Damn.

Three Rocksters are Bidenites
Trying to avoid Kryptonite
No Mamma No Pappa No Uncle Sam
Black Rock well embedded Damn.

Fink developed mortgage back securities
What drove world to brink imperiously
No Mamma No Pappa No Uncle Sam
Just the truth Damn.

Fink authored in 2008 too big to fail
Made sure whales did not travail
No Mamma No Pappa No Uncle Sam
Guess who absorbed Lehman Damn.

Finch a bird that flies through air
Fink derivative for one square
No Mamma No Pappa No Uncle Sam
Germans call wild birds Damn.

Bread and circus provided to mobs in Rome
Depot uses Blackstone 401k from throne
No Mamma No Pappa No Uncle Sam
This circus does not give a Damn.

Blackstone removed coal from much of management
Prefer to have less coal more starvation banishment
No Mamma No Pappa No Uncle Sam
Less coal less energy less people understand Damn.

As I told Washington Fink likes to smirk
Believes all rest nothing but jerks
No Mamma No Pappa No Uncle Sam
Never regulated unlike a bank Damn.

47 million reasons why Black Rock runs 401k
Pretty obvious powerful in stock way
No Mamma No Pappa No Uncle Sam
Number two shareholder get picture Damn.

Larry to Rome began with laurel crosswords
Combine with Fink laurels for wild birds
No Mamma No Pappa No Uncle Sam
SPQR on laurel does not give a Damn.

Hillary and Fink like paper and ink
Channeled thoughts she blinked
No Mamma No Pappa No Uncle Sam
Depot matches for contributions to this Damn.

Blackrock a derivative of ink and stone
Black ink and rock solid their clone
No Mamma No Pappa No Uncle Sam
Black Rock a boulder from this stone Damn.

Hypocrisy a form of greed for sale
Explain actions and beliefs beyond veil
No Mamma No Pappa No Uncle Sam
Hypocrisy bought and sold Damn.

Asked Dear Abbey following questions in home office HR
Told she real star one of the best there are a superstar
No Mamma No Pappa No Uncle Sam
Ask Dear Abbey but don't give a Damn.

Part one of their wheel taking care of people
Cutting salaries 80% more church steeple
No Mamma No Pappa No Uncle Sam
No answer no surprise Damn.

Part two passed through excellent customer service
Cuts in schedule no call-outs in play how less nervous
No Mamma No Pappa No Uncle Sam
Quiet on part two Damn.

Part three building better relationships wheel states
Abbey silent on how this grates much less berates
No Mamma No Pappa No Uncle Sam
Part three does not give a Damn.

Entrepreneurial spirit mentioned in part four
Largely ignored except to silence and gore
No Mamma No Pappa No Uncle Sam
No answer yet Abbey Damn.

Respect for all people or did Part 5 mean sheeple
Abbey more silent than hungry boll weevil
No Mamma No Pappa No Uncle Sam
Not a word Damn.

Part six pick up stix increase shareholder value
Cutting cost reducing service how true Abbey no clue
No Mamma No Pappa No Uncle Sam
Shareholder value means expense right Damn.

Doing right part seven on wheel how does this feel
Use might call it right Abbey bad deal
No Mamma No Pappa No Uncle Sam
Bad for employees no deal Damn.

Giving back part eight or Depot take back
Bring employees to knees Abbey pick up slack
No Mamma No Pappa No Uncle Sam
Give or take back don't give a Damn.

Wheel complete sections joined Abbey wrong
How to feel part of this increasing throng
No Mamma No Pappa No Uncle Sam
Abbey and crickets in play Damn.

One last shot to end interrogatory gabbies
Reaction if full-times reduced by this Abbey
No Mamma No Pappa No Answer
Too close to home right Damn.

Concerns called by Abbey wanted to discuss and touch base
Require writing later deny or misunderstanding erase
No Mamma No Pappa No Uncle Sam
Talk cheap Damn.

Objective questions deserve written answers
Depot would rather play with German panzers
No Mamma No Pappa No Uncle Sam
Panzers don't give a Damn.

New 401k offered to all today a big deal
Took pay away how should we feel
No Mamma No Pappa No Uncle Sam
Pigs in trough again Damn.

Written in good book truth shall set free
Depot denies simply flees
No Mamma No Pappa No Uncle Sam
Truth cut down does not give a Damn.

Eat fruit of their way satisfy with devices
Depot shall never appreciate these sacrifices
No Mamma No Pappa No Uncle Sam
Sacrificed in vain Damn.

Backsliding simple inside corporate temple
Careless ease one day will cease be simple
No Mamma No Pappa No Uncle Sam
This temple does not give a Damn.

Righteousness not number on screen
Probably why at Depot rarely seen
No Mamma No Pappa No Uncle Sam
Numbers right not righteous Damn.

Justice at Depot often obscene screams
Profit at any price so it seems
No Mamma No Pappa No Uncle Sam
Justice might reduce profit Damn.

Lack of discipline no constancy of purpose
These follies turn Depot into sad circus
No Mamma No Pappa No Uncle Sam
Folies Bergère don't give a Damn.

Part-time at Depot like Ox to slaughter
Fettered correction dog muzzled why bother
No Mamma No Pappa No Uncle Sam
Part-times nothing but pets Damn.

Whirlwind comes and does as pleases
Vinegar to teeth smoke to eyes releases
No Mamma No Pappa No Uncle Sam
Whirlwinds don't give a Damn.

Righteous have hope wicked only dope
Depot descending this slippery slope
No Mamma No Pappa No Uncle Sam
Dope does not give a Damn.

Swelling with pride emptiness and shame
Humbled by trial and travail preferred aim
No Mamma No Pappa No Uncle Sam
Swelling not selling Damn.

Merciful kind and generous benefits all
Depot callous willful indifferent fall
No Mamma No Pappa No Uncle Sam
Depot chose their path Damn.

Depot like ring of gold to pig's snout
Never can learn exactly what about
No Mamma No Pappa No Uncle Sam
Ring of gold does not give a Damn.

Confident in wealth riches become wretches
Business moving rapidly toward ditches
No Mamma No Pappa No Uncle Sam
Rich to wretch and don't give a Damn.

Management way always right in their eyes
Just read numbers strive live and lie
No Mamma No Pappa No Uncle Sam
Good on numbers Damn.

Corporate pride and insolence build contention
Explains absence of part-time retention
No Mamma No Pappa No Uncle Sam
Pride does not give a Damn.

Unjust gain never remains dwindles away
Greater powers in play have much to say
No Mamma No Pappa No Uncle Sam
Unjust gain greed Damn.

Corporate pride disgusting hateful really offensive
Employees need to raise some tall fencing
No Mamma No Pappa No Uncle Sam
Raise high fence beams carpenters Damn.

Depot makes great revenues often injustice
Not afraid to take moment and bust us
No Mamma No Pappa No Uncle Sam
Injustice and profit don't give a Damn.

Depot huge dam full of water crack and trickle
Crack becomes fissure causes real pickle
No Mamma No Pappa No Uncle Sam
Happened in Inner Mongolia too Damn.

Bean Counter little time for understanding
Promoting personal opinions and branding
No Mamma No Pappa No Uncle Sam
Mouth his ruin Damn.

Corporate no vision must soon perish
Only blind rule over this parish
No Mamma No Pappa No Uncle Sam
No vision and who gives a Damn.

Mistreat employees because you can
Never listen again do you understand
No Mamma No Pappa No Uncle Sam
Deaf forever understand Damn.

Bartolome de Las Casas opened store for knaves
Employees at Depot understand betrayed
No Mamma No Pappa No Uncle Sam
This house not a home Damn.

Abbey Hall came off wall emailed Bard not in free fall
Answered to penny involving numbers plenty appall
No Mamma No Pappa No Uncle Sam
Very precise on numbers only Damn.

Said scheduled to meet customer needs
Flex part-times bring to their knees
No Mamma No Pappa No Uncle Sam
Part-times brought to knees don't give a Damn.

Hours ebb instead of flow part-times dread
Full-times never get into this bed
No Mamma No Pappa No Uncle Sam
Slow does not give a Damn.

Hall said flexibility of part-times appreciated
Have no choice except leave or be terminated
No Mamma No Pappa No Uncle Sam
These appreciated don't give a Damn.

Two bullet points written by legal a third for numbers
Ignored all rest managed deep slumber
No Mamma No Pappa No Uncle Sam
Don't answer Damn.

Ignored 80% cut impact on customers or why come in at all
Afraid if answered might walk plank or be keelhauled
No Mamma No Pappa No Uncle Sam
Job security right Damn.

Taking care of some people that is for sure
Rest unimportant not quite human assured
No Mamma No Pappa No Uncle Sam
Orwell and Animal Farm at Depot Damn.

Customer service ignored by numbers reduction
Failed to explain how to make this function
No Mamma No Pappa No Uncle Sam
Customer service laugh Damn.

Shareholder value might make right giving back
Expense not value might not right taking from others smack
No Mamma No Pappa No Uncle Sam
No values practiced here Depot Damn.

Leadership by example why full-times not cut
Do as we say not as we get answer in rut
No Mamma No Pappa No Uncle Sam
This rut does not give a Damn.

How would feel be one of these eels
Probably Abbey then kicks up heels
No Mamma No Pappa No Uncle Sam
So why are we to work together Damn.

Bean Counter likes to offer this is our store
Answer now not for part-times anymore
No Mamma No Pappa No Uncle Sam
Full-times only in this store right Damn.

Abbey and management have writing
Part-times know for sure not inviting
No Mamma No Pappa No Uncle Sam
It did not have to be this way Damn.

Mark of any organization treatment of least
Depot always bullies uses mark of beast
No Mamma No Pappa No Uncle Sam
This beast does not give a Damn.

Jesse blue hair complete wearing granny's red dress
Combed back looked like Aunt Bess
No Mamma No Pappa No Uncle Sam
Skin still porcelain Damn.

Sign of times in tattoos and body carvings
Women replaced men with these markings
No Mamma No Pappa No Uncle Sam
Women tattooed more than men Damn.

April hot topics growing cold turning to mold
Seems all forgotten possibly rotten now old
No Mamma No Pappa No Uncle Sam
More empty letters who gives a Damn.

New letter appeared stating cashiers now accountable
Accountability anywhere in store jest insurmountable
No Mamma No Pappa No Uncle Sam
Accountability at Depot a laugh Damn.

Cashiers cannot count change much less explain
How then tantamount to count account no brain
No Mamma No Pappa No Uncle Sam
No brain does not give a Damn.

New health rules put out by Depot fools
Not a clue act like dumb mules
No Mamma No Pappa No Uncle Sam
Dumb mules don't give a Damn.

Judgement and discernment at Depot assure internment
Thinking and planning a danger to policy dad burn it
No Mamma No Pappa No Uncle Sam
These dads burned Damn.

Inclusive when convenient when not pretend
How justify schedule and pay intend
No Mamma No Pappa No Uncle Sam
Inclusive yes if win for Depot only Damn.

Schedule four eight or twelve not to appreciate
Depot likely close gate completely obfuscate
No Mamma No Pappa No Uncle Sam
Just be flexible right Damn.

Brandon reappeared in store after three months
Struggling to defeat medical behemoth
No Mamma No Pappa No Uncle Sam
Great to have Brandon back Damn.

Money offered HR squared for Sav affliction
Replied not allowed in Depot's jurisdiction
No Mamma No Pappa No Uncle Sam
This jurisdiction does not give a Damn.

No aid regardless of need said Melanie
Samaritan verse Pharisee felony
No Mamma No Pappa No Uncle Sam
Leave her in street to die Damn.

Have a nice day Melanie did say took leave
Responded don't patronize nor cause to heave
No Mamma No Pappa No Uncle Sam
Just step over employee in need Damn.

Hitching star to Bean Counter wagon
Missing cliff and coming chasm
No Mamma No Pappa No Uncle Sam
Bye bye Melanie Damn.

Melanie repeated leaving mess unheeded
Have day deserved life earned repeated
No Mamma No Pappa No Uncle Sam
And enjoy White Throne Melanie Damn.

Kimme in front wearing mask for Lisa support
Promised to get funds to Sav make a report
No Mamma No Pappa No Uncle Sam
Kimme has big heart Damn.

Throw in with Depot be their brother
Fill house with goods taken from another
No Mamma No Pappa No Uncle Sam
Sheol and Depot similar Damn.

Greedy of gain run to evil unrestrained
Depot ambushed none will remain
No Mamma No Pappa No Uncle Sam
Unrestrained does not give a Damn.

Scoffers scoff hate knowledge
How graduate from Depot college
No Mamma No Pappa No Uncle Sam
Scoffers don't give a Damn.

Backsliding ease of simple employ
Careless ease shall destroy corduroy
No Mamma No Pappa No Uncle Sam
Depot ease and backsliding Damn.

Righteousness justice fair dealing right path
Perverse to Depot brings great wrath
No Mamma No Pappa No Uncle Sam
Perverse does not give a Damn.

Crooked wayward devious worse than mischievous
Wicked cut off from business treasure Vesuvius
No Mamma No Pappa No Uncle Sam
Just ask Pompeii Damn.

Mercy forgiveness at Depot forsaken forgotten
Hypocrisy greed falsity rule rotten
No Mamma No Pappa No Uncle Sam
Hypocrites don't give a Damn.

Depot inequities ensnared wickedness in cords
Perish for lack of instruction folly astray lords
No Mamma No Pappa No Uncle Sam
Cords do strangle Damn.

Reprove fool hated at Depot bruised
Do for wise greatly approved
No Mamma No Pappa No Uncle Sam
Simple scorner Depot Damn.

Management greedy for unjust gain
Makes it likely one day shamed
No Mamma No Pappa No Uncle Sam
This management does not give a Damn.

Bad things in Garden came as three
Now stop leave it be new plea
No Mamma No Pappa No Uncle Sam
Stop at three Damn.

Schedule received hours returned to twelve
Clap like a seal say swell
No Mamma No Pappa No Uncle Sam
Eight or twelve who gives a Damn.

Hours increased after exchange with home office HR
Pulled file EEOC tag present raised bar
No Mamma No Pappa No Uncle Sam
Employee file tagged Damn.

Sav living in bondage probably true
Now has medical bills overdue
No Mamma No Pappa No Uncle Sam
No compassion no help Damn.

Keats saw world in grain of sand
Depot sells and pounds no strand
No Mamma No Pappa No Uncle Sam
Sand in eyes Damn.

Never believe do as Depot may please
Not enough to create breeze more wheeze
No Mamma No Pappa No Uncle Sam
As you please Damn.

Tragic to see so many ground into dust
Won't escape endless rush
No Mamma No Pappa No Uncle Sam
The crushed don't give a Damn.

Lords and ladies leap in Byzantium
Have neither sword nor Chrysanthemum
No Mamma No Pappa No Uncle Sam
Just more markets right Damn.

Maud Gonne for Yeats neigh went away
Depot with part-times likes to play
No Mamma No Pappa No Uncle Sam
Maud does not give a Damn.

Cold as ice full of vice not quite nice
Depot dispenses useless advice
No Mamma No Pappa No Uncle Sam
Vice does not give a Damn.

Chair kicked over noose around neck
Required intervention this action correct
No Mamma No Pappa No Uncle Sam
Leave management swinging never hanging Damn.

Promised part-time HC not anointed nor published
Maybe decided to throw in rubbish
No Mamma No Pappa No Uncle Sam
No part-time HC Damn.

Friday nights for high school football gateway
At Depot just vacant aisles and empty bays
No Mamma No Pappa No Uncle Sam
Friday night lights don't give a Damn.

Waiting on EEOC to march not yet in line
Wonder if might find way to spend dime
No Mamma No Pappa No Uncle Sam
EEOC not on time Damn.

Store a tinderbox of kindling and wrap
Management completely unaware of trap
No Mamma No Pappa No Uncle Sam
Traps don't give a Damn.

Open hearth steelmaking not process used
Bone marrow dried Depot similarly abused
No Mamma No Pappa No Uncle Sam
Even marrow dried Damn.

Returning after forced four-day sojourn
Bard learns how to intern upon return
No Mamma No Pappa No Uncle Sam
What has been missed Damn.

Steve in paint said schedule brown out not last long
Bard responded neither will he when subjected to wrong
No Mamma No Pappa No Uncle Sam
Won't last long Damn.

Depot abused three quarter of million
Really bad marketing almost crocodilian
No Mamma No Pappa No Uncle Sam
Part-times abused make bad customers Damn.

Uncola successful marketing ploy
Unservice latest from Depot deployed
No Mamma No Pappa No Uncle Sam
The New House of Unservice Damn.

Employees empty made of straw hollowed
Consumed of spirit soul in woe swallowed
No Mamma No Pappa No Uncle Sam
And eyes that never blink don't give a Damn.

Small talk and greetings balm for pain
Never confused to mean any sort of gain
No Mamma No Pappa No Uncle Sam
No past less future only present Damn.

A schedule a schedule until not
Sometimes Depot prefers to have it rot
No Mamma No Pappa No Uncle Sam
Who needs a schedule Damn.

Mandy covered in tattoos heavy metals flowing through
Took second shot went to pot now at home sick unglued
No Mamma No Pappa No Uncle Sam
Heavy metals and vaccine mixed Damn.

Wasco boiling in light heat beaten Garden
Come in before collapse beg your pardon
No Mamma No Pappa No Uncle Sam
Chris struggling with heat Damn.

Erica on phone in flooring seat
Looked like she had customer beat
No Mamma No Pappa No Uncle Sam
Erica taking care of business Damn.

Joyce holding court in locker room
Not interested in lowering boom
No Mamma No Pappa No Uncle Sam
Joyce cutting up great Damn.

Customers continue to greet Bard come to tent
Some act as if heaven sent want to repent
No Mamma No Pappa No Uncle Sam
Just acknowledge them as human Damn.

Nick victim always done to never for
Understand then why glum finds life chore
No Mamma No Pappa No Uncle Sam
Nick a victim Damn.

Maxed out revenue share for all employees receive
Of course remember cut hours like thieves
No Mamma No Pappa No Uncle Sam
Spend it at Starbucks Damn.

Mandy overcoming second shot
Cut hair resumed spot
No Mamma No Pappa No Uncle Sam
Inoculations don't give a Damn.

Management spends day on empty schemes
Commotion and confusion normally themes
No Mamma No Pappa No Uncle Sam
These themes don't give a Damn.

Olive back from opera city
Said fling bang bang chitty
No Mamma No Pappa No Uncle Sam
Chitty chitty bang bang does not give a Damn.

Negotiated plan revision with Olive as HC
Stay in Garden to close then break free
No Mamma No Pappa No Uncle Sam
Out the door very smooth Damn.

Ex-military in store to try and steal
What is up with this stupid spiel
No Mamma No Pappa No Uncle Sam
Military no better than that Damn.

You would think a phrase often spoken
You would and think never connect broken
No Mamma No Pappa No Uncle Sam
Not at Depot for real Damn.

Garden party very quiet tonight
Nobody around to cause fright
No Mamma No Pappa No Uncle Sam
Quiet in Garden again Damn.

Say to management on parade instructed
Serve employees never be obstructed
No Mamma No Pappa No Uncle Sam
Employees not obstructed might give a Damn.

Tina in Service discussed Lisa chemo trek
Sick and weak fewer hours a wreck
No Mamma No Pappa No Uncle Sam
Lisa needs intervention Damn.

How increased trouble and woe
When management truth does not bestow
No Mamma No Pappa No Uncle Sam
Trust no one Damn.

Depot turns honor into shame
Vanity and lies sought to blame
No Mamma No Pappa No Uncle Sam
Honor at Depot for sale on aisle 4 Damn.

Joy and rejoice in job each day
If only understood this ballet
No Mamma No Pappa No Uncle Sam
This ballet does not give a Damn.

Donna with glowing orange tennis shoes
Quite sight as walks through
No Mamma No Pappa No Uncle Sam
Glow in dark orange Damn.

Jesse asked Bard how left Middle
Told her to find solution to riddle
No Mamma No Pappa No Uncle Sam
Middle open who gives a Damn.

April told Bard never cover SCO and Middle
Later did both and played the fiddle
No Mamma No Pappa No Uncle Sam
Fiddle away and don't give a Damn.

Bard in Middle alone on Saturday only register doing cash
Two replaced like new puppeteers mad dash
No Mamma No Pappa No Uncle Sam
When Bard one when not use two Damn.

Explained new training system in detail
Believe Depot off rails beyond pale
No Mamma No Pappa No Uncle Sam
Schedule or forget management Damn.

No one in Garden to provide service
May fates allow to preserve us
No Mamma No Pappa No Uncle Sam
Just program and send to Customer Service Damn.

Jimmy limping in pain helped load washer
About to go to doctor knows it disaster
No Mamma No Pappa No Uncle Sam
On one leg loading a washer Damn.

Dre came by asked if had his phone
Needs company device forgot groan
No Mamma No Pappa No Uncle Sam
Might be nice to wear phone Damn.

Customers asked about heat concerned with doubt
Explained most expendable in this redoubt
No Mamma No Pappa No Uncle Sam
Bard most expendable Damn.

Temperature 102 left cashier alone to melt
Bard insisted replace her life belt
No Mamma No Pappa No Uncle Sam
No rotation and leave them out there Damn.

Wasco with heat prostration when passing Garden aeration
Asked how hotter for him than cashier on station
No Mamma No Pappa No Uncle Sam
Only matter if they affected right Damn.

Christy pale as ghost in paint
Indicated dinner with boyfriend restraint
No Mamma No Pappa No Uncle Sam
Christy looking like Casper Damn.

Referred to significant other as fiancée
After three years oh brother fantasy
No Mamma No Pappa No Uncle Sam
Fiancée for life Damn.

Little Christy in Garden at end extend
Turned on wind tunnel sat on bucket begin
No Mamma No Pappa No Uncle Sam
A real sight in the heat Damn.

Roland nixed any call ins as policy
None answered Lot roundup audibly
No Mamma No Pappa No Uncle Sam
Save those nickels and don't give a Damn.

Shannon defiant not under Christy
Job functions risky prefers reach for whiskey
No Mamma No Pappa No Uncle Sam
On the clock Damn.

Customer paid cash from huge stash
Flashing roll more than rash
No Mamma No Pappa No Uncle Sam
Not real smart Damn.

No water bottles in refrigerator
Made it feel more like an incinerator
No Mamma No Pappa No Uncle Sam
No water and who gives a Damn.

Pray for clouds to stop sun heat on metal roof
Sky simply rained only reproof
No Mamma No Pappa No Uncle Sam
Sun beating down Damn.

RVP to appear in store this Tuesday first time ever
Megan Area Manager instructing supervisors forever
No Mamma No Pappa No Uncle Sam
Why would RVP come to forgotten store Damn.

Megan and Bean Counter tied at hip
Helped bring lumber cart to slip
No Mamma No Pappa No Uncle Sam
Something big this way coming Damn.

Said hello to Bean Counter in front of Megan
Responded with hello Mr. very respectful vegan
No Mamma No Pappa No Uncle Sam
They call me Mister Tibbs wow Damn.

Noah in Lot a bit damaged needs more training
April helping to be responsible for maintaining
No Mamma No Pappa No Uncle Sam
He can do this and will Damn.

OU and Longhorns joining SEC very strange
Could this be part of Depot shake-up or change
No Mamma No Pappa No Uncle Sam
0884 may never be the same Damn.

Bean Counter on floor first time in nearly a month
Caused whole lot of employees to provide lunch
No Mamma No Pappa No Uncle Sam
On the floor again Damn.

Asked April why Megan in store on Sunday
Coach FSE what to say RVP comes this way
No Mamma No Pappa No Uncle Sam
Wonders never cease Damn.

Management acting like cats scalded
Employees wondering what appall did
No Mamma No Pappa No Uncle Sam
Scalded cats pitiful Damn.

Bard not scheduled during RVP Preacher visit
April smiled said thanks for this tidbit
No Mamma No Pappa No Uncle Sam
April very funny Damn.

Little Christy eaten up with stress over car distress
Unable to make Door Dash delivery express
No Mamma No Pappa No Uncle Sam
Car broke in distress Damn.

Depot customers simply cannot be beat
Expectation of service zero appreciate any neat
No Mamma No Pappa No Uncle Sam
Great customers Damn.

Why RVP coming to end of line in Decatur
Never before in history witnessed curator
No Mamma No Pappa No Uncle Sam
RVP may give a Damn.

Catherine grew very red at customer service
Pulled hair back to cool meet customer circus
No Mamma No Pappa No Uncle Sam
A ring mistress needs a whip Damn.

Raining like cats running from dogs
Crossed parking lot filled like bog
No Mamma No Pappa No Uncle Sam
Water rising Damn.

Sullins asked if wanted to wade through deluge
Not a turkey will keep head down reach refuge
No Mamma No Pappa No Uncle Sam
Bring umbrella and galoshes next time Damn.

Chance and Amanda working on pallet cream puff
Wrapped plastic looked like icicles tough
No Mamma No Pappa No Uncle Sam
Used a lot of plastic but wow Damn.

Josh with Chris in tow came by PRO for energy
Gathering of weekend stevedores great synergy
No Mamma No Pappa No Uncle Sam
First energy drink on me Damn.

Dre rechristened cool pup as title
No matter what maintains cool vital
No Mamma No Pappa No Uncle Sam
Cool pup cool Damn.

Bags about to end not where to begin
None arrive soon be at another end
No Mamma No Pappa No Uncle Sam
Ask why no bags again Damn.

Closed cash option at SCO oh no dear
Now all cash goes through middle cashier
No Mamma No Pappa No Uncle Sam
Middle cashier just dumped on Damn.

When Bard middle cashier all others absent
Handles all cash just like savant
No Mamma No Pappa No Uncle Sam
Everyone else works with two not alone Damn.

Customer with dog in buggy treated Bard ugly
Sprayed spit while pulling items from cart smugly
No Mamma No Pappa No Uncle Sam
Spit on by a dog Damn.

Paul guinea pig for big pharma
Stated all sick unvaccinated bad karma
No Mamma No Pappa No Uncle Sam
And Israelis say otherwise Paul Damn.

Employee at Tennessee store lived in trailer
Three ducks inside family in lot retailer
No Mamma No Pappa No Uncle Sam
Depot employee living with ducks Damn.

April arrived to close PRO let Bard go
Amazed at customer load made flow
No Mamma No Pappa No Uncle Sam
How did he do that Damn.

Orange cart with customer accessories
Rain came made intercessory
No Mamma No Pappa No Uncle Sam
Brown paper drowned in rain Damn.

Covid red virus and barcodes much in common
Both disrupt neither fixed by cobalamin
No Mamma No Pappa No Uncle Sam
Cobalamin will not work Damn.

Barcodes AWOL for whatever reason all evening
Wish management could stop unreasoning
No Mamma No Pappa No Uncle Sam
No barcodes and don't give a Damn.

Very thirsty with large purchase
Give them free water watch surface
No Mamma No Pappa No Uncle Sam
Free bottled water gold to them Damn.

Made it through another weekend crusher
How men must have felt inside Thresher
No Mamma No Pappa No Uncle Sam
Legs feel like crushed bulkheads Damn.

PRO phone closed on weekends
Why then rings off hook no stipends
No Mamma No Pappa No Uncle Sam
Let her ring and don't give a Damn.

Jimmy strolled by with knee not limping
Still hurt but no longer crimping
No Mamma No Pappa No Uncle Sam
Just walk on it Damn.

Brianna more than done in southern sun
Fleeing back to Michigan have more fun
No Mamma No Pappa No Uncle Sam
Brianna will be missed Damn.

Why call almond milk almond milk
Nut juice just more management silt
No Mamma No Pappa No Uncle Sam
Stew in your own nut juice at Depot Damn.

Proverbial Jimme takes what you Gimme
At Depot often like climbing chimney
No Mamma No Pappa No Uncle Sam
Gimme does not give a Damn.

April working with Noah in lot to do more
Had to show how to bring carts through door
No Mamma No Pappa No Uncle Sam
Good luck with this April Damn.

Ethan departing for JSU land in week
Looking forward to not working this beat
No Mamma No Pappa No Uncle Sam
Going to school good for him Damn.

Drinks and cases now normally filled
Lot guys have created amazing thrill
No Mamma No Pappa No Uncle Sam
Drinks in cases who knew wow Damn.

Ryan asleep head down in locker room
Exhausted by work in this Khartoum
No Mamma No Pappa No Uncle Sam
Chinese Gordon does not give a Damn.

Eat not of spread Depot provides on occasion
Begrudge cost not happy with equation
No Mamma No Pappa No Uncle Sam
Begrudged even morsels Damn.

Depot orange wine sparkling in glass
Bites like adder in demitasse
No Mamma No Pappa No Uncle Sam
Don't drink the wine Damn

Management may plot oppression and trouble
Envy and strife then treble incredible
No Mamma No Pappa No Uncle Sam
Trouble is trouble right Damn.

Employees protest did jobs
How come store overrun by mobs
No Mamma No Pappa No Uncle Sam
Just do your job whatever Damn.

Depot at times opposed to natural law
Calamity shall come then freefall
No Mamma No Pappa No Uncle Sam
Obey natural law Damn.

Expediency glue binds Depot blind
Whatever makes profit matters most in mind
No Mamma No Pappa No Uncle Sam
These blinds don't give a Damn.

Like snow in summer or rain at harvest
Honor not fitting for Depot con artist
No Mamma No Pappa No Uncle Sam
Honor and Depot Damn.

As a door turns on hinges
So cashier statue cringes
No Mamma No Pappa No Uncle Sam
Cashier frozen does not give a Damn.

Restrain Depot like stopping wind
Iron sharpens iron not hot air skinned
No Mamma No Pappa No Uncle Sam
Hot air skinned Damn.

Weary with groaning employees look to stoning
Eyes grow dim never see atoning
No Mamma No Pappa No Uncle Sam
How can weary give a Damn.

Bean Counter wise to do following
Order lunch for all surprise hollowing
No Mamma No Pappa No Uncle Sam
Make a real impression Bean Counter Damn.

Wicked iniquity lies too often victims cry
Pretty soon into pit will fly
No Mamma No Pappa No Uncle Sam
Moral turpitude does not give a Damn.

Abuse of part-times rests on their head
At Depot a moment of approaching dread
No Mamma No Pappa No Uncle Sam
Dread does not give a Damn.

RVP and pie in sky just spit in eye
No one knows what may fly
No Mamma No Pappa No Uncle Sam
Fly away maybe Damn.

Woman unmasked ignored leased ship
Claims 70% made in American tidbit
No Mamma No Pappa No Uncle Sam
Believe and buy stock Damn.

If these goods made in America
Why lease ship for Red China esoterica
No Mamma No Pappa No Uncle Sam
Esoterica does not give a Damn.

RVP came saw and rend still standing employees spent
RSVP not received employees grieved store really bent
No Mamma No Pappa No Uncle Sam
Put up the orange carpet Damn.

Young'uns leaving store by drove
Time for school treasure trove
No Mamma No Pappa No Uncle Sam
Off to school goodbye Damn.

Jesse eyes ablaze explained coming school apocalypse
No longer available for hours days or even grip
No Mamma No Pappa No Uncle Sam
Off to school again Damn.

Reviewed all work performed under roof
RVP Preacher toil burden of proof
No Mamma No Pappa No Uncle Sam
Profit and toil don't give a Damn.

Stephanie not reappearing after rotator surgery
Some believe may have performed perjury
No Mamma No Pappa No Uncle Sam
Four plus months what is happening Damn.

Reduced hires part-times start to droop
Others simply decide to flee coop
No Mamma No Pappa No Uncle Sam
And who cares Damn.

Depot going code blue thwart thief review
Bluetooth sings tune of tool on cue
No Mamma No Pappa No Uncle Sam
Better than spider wraps for sure Damn.

Lisa long road to trudge alone chemo three days a week
Tougher than nails still made hollowed cheeks
No Mamma No Pappa No Uncle Sam
Pray for Lisa and give a Damn.

Store that has been will be again
Has been done so too shall not abstain
No Mamma No Pappa No Uncle Sam
An endless silo does not give a Damn.

Rivers run into sea yet unfilled
So too consequences drilled
No Mamma No Pappa No Uncle Sam
Unfilled is unfilled Damn.

Remembrance of things past unlikely nothing new
What done not remembered now Lulu
No Mamma No Pappa No Uncle Sam
Lulu not remembered Damn.

Preacher RVP over region store 0884 fine
Sold Wisdom for gelt expanded waistline
No Mamma No Pappa No Uncle Sam
Gelt for Wisdom not good Damn.

Striving in tent nothing but vanity
Straightening crooked pure insanity
No Mamma No Pappa No Uncle Sam
Vanity and insanity don't give a Damn.

Power of home office enters RVP counsel late
Preacher wisdom great from respective slates
No Mamma No Pappa No Uncle Sam
Hubris not smart Damn.

Folly and madness found at every turn
Often used to crank store churn
No Mamma No Pappa No Uncle Sam
Just plain crazy Damn.

Regaled with mirth provided pleasure
Ledger reviewed very great treasure
No Mamma No Pappa No Uncle Sam
Pleasure in ledger does not give a Damn.

What did visit from Preacher accomplish
Miles Smith did not find Pocahontas
No Mamma No Pappa No Uncle Sam
Pocahontas does not give a Damn.

Research mind cheer body with wine
Preacher promises will be fine
No Mamma No Pappa No Uncle Sam
Make it red Damn.

Preacher great works see spreadsheets
Never will end in anything but dead heat
No Mamma No Pappa No Uncle Sam
Dead heat and who gives a Damn.

Gathered together half trillion of gold and silver
Depot not parted with even a sliver
No Mamma No Pappa No Uncle Sam
Sliver does not give a Damn.

So much wealth amassed what waste
Long since forgotten how to remain chaste
No Mamma No Pappa No Uncle Sam
Chaste does not give a Damn.

Who will remember Preacher's visit done
At Depot fun preferred over bofors gun
No Mamma No Pappa No Uncle Sam
Bofors gun does not give a Damn.

Gather and heap up remain stuck up
Trails and tribulations will soon erupt
No Mamma No Pappa No Uncle Sam
Stuck up and don't give a Damn.

I Am that I Am no rhyme nor reason only confusion
No beginning nor end much less conclusion
No Mamma No Pappa No Uncle Sam
I Am that I Am no more to say today Damn.

0884's pin pulled from Orange Life's chart
No hope for rest to sea as Lemmings march
No Mamma No Pappa No Uncle Sam
This Lemming won't give a Damn.

Part-times treated rougher and tougher
Management makes no attempt to buffer
No Mamma No Pappa No Uncle Sam
Buffer suffer who gives a Damn.

Depot nourished matured made great exalted
One day soon ripe rotten defaulted
No Mamma No Pappa No Uncle Sam
Defaults don't give a Damn.

Shareholders know shares and paper
Depot not know what in this shaker
No Mamma No Pappa No Uncle Sam
Depot and shareholders don't give a Damn.

Full of contempt rent and unkempt
Many will see this rude attempt
No Mamma No Pappa No Uncle Sam
Unkempt does not give a Damn.

Employees punished revolt to follow
Soon company will find hard to swallow
No Mamma No Pappa No Uncle Sam
Choking for sure Damn.

No soundness found in this corporate body
Sick faint nauseated not appreciated bawdy
No Mamma No Pappa No Uncle Sam
Bawdy and body don't give a Damn.

People perish for lack of knowledge
Depot excels at attending this college
No Mamma No Pappa No Uncle Sam
This college won't give a Damn.

What purpose served by profit
Better finished if but chocolate
No Mamma No Pappa No Uncle Sam
Chocolate desirable right Damn.

Emptiness vanity pride offered in futility
Who can possibly serve much less enjoy imbecility
No Mamma No Pappa No Uncle Sam
Imbeciles do not give a Damn.

Do right not what you can to weak
Then watch sales jump profit peak
No Mamma No Pappa No Uncle Sam
Serve weak and flourish Damn.

Wine mixed with water silver turned to dross
Home Depot unable to hide gathering loss
No Mamma No Pappa No Uncle Sam
Dross worthless Damn.

Princes like thieves seek compensation and award
Take what you can put nothing in reframe on boards
No Mamma No Pappa No Uncle Sam
Put nothing in and don't give a Damn.

Wrong things done right a deadly spell
Assures a slow descent into a very hot Hell
No Mamma No Pappa No Uncle Sam
No water in Hell Damn.

Where has vision and certainty gone
Sold for profit to Mahanaim before dawn
No Mamma No Pappa No Uncle Sam
Mahanaim does not give a Damn.

Balsam myrrh and spice very nice
Depot usually prefers to roll dice
No Mamma No Pappa No Uncle Sam
Dice do not give a Damn.

A lily among thorns this store in season
Compare to others located in region
No Mamma No Pappa No Uncle Sam
Thorns do not give a Damn.

Evil may come upon Earth
Depot hopes does not take berth
No Mamma No Pappa No Uncle Sam
Just embrace evil Depot Damn.

Depot sells but never sows seed
One day will have no crop to feed
No Mamma No Pappa No Uncle Sam
No seed no crop no feed Damn.

Lust ends sorrow and vexation
For Depot appointed destination
No Mamma No Pappa No Uncle Sam
This destination a one-way ticket Damn.

Gentle spirit turns away wrath and indignation
Evil from ruler practiced Depot nation
No Mamma No Pappa No Uncle Sam
Indignation does not give a Damn.

Training ends in wicked madness
No end to this everlasting sadness
No Mamma No Pappa No Uncle Sam
Sadness does not give a Damn.

Management prognosis causes neurosis
Employees respond cryptobiosis
No Mamma No Pappa No Uncle Sam
Cryptobiosis completed may give a Damn.

Valid and consensus mandated regardless of truth
Scientific validity and fact established forsooth
No Mamma No Pappa No Truth
They decide truth right Damn.

Appeal to authority consensus management abound
Right and wrong no longer matter under this Crown
No Mamma No Pappa No Uncle Sam
This Crown does not give a Damn.

Flip-flop and politically positioned
A great way to run this inquisition
No Mamma No Pappa No Uncle Sam
Flip-flop and don't give a Damn.

Policy says no more than two hours in Garden
Why then four required no pardon
No Mamma No Pappa No Uncle Sam
102 and no one gives a Damn.

Groupthink rules over individual self-determination
Price of admission to Ya-Ya Depot Nation
No Mamma No Pappa No Uncle Sam
Ya-Ya Sisterhood does not give a Damn.

Consensus thought removes thought no appellate
Employee no longer fit to yell it
No Mamma No Pappa No Uncle Sam
No appellate and don't give a Damn.

Hobgoblin of minds equals oppression
Employees that think seek secession
No Mamma No Pappa No Uncle Sam
Oppression secession Damn.

Employees beginning to band together
Depot would be wise to loosen tether
No Mamma No Pappa No Uncle Sam
Tethered employees don't give a Damn.

Creating silence calling it peace
Does not help Depot management in least
No Mamma No Pappa No Uncle Sam
This peace shall end Damn.

Treat others as Depot chooses proven view
When done in reverse deemed askew
No Mamma No Pappa No Uncle Sam
Treatment should run both ways right Damn.

Whopper Sand buried deep in Gulf
Depot will never get to shelf
No Mamma No Pappa No Uncle Sam
More sand than can be bagged Damn.

Barcodes on discounts not always work
Puts cashier in position of being jerk
No Mamma No Pappa No Uncle Sam
Have to get creative with this right Damn.

Dinosaurs like Depot once ruled Earth
Now nothing more than bones in turf
No Mamma No Pappa No Uncle Sam
Depot would be wise to learn Damn.

Employees endless cerebellum
Why then Depot yelling at them
No Mamma No Pappa No Uncle Sam
Don't use their minds right Damn.

Employee diamonds often unseen much less cut
Depot blind to opportunity presented by strut
No Mamma No Pappa No Uncle Sam
Diamonds abound and don't give a Damn.

Natural law righteous requires a Giver
Depot would do well to quiver
No Mamma No Pappa No Uncle Sam
Natural law does give a Damn.

Perverseness error confusion required inclusion
Three legs of Depot stool foments delusion
No Mamma No Pappa No Uncle Sam
Delusion does not give a Damn.

Natural law and Depot completely out of sync
Employees may throw in kitchen sink
No Mamma No Pappa No Uncle Sam
Kitchen sinks don't give a Damn.

EEOC on brink for complaint to file
Be patient still may take awhile
No Mamma No Pappa No Uncle Sam
On brink does not give a damn

Bluetooth and chip make tools wink
Stolen from owner they can close in blink
No Mamma No Pappa No Uncle Sam
This blink winks not Damn.

Old and grey warriors from Vietnam in line
Don't know how to qualify for discount fine
No Mamma No Pappa No Uncle Sam
No discount for real war vets Damn.

Want to serve vet make better
Create in store means to register
No Mamma No Pappa No Uncle Sam
These vets do deserve a Damn.

Barcode malaprops not getting better
Perhaps entire process under bad weather
No Mamma No Pappa No Uncle Sam
Malaprops do not give a Damn.

Ronald McDonald out of favor no work
Now employed as CEO's soda jerk
No Mamma No Pappa No Uncle Sam
Giving old Ronald real bad name Damn.

Discounts and reductions flood card emails
Why needed with sales increasing details
No Mamma No Pappa No Uncle Sam
Makes mess at register Damn.

HR squared back on job easy to see
Scheduling continues to sink endlessly
No Mamma No Pappa No Uncle Sam
Welcome back Melanie Damn.

Review and evaluation needed for all
Easier to find walk-in hall
No Mamma No Pappa No Uncle Sam
No review less evaluation who gives a Damn.

Bo Peep traveled to Miami on vacation
Returned with Red virus according to PCR notation
No Mamma No Pappa No Uncle Sam
PCR tests don't work CDC Damn.

No HC until close walked to paint for Christy
Asked to open drawer for cash and quarters nifty
No Mamma No Pappa No Uncle Sam
Discovered she did not have key Damn.

Bard tried to be part HC for eves like this
Instead management pushed over abyss
No Mamma No Pappa No Uncle Sam
Serves them right Damn.

Joyce arrived at close to empty registers
Appeared she preferred Rochester
No Mamma No Pappa No Uncle Sam
Joyce came through Damn.

Christy tried to help with money and belt
Really appreciated all efforts heartfelt
No Mamma No Pappa No Uncle Sam
Took drawer key away from her Damn.

Ethan overwhelmed by triple digit heat and humidity
Wasco walking death not feeling serendipity
No Mamma No Pappa No Uncle Sam
Hundred degrees get over it Damn.

Customer with tie wanted 104 boards at eight thirty
Joyce interceded made Rocky get dirty
No Mamma No Pappa No Uncle Sam
Watch out if Joyce looks for you Damn.

Paid a large compliment to Bard sparred
Wondered if once been cashier at her bar
No Mamma No Pappa No Uncle Sam
One of Joyce's boys Damn.

Caesar alone in Lumber no Paul
Kept customers moving without pause
No Mamma No Pappa No Uncle Sam
Caesar a one-man band Damn.

Stephanie visiting Roland astride tow motor
Looking for help maybe a promoter
No Mamma No Pappa No Uncle Sam
Making progress but not yet back Damn.

Phyllis brought sticky note to Bard assigning PRO
Only cashier in middle so how to know
No Mamma No Pappa No Uncle Sam
Sticky note management who gives a Damn.

Called Millie in Garden when lightning streaked
Close it now or risk becoming a freak
No Mamma No Pappa No Uncle Sam
Millie glad Bard cared Damn.

Two kids with parents in tow given candy to go
Mom took them to candy bought only a sucker whoa
No Mamma No Pappa No Uncle Sam
Kids don't want candy bars Damn.

Doughnuts from Daylight left in PRO tonight
Gave to Ethan to help bring him delight
No Mamma No Pappa No Uncle Sam
Never too hot to eat a doughnut Damn.

Gave customer waiting water for contemplating
Discovered made him more scintillating
No Mamma No Pappa No Uncle Sam
Small gestures count Damn.

Mary alone no one in Middle marooned at SCO
Every customer served great thrill show
No Mamma No Pappa No Uncle Sam
Autistic alone and did great Damn.

Bo Peep with mask and sanitizer replete
Found as Bard warned could not compete
No Mamma No Pappa No Uncle Sam
Get well and tend your sheep Damn.

Customer bought wood and items
Picked up butt outside to smoke frightened
No Mamma No Pappa No Uncle Sam
Picks up used cigarette Damn.

Short turnaround then back into heat
Pretty tough on an old man this beat
No Mamma No Pappa No Uncle Sam
Suck it up Buttercup Damn.

Sylvia nails for gun missing half price
Customer tried to remove not nice
No Mamma No Pappa No Uncle Sam
Not what Sylvia intended Damn.

Mighty hand of Depot shown Associates
Thieves enter store merchandise felonious
No Mamma No Pappa No Uncle Sam
Hand does not give a Damn.

Steve relieved tired Christy in paint
Ready to act as patron saint
No Mamma No Pappa No Uncle Sam
Steve has Christy's back Damn.

Common sense rarely applied there a reason
Such never fit in any spreadsheet adhesion
No Mamma No Pappa No Uncle Sam
Common sense never on spreadsheet Damn.

Brought three cases of warm bottled water to Garden
Jessie showed recission thanked for free pardon
No Mamma No Pappa No Uncle Sam
Why not filled already Damn.

Only two cashiers Friday eve
Made delivering water make-believe
No Mamma No Pappa No Uncle Sam
Why no water Damn.

Stupidity and duplicity go hand in hand
At Depot well-regarded members of band
No Mamma No Pappa No Uncle Sam
Stupid duplicit and don't give a Damn.

Jessie sensitive wasp sting ended Garden fling
Came inside for Benadryl then crying thing
No Mamma No Pappa No Uncle Sam
Jessie in tears from stings Damn.

Charlie heard of wasp affliction
Said allergic no place in Garden benediction
No Mamma No Pappa No Uncle Sam
Just kill the wasps Damn.

April told Bard did not like her much
Loaded tank onto truck any question shucks
No Mamma No Pappa No Uncle Sam
Job needs doing right Damn.

Reminded April Bard fit as part-time HC
Really a need for this role on Friday Eve
No Mamma No Pappa No Uncle Sam
Enjoying that battleax now April Damn.

Worked four straight headed for break
April said be late finish Garden plate
No Mamma No Pappa No Uncle Sam
April worried about Bard Damn.

No tubes in Garden register full of cash
April made dash checked on Bard in flash
No Mamma No Pappa No Uncle Sam
Thanks for giving a Damn.

No lot coverage in twenty-four no manager in store
Just another Saturday to fully explore
No Mamma No Pappa No Uncle Sam
Managers don't even come to work Damn.

Buggies and carts vagabonds all over lot
Makes hard finding a parking spot
No Mamma No Pappa No Uncle Sam
110 over macadam forget it Damn.

Andrea pensive and quiet on register seven
Tired not enjoying this shift's leaven
No Mamma No Pappa No Uncle Sam
Always quiet now sphinx Damn.

Fiasco building over sod in hand other than Bermuda
No one telling cashiers receiving Barracuda
No Mamma No Pappa No Uncle Sam
Don't disclose name of sod Damn.

Melisha appeared in Garden fifteen before end
April trying to watch out for Bard again
No Mamma No Pappa No Uncle Sam
Thanks April Damn.

Christy reading book walking out store
Bard blocked path caused to see more
No Mamma No Pappa No Uncle Sam
Does not want eye contact Damn.

Warpaint by Indians serious in west
Christy wearing stronger perfume best
No Mamma No Pappa No Uncle Sam
Just sniff Damn.

Time clock not acknowledging numbers on pane
Put fist to glass remembered names under pain
No Mamma No Pappa No Uncle Sam
Make Time Clock accede and give a Damn.

Two cashiers in middle except when Bard holding fort
Does work of two plus SCO cash no retort
No Mamma No Pappa No Uncle Sam
Different allocation when Bard in Middle Damn.

Sniffed out air conditioners and tool boxes
Christy helping customers as if sly foxes
No Mamma No Pappa No Uncle Sam
Just follow the scent Damn.

Skylar scheduled four but cashiers poor
Bo Peep out Jesse floored asked to stay more
No Mamma No Pappa No Uncle Sam
Great team player just like Bard once Damn.

Military discount day with many customers
No war won in very long day GI hustlers
No Mamma No Pappa No Uncle Sam
Thanks for never winning Damn.

Not-so-smart customers wearing face diapers
Fear and terror in place of reason deadly Ypres
No Mamma No Pappa No Uncle Sam
Remember when America home of the brave Damn.

No coverage in lot Bri came to help load
April assist Bard said desist in abode
No Mamma No Pappa No Uncle Sam
April not lifting ever Damn.

Culvers ice cream on Melisha's mind
Wanted to jump in pile spend a dime
No Mamma No Pappa No Uncle Sam
Heat makes for great fantasy Damn.

Toward end Bard found water no longer satisfied
Bloated in heat knew time to treat liquid apartheid
No Mamma No Pappa No Uncle Sam
Drank too much water Damn.

Turned off wind tunnel fan in heat
Understood when customers spoke neat
No Mamma No Pappa No Uncle Sam
Wind tunnels don't give a Damn.

Barcode choked customer took note
Bard fixed without breaking stride anecdote
No Mamma No Pappa No Uncle Sam
Barcodes not Customer problem Damn.

Wasps like moisture and flowers
Why not drain water each hour
No Mamma No Pappa No Uncle Sam
How hard is this Damn.

Walked to car buggies carts abandoned
Spread over lot tossed about useless propaganda
No Mamma No Pappa No Uncle Sam
Hey ASM and Bean Counter your play Damn.

Ryan helped load with Bard in tow
Made very large hot water heater go
No Mamma No Pappa No Uncle Sam
Ryan a big help when needed Damn.

Rare exotic obscure not part of Depot view
Recherche never found in their sachet brew
No Mamma No Pappa No Uncle Sam
Obscure does not give a Damn.

April admitted heat made hair frizzled
Appreciated Bard wading into sizzle
No Mamma No Pappa No Uncle Sam
Sizzled and give a Damn.

Skylar arrived as Bard said goodbye
Thanked again for helping tribe
No Mamma No Pappa No Uncle Sam
Skyler true blue Damn.

Jesse a bit OCD when bored in PRO station
Arranged suckers by color beautiful sensation
No Mamma No Pappa No Uncle Sam
Made sucker display beautiful Damn.

Wear masks required box says don't work
Depot promoting fear being a jerk
No Mamma No Pappa No Uncle Sam
Face diapers do not work that is science Damn.

Company flies with birds of a feather
Black Rock McKenzie Allstate CDC bellwether
No Mamma No Pappa No Uncle Sam
No integrity here for sure Damn.

RVP brought to store for review of excellence
Hard to believe stupidity and arrogance
No Mamma No Pappa No Uncle Sam
Once again House of Stupidity rules Damn.

Inventory audit came undone so rumored
Few employees had good humor
No Mamma No Pappa No Uncle Sam
Good Humor ice cream Damn.

Brad retired arrived wearing Depot shirt
Pressed into service just like a clerk
No Mamma No Pappa No Uncle Sam
No employee would answer Damn.

Kevin said RVP Preacher came selling
Brought here by District fortune telling
No Mamma No Pappa No Uncle Sam
Drinks own bathwater Damn.

Fifteen customers at PRO with Bard alone
Jesse returned said hold phone
No Mamma No Pappa No Uncle Sam
Jumped on register and helped Bard Damn.

April told Bard in middle to fly away
No more help coming to replace today
No Mamma No Pappa No Uncle Sam
No in Middle for Sunday eve typical Damn.

Lunchroom conversation with April over Christy
Indicated much happier now less risky
No Mamma No Pappa No Uncle Sam
Christy much more content now Damn.

Christy in paint hardware laminate cabinets
Roams store fewer reports more gladness
No Mamma No Pappa No Uncle Sam
Having fun again Damn.

Cherry matching paint in store looking red
Customers know can approach her spread
No Mamma No Pappa No Uncle Sam
Cherry a very valuable classic Damn.

Behr over store in sweat from humidity
Not yet recovered from weekend festivities
No Mamma No Pappa No Uncle Sam
Knows how to party down Damn.

Moved register box to check connections
Found three tape measures more confections
No Mamma No Pappa No Uncle Sam
Hard to believe behind box Damn.

Three tube warning then two then one
Bard reminding to have fun
No Mamma No Pappa No Uncle Sam
Three two one Damn.

Bags about gone receipt tapes a memory
See some more sometime this century
No Mamma No Pappa No Uncle Sam
Tapes and bags do not matter right Damn.

Autism not job required at Depot
Similar to aluminum and Alcoa
No Mamma No Pappa No Uncle Sam
Autism and Depot perfect Damn.

No lot coverage for twenty-four Behr arrived to skin
Makes sense to notify everybody's next of kin
No Mamma No Pappa No Uncle Sam
What a mess in lot for this Behr Damn.

Brandon in Locker room worked on break
Said hi to Bard made feel like mooncake
No Mamma No Pappa No Uncle Sam
Thanks Brandon for giving a Damn.

Hypocrisy like clouds of smoke arrive for folks cliche
Not paying health hazard demand face diapers in play
No Mamma No Pappa No Uncle Sam
Insufferable hypocrites don't give a Damn.

He has a controversy with Depot wrongs
Much worse than banging gongs
No Mamma No Pappa No Uncle Sam
Not a good place to be Damn.

Ineptitude systemic great clinic
Only true don't be a cynic
No Mamma No Pappa No Uncle Sam
The inept never give a Damn.

Utter incompetence employed mystical spell
Served to all employees at dinner bell
No Mamma No Pappa No Uncle Sam
Incompetence does not give a Damn.

Colossal stupidity matched only by frigidity
Hard to stand rigidly in all this humidity
No Mamma No Pappa No Uncle Sam
Stupid is as stupid does Damn.

Cream rises to top an old adage view
At Depot more like spoiled milk PU
No Mamma No Pappa No Uncle Sam
Spoiled milk rises too right Damn.

Remember management deep horror
Treat employees like corn borer
No Mamma No Pappa No Uncle Sam
Corn borer does not give a Damn.

HR squared Melanie plays role repeated every scene
In one ear out other no process between very keen
No Mamma No Pappa No Uncle Sam
Accomplished talent in this role Damn.

Reminisced about missing Dan did April
Drives past home truck parked unstable
No Mamma No Pappa No Uncle Sam
Dan not in truck Damn.

Come let management decide issues between us
Probably means will be mean to us
No Mamma No Pappa No Uncle Sam
Just be mean right Damn.

Strengthen weak hands make firm from feeble
More likely at Depot to find a Bald Eagle
No Mamma No Pappa No Uncle Sam
Shoot the strays Damn.

Fear and hasty heart Depot's answer to smart
Wonder when will publish this work of art
No Mamma No Pappa No Uncle Sam
Andy Warhol did not do this Damn.

Trust and rely on Depot as provider
Rarely sell this apple cider
No Mamma No Pappa No Uncle Sam
Trust Depot you must be mad Damn.

Keep still answer nil Depot favorite drill
Employees learn to avoid this thrill
No Mamma No Pappa No Uncle Sam
No thrill here Damn.

Have you not heard what planned long ago
Raging against employees arrogance hook in nose
No Mamma No Pappa No Uncle Sam
Hooked again Damn.

Customer ten percent off price matched Lowes
April told her low as Depot goes
No Mamma No Pappa No Uncle Sam
Price match not discounted Damn.

Employees nothing before Depot majesty
Suffer greatly from recurring tragedy
No Mamma No Pappa No Uncle Sam
Travesty does not give a Damn.

Lebanon forests less than Depot's lumber budget
Management hoping to find charge off fudget
No Mamma No Pappa No Uncle Sam
Fudget and charge off do not give a Damn.

Depot prone to worship golden calf
Convinced works on their behalf
No Mamma No Pappa No Uncle Sam
Sell the gold right Damn.

Chaos includes emptiness falsity and futility
Management effectiveness an impossibility
No Mamma No Pappa No Uncle Sam
Futility does not give a Damn.

Giving power to faint and weary
For Depot an unlikely inquiry
No Mamma No Pappa No Uncle Sam
An enquiry does not give a Damn.

Depot quickly swallowed up alive
Employees learn applies to hide
No Mamma No Pappa No Uncle Sam
Swallowed alive who gives a Damn.

Customer buys material to build house
Employees know quickly never joust
No Mamma No Pappa No Uncle Sam
Can't quite do this after all Damn.

Afflicted many times by Management in line
Made sure all employees do time pay fines
No Mamma No Pappa No Uncle Sam
Not an incentive Damn.

Haughty heart lofty eyes target for woe
Promotion at Depot makes all this go
No Mamma No Pappa No Uncle Sam
Lofty eyes don't give a Damn.

Olive declines eyes to sleep before store keep
Explains why little rest in heap
No Mamma No Pappa No Uncle Sam
Rest and heap do not give a Damn.

Depot full of ample provision all season
Decline to share like ungrateful demons
No Mamma No Pappa No Uncle Sam
Payroll not very good Damn.

Depot selling fear with diapers and wash
Promotes lockdowns sales profit isochronous
No Mamma No Pappa No Uncle Sam
Become only game in town this way Damn.

Rigid controlled uniformity established Depot normality
Standardization repression forced sterilization reality
No Mamma No Pappa No Uncle Sam
Messerschmidt Gleichschaltung in Depot Damn.

Conformity to Depot like pasteurized milk
Equal identical forced switch sour buttermilk
No Mamma No Pappa No Uncle Sam
Just love those Orange shirts Damn.

Rahab and Gideons need to appear and stand
Home of Brave and Free extinct in Depot land
No Mamma No Pappa No Uncle Sam
Brave required for free Damn.

Carpenters employ orthotomeo bankers dokimo
Depot does neither prefers Aruba and Kokomo
No Mamma No Pappa No Uncle Sam
Depot compromised no surprise Damn.

Counsel and confession never in Depot procession
Count beans make lean answer to any recession
No Mamma No Pappa No Uncle Sam
No good much less right only profit Damn.

Secular counsel advice plans and purpose
Mockers scorn gather Depot circus
No Mamma No Pappa No Uncle Sam
Scorned don't give a Damn.

Disobedient wicked chaff never laugh
Cash and profit fail before His staff
No Mamma No Pappa No Uncle Sam
Judgement twenty-four seven Damn.

Profit and gain without justice no standing
What happens when end comes no landing
No Mamma No Pappa No Uncle Sam
Profit alone leads to perish Damn.

Empty schemes not well-laid plans
Depot one day be Rosencrantz
No Mamma No Pappa No Uncle Sam
Rosencrantz and Guildenstern are dead Damn.

Depot management act wisely rulers of geld
Serve employees well lest wrath beheld
No Mamma No Pappa No Uncle Sam
Wrath does not give a Damn.

Turning honor and glory into profane shame
Vanity futility lies Depot plays awful game
No Mamma No Pappa No Uncle Sam
Does not matter right Damn.

Accountability for designs cast them out
Depot never will accept this rout
No Mamma No Pappa No Uncle Sam
These designs don't give a Damn.

When profit and sales plummet Sheol ascends summit
Depot groaning in grief bitter buffet whodunit
No Mamma No Pappa No Uncle Sam
Numbers go up and down Damn.

Depot dominion over employee hands
Believe extends to feet understand
No Mamma No Pappa No Uncle Sam
Just a job really Damn.

About to trip and fall into pit
Depot may never return from this trip
No Mamma No Pappa No Uncle Sam
This pit self-made Damn.

Forget frail nature practice hubris and pride
Depot soon fail history provides guides
No Mamma No Pappa No Uncle Sam
History does not give a Damn.

Depot management assumes no want nor adversity
Much less true than accepting biodiversity
No Mamma No Pappa No Uncle Sam
Biodiverse does not give a Damn.

Use card lie for poor helpless and unfortunate
Like Lion in thicket looking to trick importunate
No Mamma No Pappa No Uncle Sam
A pound of flesh Damn.

Crush employees sink down Orange life
Depot marches and plays fife
No Mamma No Pappa No Uncle Sam
And Hamlin does not give a Damn.

Foundations crumbling management stumbling
Depot headed toward big humbling
No Mamma No Pappa No Uncle Sam
Humbled still don't give a Damn.

Words without use spoken flattering deceit
Management excels indefensible downbeat
No Mamma No Pappa No Uncle Sam
Downbeat does not give a Damn.

Vileness exalted in endless pride baseness exalted
One day soon shall become defaulted
No Mamma No Pappa No Uncle Sam
Exalted don't give a Damn.

Abominable deeds often creed not fine much less right
Doing good lost to pure might in Depot flight
No Mamma No Pappa No Uncle Sam
This flight does not give a Damn.

Extorting interest from innocent pretense
No defense much less ten cents
No Mamma Pappa No Uncle Sam
Ten cents does not give a Damn.

Aerarium militare to Rome for Depot Essential
Expect bust very soon consequential
No Mamma No Pappa No Uncle Sam
Essential does not give a Damn.

Worthless pedagogical hypocriticals burdened
Better for employees to receive orange turban
No Mamma No Pappa No Uncle Sam
Burdened do not give a Damn.

Mountain of debt one day regret
Depot shall never overcome awful bet
No Mamma No Pappa No Uncle Sam
Wagering does not give a Damn.

Customs promulgated soothsayers foretell
Depot pledges strike hands alien bands Noel
No Mamma No Pappa No Uncle Sam
Foretell foreboding Damn.

Idols and idiots rule supreme Depot regime
Common man bowed down humbled cream
No Mamma No Pappa No Uncle Sam
Idols do not give a Damn.

Nobody doesn't like Sara Lee sweet confection
Christy Lea no relation no confession
No Mamma No Pappa No Uncle Sam
Christy not Sara Damn.

Eternal fiancée of Christy plays Othello
Fights Cyrus Black sheep poor fellow
No Mamma No Pappa No Uncle Sam
This Moor not married to Desdemona Damn.

Land of free and home of the brave
Not found nor practiced among Depot slaves
No Mamma No Pappa No Uncle Sam
Slaves are not brave nor free Damn.

Mindless fear stirred in pot
Pretty hard to drink that slop
No Mamma No Pappa No Uncle Sam
No faith have fear don't give a Damn.

Rumor has it new bags bit thicker
Management fails to place on ticker
No Mamma No Pappa No Uncle Sam
Bags not ordered again Damn.

Last week store busy with school sales
Tizzy looking for Tin Lizzy filled sails
No Mamma No Pappa No Uncle Sam
And Model T does not give a Damn.

Mamma don't raise your child to be Depot possession
Why would have them ever join this procession
No Mamma No Pappa No Uncle Sam
Do better than this for them Damn.

Tamerlane in Samarkand built empire
Iron for sale Depot seeks respire
No Mamma No Pappa No Uncle Sam
Tamer the lame does not give a Damn.

Amber HC tonight came to relieve
Told stories of Roland hard to believe
No Mamma No Pappa No Uncle Sam
Amber telling it like it is Damn.

Rooster Isaac refused to leave hen house
Garden break too hot to take louse
No Mamma No Pappa No Uncle Sam
Just send him home Damn.

April responded with letter to all HCs
Not addressing problem for real please
No Mamma No Pappa No Uncle Sam
Afraid of a Rooster Damn.

Never trained nor prepared like ASM
Blame ignorance on HC say again
No Mamma No Pappa No Uncle Sam
ASM did not know either Damn.

No one in Lot three evenings in a row
Paul alone in Lumber oh no another blow
No Mamma No Pappa No Uncle Sam
Alone again Damn.

Question to Depot leaders sales and profit off charts
Why then cut hours employees and all fine arts
No Mamma No Pappa No Uncle Sam
Greed greed greed Damn.

Paul unable to pull large order of wood
Had no flagger left customer misunderstood
No Mamma No Pappa No Uncle Sam
No staff to fill orders Damn.

Sam arrived with pallet unknown
Left box and pulley in aisle bemoan
No Mamma No Pappa No Uncle Sam
Just leave it in the aisle Damn.

Paul needed flagger for orders to pull
Shanghaied Sam I Am great help in full
No Mamma No Pappa No Uncle Sam
Sam helped Paul out of a jam Damn.

Amber returned to PRO at close
Wait and watch customers adios
No Mamma No Pappa No Uncle Sam
And three strips and no tubes Damn.

Lights dimmed door locked Amber goodbye
Sometimes she does closing easy as pie
No Mamma No Pappa No Uncle Sam
Fun to have her as HC Damn.

Sought Rocky for cutting merchandise
ASM found somewhere beyond Paradise
No Mamma No Pappa No Uncle Sam
ASM ran the saw Damn.

Run on lumber this eve beyond span of control
Sold by pallet no end to parade and parole
No Mamma No Pappa No Uncle Sam
Span of control a joke Damn.

Customer arrived asked for service
Explained no employees preserve us
No Mamma No Pappa No Uncle Sam
They just want to buy and pay Damn.

Shannon in Lumber abandoning ship shift complete
Wasco wanted her to stay perform repeat
No Mamma No Pappa No Uncle Sam
Not happening Chris get real Damn.

Thanked customers for not wearing masks at register
Glad some have courage intelligence and character
No Mamma No Pappa No Uncle Sam
A few Natural Born citizens Mr. Jefferson Damn.

Started to leave over diaper wearing
Glad stayed watched forbearing
No Mamma No Pappa No Uncle Sam
Forbearing does not give a Damn.

Mandy once in bookkeeping now paranoid flourish
Wraps receipts in paper around drink purchased
No Mamma No Pappa No Uncle Sam
Wrap receipt around drink Damn.

Beasts of burden names remembered uncertain
Depot management oblivious behind curtain
No Mamma No Pappa No Uncle Sam
Nothing behind this curtain worth a Damn.

Phyliss asked about Christy endless fiancée
Can't imagine mother living there touché
No Mamma No Pappa No Uncle Sam
Phyliss can't understand Damn.

Son growing up with this endless skein
Hard to imagine what may have seen
No Mamma No Pappa No Uncle Sam
First mom now son Damn.

Does man know Christy believes betrothed
Maybe painting like Vincent van Gogh
No Mamma No Pappa No Uncle Sam
And impressionism does not give a Damn.

Shift ended in PRO no end nor belief
Called to beef Amber no relief
No Mamma No Pappa No Uncle Sam
April left Amber in a jam Damn.

Called April trash not emptied in four days
Management might decide to end malaise
No Mamma No Pappa No Uncle Sam
Why empty trash in this store Damn.

Christy loaded down half-ton on pallet jack
No one available for tow motor sad sack
No Mamma No Pappa No Uncle Sam
Christy twisted like broken pretzel Damn.

Self-induced purgatory Christy's great glory
Emerged found much to make hoary
No Mamma No Pappa No Uncle Sam
Deserves better than that Damn.

Depot tells employees to only work schedule
Expect employee to extend shift bedevil
No Mamma No Pappa No Uncle Sam
A one-way street only Damn.

When calling overhead use titles or location
No one's name under Thracian incantation
No Mamma No Pappa No Uncle Sam
Thrace does not give a Damn.

Thanking customers for not wearing diapers
Asked to tell Home Office gripers
No Mamma No Pappa No Uncle Sam
Real Americans mean no Damn.

Buggies not moved in two days
Told April news then moved no delays
No Mamma No Pappa No Uncle Sam
Lot abandoned again Damn.

Store honored for excellent achievement
Tell management empty garbage frequent
No Mamma No Pappa No Uncle Sam
Garbage unemptied and who gives a Damn.

$887 check for employees total from usury sales
Split up melts away another Depot fail
No Mamma No Pappa No Uncle Sam
Keep the pennies Depot Damn.

Closed restaurant not essential over Red virus
Depot more infected ignored too desirous
No Mamma No Pappa No Uncle Sam
Depot and Red Virus essential Damn.

Melisha and Jesse said Bard mean to them
Failed to see back covered still condemned
No Mamma No Pappa No Uncle Sam
Does not matter Damn.

April slipping as supervisor
Door knock becoming chief advisor
No Mamma No Pappa No Uncle Sam
Ashley next in line fine Damn.

Christy likes paint more than flooring
Conversation there easier less exploring
No Mamma No Pappa No Uncle Sam
Easy to control dialog at paint Damn.

Worked for cashiers not store management
Contempt for all but employees laminate
No Mamma No Pappa No Uncle Sam
Can't leave then in a bind Damn.

Barcodes in Lumber too often broke
Very hard to checkout customer folk
No Mamma No Pappa No Uncle Sam
Too busy for working barcodes Damn.

Offered corporate donuts from Krispy Kreme
Junk food employees obese not dream
No Mamma No Pappa No Uncle Sam
Kill off the morbidly obese Damn.

Sight never seen ASM on register
Nowhere to cover these characters
No Mamma No Pappa No Uncle Sam
ASM on register not happening Damn.

Safe to say no one wants FSM nor HC job
Free to do what they want be a slob
No Mamma No Pappa No Uncle Sam
Do what you want Damn.

Treadmill moving slowly inside collapsing silo
Hollow Depot very far from wearing halo
No Mamma No Pappa No Uncle Sam
Fallen halo Depot Damn.

When customer asks explain why no service
Coverage cut hours reduced cursed excursus
No Mamma No Pappa No Uncle Sam
Excursus does not give a Damn.

Excuses and reasons reign supreme
Results never their fair endgame
No Mamma No Pappa No Uncle Sam
And who cares about hot air Damn.

Fortress of steel and lock in back
Helps management hide never knock
No Mamma No Pappa No Uncle Sam
Safe in safe right Damn.

ASMs like roaches in behavior of fear
On floor after dark when customers clear
No Mamma No Pappa No Uncle Sam
Roaches don't give a Damn.

April beginning to shutdown functions suasible
Realizing no outcome nor progress possible
No Mamma No Pappa No Uncle Sam
And playing for benefits Damn.

Found a note with typos galore signed by management
In this store are you serious simply entertainment
No Mamma No Pappa No Uncle Sam
And this urban legend does not give a Damn.

Three enemies faced by employees perhaps even four
Lowes up street Home Office beat management abhor
No Mamma No Pappa No Uncle Sam
And number four scheduling Damn.

Depot app endless comedy and charade
Tell customers to never believe parade
No Mamma No Pappa No Uncle Sam
No one knows what is in store Damn.

Percival Lowell saw canals on Mars
Depot believes they really stars
No Mamma No Pappa No Uncle Sam
And Grauman's Chinese does not give a Damn.

Melisha brought Bard a cheap Depot pin
Bard threw in trash bin
No Mamma No Pappa No Uncle Sam
Thanks for cheap Damn.

Increasing days and hours to three and twelve respectively
Wonder who conjured up these spells collectively
No Mamma No Pappa No Uncle Sam
Who gives a Damn.

Employees mad and rage over wage
Better to remain quiet and stealth engage
No Mamma No Pappa No Uncle Sam
Engage and don't give a Damn.

What would Depot do if all 2,300 stores called out
How much suffering would then come about
No Mamma No Pappa No Uncle Sam
Pick random days and call out Damn.

Register in PRO new mural covering transaction
Ring up numbers unseen no satisfaction
No Mamma No Pappa No Uncle Sam
And another wonder boy idea Damn.

So disheartening on weekend in PRO
Tell customers returns must go to Service slow
No Mamma No Pappa No Uncle Sam
Not fair to customer nor Customer Service Damn.

Contractors buy more than need bulk discount
Return excess for slow recount
No Mamma No Pappa No Uncle Sam
Does not make sense but who gives a Damn.

Associates robbed and plundered snared in concrete bondage
Management makes prey and spoil appendage fondness
No Mamma No Pappa No Uncle Sam
Bondage does not give a Damn.

Depot remembers not former things nor old
Impaled on golden cross foreboding abode
No Mamma No Pappa No Uncle Sam
And build a bed with no rest Damn.

Rarely honor much less respect employees
Management denies access to freebies
No Mamma No Pappa No Uncle Sam
No respect nor honor Damn.

Sweet cane money or fat from sacrifice
Depot weighs employee edifice
No Mamma No Pappa No Uncle Sam
Burdened do not give a Damn.

Depot Associate not formed nor molded
Prefer to practice ignorance and scolding
No Mamma No Pappa No Uncle Sam
Never prepared and don't give a Damn.

Depot house of graven idols profit delight
Confusion chaos worthless incite
No Mamma No Pappa No Uncle Sam
These idols don't give a Damn.

Numbers on a screen belie belief unseen
Employees know these one-day scream
No Mamma No Pappa No Uncle Sam
Numbers on a screen don't give a Damn.

Management besmeared cannot see
No difference between forest nor tree
No Mamma No Pappa No Uncle Sam
Besmeared simply blind Damn.

Never consider in mind eating seed
Believe just more feed from greed
No Mamma No Pappa No Uncle Sam
Seed consumed lost Damn.

Woe to Depot for employees begotten
Management caused to become rotten
No Mamma No Pappa No Uncle Sam
Employees made rotten do not give a Damn.

In Depot trust turned to dust
Employees know full of rust
No Mamma No Pappa No Uncle Sam
No trust left Damn.

Plan end from beginning strategy winning
Depot plans beginning after end imprinting
No Mamma No Pappa No Uncle Sam
Plan from behind and don't give a Damn.

Trusted wickedness and darkness unseen
Knowledge and wisdom astray obscene
No Mamma No Pappa No Uncle Sam
Unseen revealed don't give a Damn.

Management absent mercy provides heavy yoke
Soon becomes woke followed by broke
No Mamma No Pappa No Uncle Sam
Yolk unburdened Damn.

Persist spreadsheet charms and sorcery
Disaster exposing chicanery and forgery
No Mamma No Pappa No Uncle Sam
Built on spreadsheets Damn.

Employees refined like silver furnace affliction
Management promotes terrible malediction
No Mamma No Pappa No Uncle Sam
The afflicted in this furnace don't give a Damn.

Greed and avarice ensconced inside
Desolation and destruction lurk hide
No Mamma No Pappa No Uncle Sam
Better hide for sure Damn.

Cup staggering intoxication filled to brim
Management drains every whim
No Mamma No Pappa No Uncle Sam
Sober not here Damn.

Staggering toward pit yawning for sport Dugged
Feet in net hidden ensnared work drugged
No Mamma No Pappa No Uncle Sam
Dugged management does not give a Damn.

Dixie fire close to heart of Depot management
Building material sales reap embellishment
No Mamma No Pappa No Uncle Sam
And burn baby burn equals profit Damn.

Storms in Atlantic or Gulf hit coast
Depot ghouls feast on meat and roast
No Mamma No Pappa No Uncle Sam
Depot worships mother nature Damn.

No knowledge rabid dogs never enough
Shepherds way not understood tough
No Mamma No Pappa No Uncle Sam
Packs of dogs don't give a Damn.

Ears uncircumscribed cannot hear much less feign
Covetousness unjust gain more profit sustain
No Mamma No Pappa No Uncle Sam
Uncircumscribed don't give a Damn.

Trust not nor rely on figures that lie
Management better learn fast to survive
No Mamma No Pappa No Uncle Sam
They won't learn Damn.

Brutes irrational stupid no rebuke
Imprudent scattered profit fluke
No Mamma No Pappa No Uncle Sam
Stupidity does not give a Damn.

Mercedes Ricardo rolled out EEOC enforcement
Providing assistance endorsed reinforcement
No Mamma No Pappa No Uncle Sam
Rolling out the Mercedes Damn.

When papers arrive and served
Wonder who receives preserved
No Mamma No Pappa No Uncle Sam
Home Office might give a Damn.

EEOC using big cannon for a gnat
Are they hunting for much bigger cat
No Mamma No Pappa No Uncle Sam
This cat may be in the bag Damn.

Oh to be fly on wall when papers arrive
Will pillars withstand plans contrived
No Mamma No Pappa No Uncle Sam
Flies really don't give a Damn.

Bryan trained and hired for PRO
Arrived at work saved him from Garden blow
No Mamma No Pappa No Uncle Sam
Bryan a doormat Damn.

Promoted to full-time and trained for PRO functions
Bryan uniquely gifted help Sylvia instructions
No Mamma No Pappa No Uncle Sam
Go PRO Bryan Damn.

Sent Bryan to PRO went to Garden
Explained to Amber real bargain
No Mamma No Pappa No Uncle Sam
Sylvia alone in PRO needs Bryan Damn.

Argued to send to PRO because Bryan first to leave
No difference in PRO nor Garden think reprieve
No Mamma No Pappa No Uncle Sam
Can they not count Damn.

Arrived in Garden Customer wanted twenty bags
Parked in road drive through locked more drags
No Mamma No Pappa No Uncle Sam
Drive-thru locked eight hours later Damn.

Finished shift at PRO after Bryan left
$7,000 drywall special order uncovered bereft
No Mamma No Pappa No Uncle Sam
Special order does not give a Damn.

Broke rule called Donna told rain coming
Drywall exposed wind and water forthcoming
No Mamma No Pappa No Uncle Sam
Rain and drywall not good Damn.

Donna excited sent Kolby not cheese
Small wrap to cover pallets oh please
No Mamma No Pappa No Uncle Sam
Still uncovered and thundering Damn.

Joey and Missy told to fix previous eve
Missy took leave Joey did not believe
No Mamma No Pappa No Uncle Sam
Sylvia looked but did not see Damn.

Hollywood and Behr made appearance to square
Found wrap covered drywall nothing left bare
No Mamma No Pappa No Uncle Sam
All this to keep a special-order secure Damn.

Wasps assaulting Garden Party
Flew up Bard's leg not least jolly
No Mamma No Pappa No Uncle Sam
Wasps do sting Damn.

Sprayed area killed seven drove more Leaven
Wasps decided Garden seventh heaven
No Mamma No Pappa No Uncle Sam
Keep Jesse away from this Damn.

Donna lost cart and phone
Acted more than a little stoned
No Mamma No Pappa No Uncle Sam
Stoned actors don't give a Damn.

Nobody answered Garden phones
Amber released many drones
No Mamma No Pappa No Uncle Sam
No coverage in Garden typical Damn.

Wasco answered Amber's page saying busy loading
Amber told Bard Wasco come foreboding
No Mamma No Pappa No Uncle Sam
Take coverage and use it on inventory Damn.

Customer in PRO had coupon that did not work
Sent to Customer Service coupon fraud berserk
No Mamma No Pappa No Uncle Sam
Restock lumber yet again Damn.

Spending thousands electrician thanked and recognized
Provided discount thought gold received as prize
No Mamma No Pappa No Uncle Sam
First to ever say thanks to him Damn.

Amber brought tube to PRO to say
Promised Bard Andrea on way
No Mamma No Pappa No Uncle Sam
Amber helping Bard Damn.

Christy holding court in Paint this afternoon
Controlling narrative at ease making sport croon
No Mamma No Pappa No Uncle Sam
Christy having fun at work Damn.

Emptiness occurs when staff and hours cut
Forces customers to often choose very bad rut
No Mamma No Pappa No Uncle Sam
Customers in a rut leave Damn.

Lights at half mast inside darkening storm arrived
Cinemas better lucidity Depot deprived
No Mamma No Pappa No Uncle Sam
Someone just play Taps Damn.

Overhead door blocked outside pallets around
Unable to use tow motor lift Ballymore bound
No Mamma No Pappa No Uncle Sam
Try to fill orders now Damn.

Two customers pulled orders said no wait
Never did see them return restocked great
No Mamma No Pappa No Uncle Sam
Put wood on cart then abandon Damn.

Older customer in Garden knew Depot well
Stayed long enough for help with rocks swell
No Mamma No Pappa No Uncle Sam
Patience did pay off in the end Damn.

Explained to another about deployment
Stated exhausted give healing ointment
No Mamma No Pappa No Uncle Sam
Thinking straight hard Damn.

Management struts around promoting vile
Day shall come surrounding peristyle
No Mamma No Pappa No Uncle Sam
Embrace sin for profit Damn.

See Depot rage flattery deception engage
Preliminary for approaching phage
No Mamma No Pappa No Uncle Sam
Phage consumes and does not give a Damn.

Mendacity and audacity raised as plague
Truth relegated to fog and vapor vague
No Mamma No Pappa No Uncle Sam
Mendacity does not give a Damn.

Orange life through Black Rock 401k
Called to enter but corporate computer went away
No Mamma No Pappa No Uncle Sam
You cannot make this up Damn.

Stuck head into mouth of beast with Black Rock
Shareholder vested more strongly than bedrock
No Mamma No Pappa No Uncle Sam
Vested and Black Rock may give a Damn.

Called out for third time in three years
Sullins just fine Ashley in bind to switch gears
No Mamma No Pappa No Uncle Sam
Three times in three years Damn.

Money like your word incurred
Matters most who both give to preferred
No Mamma No Pappa No Uncle Sam
Word and money matter Damn.

Bo Peep returned from bout with Red virus
Struggled to move needs a thesaurus
No Mamma No Pappa No Uncle Sam
Bo Peep back Damn.

Nick at night felt very slight
Alone in Garden took a lot of might
No Mamma No Pappa No Uncle Sam
Nick feeling sorry for Nick Damn.

Customer needed 100 blocks placed in U-Haul
Nick refused help worked alone just beat all
No Mamma No Pappa No Uncle Sam
Sent Nick help refused Damn.

Nick inside passed Bo Peep at close
Told Bard she sensed attitude in pose
No Mamma No Pappa No Uncle Sam
Shepherd's hook used on attitude Damn.

Janet made cashier of month
Perfected statue pose in Garden bunch
No Mamma No Pappa No Uncle Sam
Taught her what she knows congrats Damn.

Announcement of close said reopen at six instead of eight
Bo Peep simply too much to remember on plate
No Mamma No Pappa No Uncle Sam
Bo Peep a bit flummoxed Damn.

Melisha replaced by Bard in Garden
Fatigued set in unable to focus pardon
No Mamma No Pappa No Uncle Sam
Fatigue and confusion Damn.

Later caught in PRO time to go
Three strips in register made sallow
No Mamma No Pappa No Uncle Sam
Button down unbuttoned Damn.

Bo Peep sweet to Bard told to go home
Willing to work with Skyler and none
No Mamma No Pappa No Uncle Sam
Willing to let Bard go with but one Damn.

Concerned over Sir Arthur piling on
Bard not leaving Bo Peep foregone
No Mamma No Pappa No Uncle Sam
Bo Peep takes care of sheep Damn.

Great to see Skylar again after much time apart
Really doing great job with her part
No Mamma No Pappa No Uncle Sam
Skylar just makes you glad being around Damn.

Leaving store at close Millie at Customer Service
Gave bad news Bard gone for eve not nervous
No Mamma No Pappa No Uncle Sam
Millie sad Bard leaving Damn.

Olive in Locker room provided moment of doom
Leaving store for eight straight days great gloom
No Mamma No Pappa No Uncle Sam
Store and doom joined Damn.

It just gets worse when Kimmie runs up
Getting married and this no set-up
No Mamma No Pappa No Uncle Sam
Both Kimmie and Olive gone oh no Damn.

Asked Sullins how doing said no fooling
Responded Bard in building ridiculing
No Mamma No Pappa No Uncle Sam
Sullins did laugh though Damn.

Behr hibernating after serious grueling
Heat over 100 no one gave fair ruling
No Mamma No Pappa No Uncle Sam
Behr looking for a very cold stream Damn.

I Am that I Am no rhyme nor reason only confusion
No beginning nor end much less conclusion
No Mamma No Pappa No Uncle Sam
I Am that I Am no more to say today Damn.

0884's pin pulled from Orange Life's chart
No hope for rest to sea as Lemmings march
No Mamma No Pappa No Uncle Sam
This Lemming won't give a Damn.

Afterword

Thank you for taking time to read this very long odyssey. I hope you found it enjoyable, thought provoking and at times very challenging. I read parts of it on a regular basis and continue to experience revelation and enlightenment with a sense of personal awe. On a personal level it humbles me when I see what has been written. No way I could ever write like this much less create or even have the inspiration in the natural. Very humbling and deservedly so.

The Appendix contains a brief litany of examples of some of the topics covered in the poem. Let me be clear. I doubt Home Depot is worse than other similar employers. That it is no better is the problem. I am reminded of the adage spoken by Churchill and others that said Democracy is a terrible form of government. It is just that all others are so much worst. Such is the case for Depot and system producing it.

Reform? Look in the mirror. Every system is a form of capitalism. Capitalism is merely the distribution and allocation of services and goods produced. No system is perfect, but many are worse than others.

The least worst system is a free market defined as a large number of buyers and sellers with no one controlling price, demand, or supply. It is a terrible form of economics but like above, the others are so much worse. Government's role is not participant but watch dog to see that no one does reach that position. Government is not our brother's keeper. That duty belongs exclusively to us. If a people are moral, they fill the Samaritan role. When they are not, they quickly become pharisees.

A free market requires a moral people. A moral people must have natural law and an absolute standard of conduct. They must also uphold and support a representative form of government to allow this system to flourish. It is not a coincidence that civics is not taught and held in such disrepute today across the country.

The problem then is not the cartel and oligopolistic system infecting America today. Essential, too big to fail and bailouts are but a symptom of a much greater malaise. The problem is the image in the mirror.

No morality and acceptance of Judeo-Christian principles and natural law as the absolute standard. That inexorably leads to replacement of the republic with democracy followed by rapid dissent into majority rule tyranny followed by pure tyranny. Representation replaced by rule and rule becomes force and compulsion. Dissent is ground into the dust. Republics represent. Democracies rule. Conformity replaces choice.

For business and economic system concentration into the hands of the few who then control and use government to institutionalize their cartel and or monopolistic system.

Home Depot is just a result. The Bible calls it the Beast system. Man doing what is right in his own sight can create only that in his fallen state. When I summon the courage to look in the mirror and see what is right in my own sight I do not like what stares back. . . .

Charles Ford

Glossary

FES- Front End Supervisor is the position over Head Cashiers, cashiers, and lot attendants. Christy Lea first then April fills this post during the poem.

HC- Head Cashiers that report to April the FES. Includes Amber, Ashley, Emily "Bo Peep", Isaac and Olive.

SCO- Self Check Out- Customers access this area and machines to check out with limited assistance.

ASM- Assistant Store Manager- Reports to the Store Manager. The people here are Chris, Roland, and Donna. The store manager is Josh AKA the Bean Counter. An earlier manager is named Clint and is mentioned. Another young man named Josh is also found in the poem but has no connection with this.

BTO- Bachman Turner Overdrive a rock band

HR Squared- Home Office states that the Human Resource person is their representative not an HR person hence Human resource representative HRR becomes HR squared in the poem. Shayla and Melanie are the two representatives mentioned.

PRO- Location of cash registers and desk for use by contractors when they enter the store. Missy, Sylvia, Bryan, Bob and Angela are the characters in this unit included in the poem.

Yo Yo- Nickname employed for a specific cashier employee included in poem.

0884- Home Depot assigns a number for each store. The one in Decatur, Alabama is 0884.

SKU- Stock Keeping Unit. Barcode and number supposedly on all items but often found to be missing or damaged in poem.

Wok- Acquired state of stupor and stupidity infecting occupants of America and too many Home Depot employees. How term applied in this poem.

SPQR- Symbol of Rome employed by the military legions Senator Populace of Rome is the loose translation for use in this poem.

GET- Brilliant acronym employed by Home Office that supposedly means Greet Engage and Thank.

GIT- Poetic corruption of GET into Grab Interrogate and Terrorize.

GOT- Position customer enjoys with merchandise before checkout.

Homer Fund- Company administered assistance directed to employees in need. Employees usually are main source of funding. Some of the practices are detailed in the poem.

Area 51- Specific self-checkout machine infamous for not working and often causing the other three machines to somehow follow suit. Nick named after the infamous area of Nevada. It carries the number 51. There are three other machines numbered 52, 53 and 54.

Red Virus- Nick name for Covid.

Middle- Checkout area that also includes self-checkout and register manned cash registers. Called Middle because of physical location in the store.

Index

Made in United States
North Haven, CT
09 August 2022